LOVE IS GREATER THAN AIDS

A Memoir of Survival, Healing, and Hope

REV. STEVE PIETERS

ROWMAN & LITTLEFIELD
Lanham • Boulder • New York • London

Published by Rowman & Littlefield
An imprint of The Rowman & Littlefield Publishing Group, Inc.
4501 Forbes Boulevard, Suite 200, Lanham, Maryland 20706
www.rowman.com

86-90 Paul Street, London EC2A 4NE

British Library Cataloguing in Publication Information Available

Library of Congress Cataloging-in-Publication Data

978-1-5381-8657-2 (cloth)
978-1-5381-8658-9 (electronic)

♾™ The paper used in this publication meets the minimum requirements of American National Standard for Information Sciences—Permanence of Paper for Printed Library Materials, ANSI/ NISO Z39.48-1992.

Contents

Prologue

How Did I Ever Get to This?

"STEVE, HAVE YOU EVER HAD A SEXUAL EXPERIENCE WITH A WOMAN?" I was flabbergasted by Tammy Faye Bakker's question, but no, I hadn't.

I was first called a "fairy" in second grade. I was the skinny kid with glasses, the smartest student, but sensitive and lonely. To my classmates I was an odd kid with a differentness that set me apart. My awkwardness

The author at age five at Christmas 1957, with his mother, Norma K. Pieters, his brother, Rick Pieters, and his father, Richard S. Pieters. COURTESY OF REVEREND PIETERS'S PERSONAL COLLECTION.

made it easy for them to tease me and call me names like "fairy" and "sissy." I spent a painful childhood and adolescence knowing that I was attracted to men and struggling to handle the deep shame I felt about it. When I was fourteen, I was so mortified by any sign I was a homosexual, that I sometimes wore rulers up my sleeves to keep my limp wrists stiff. When I was sixteen, I was in such despair over my secret shame that I thought about committing suicide by taking too much aspirin, but fortunately, I only swallowed a couple pills before I thought better of it.

I learned early on how to deflect criticism and be myself, largely by spending most of my time alone building a magical world in my own imagination. This world was peopled by the characters in the popular children's entertainment of the day: from *Peter Pan* to *Superman* and *Hercules,* Disney features, and endless Saturday morning cartoons and cowboy shows. I loved it all.

At the same time, all this time, another life was building inside me, a spiritual life based on faith. My paternal grandparents had been Presbyterian missionaries to Korea, and my parents were leaders in our local Congregational church. Mom and Dad raised me to be a good Christian, and through my early travels to the Holy Land and my ongoing Christian education, my faith grew.

God did not call me to the ministry at that early age. I decided early on I wanted to be a musical theater actor. From my first time on stage, as Death in a children's theater production of *The Emperor's Nightingale,* through productions at Phillips Academy in Andover, Massachusetts, where I grew up, Interlochen National Music Camp, and Northwestern University, as well as five summers of summer stock, I thrived on performing. It was the place I felt most at home. Between the ages of fifteen and twenty-three, I did over seventy productions, mostly musicals, and most of them in principal character roles. The exhilaration I felt onstage countered the shame I felt about being a homosexual.

When I graduated from Northwestern, it seemed as if all the doors in professional theater kept slamming in my face. If casting directors wanted a character actor, they hired a person the age of the character, usually older than I. Discouraged, I soon didn't try very hard to get to auditions. Instead, I answered a call to the ministry. Even after being diagnosed with AIDS (acquired immunodeficiency syndrome) a few years later, I continued to follow my call to preach and teach.

In 1985, as the AIDS epidemic began to surge through the United States, Tammy Faye Bakker of the evangelical PTL (Praise the Lord) television network decided she wanted to be the first televangelist to interview a gay man with AIDS. It was a bold and controversial move on her part, and the repercussions of that unlikely twenty-four-minute interview would reverberate for years.

Tammy Faye and her husband, Jim Bakker, were conservative televangelists with the largest Christian broadcasting network in the world. The Bakkers also built a Christian theme park and time-share hotel called Heritage USA, just outside Charlotte in Fort Mill, South Carolina. My friend Lucia Chappelle and I watched their programs from time to time, and when we weren't stunned by their conservative theology, we often laughed at their theatrics. We watched Jim and Tammy more for entertainment than for inspiration.

In November 1985, the PTL producers contacted Rev. Ken South, the executive director of the AIDS social service agency in Atlanta, Georgia, to ask if he knew of a gay man with AIDS who would be willing to be interviewed by Tammy Faye. They told him they had looked all over the South but had not been able to find anyone willing to come on her show. Ken told them he had a friend "who might be perfect."

I was living in Los Angeles at the time, a thirty-three-year-old gay pastor with AIDS doing my best to manage my own illness while ministering to others who were suffering with the "gay plague," as they called it then. When the producer called me, I had already been sick for three years and had done any number of interviews about being a gay man with AIDS. I agreed to go on the show, on the condition that the interview be live, so they couldn't edit it to suit their purposes. She assured me it would go out live. I was nervous and excited, but I looked on it as a great opportunity to talk to an audience I never would reach otherwise.

The producer said she would send me a round-trip ticket to Charlotte, where I would stay at the Heritage Village Hotel and be interviewed by Tammy Faye in their TV studio. I told her I was weak due to an experimental chemotherapy, and I would appreciate it if she would send me two tickets, so that I could bring Rev. Nancy Radclyffe, my chaplain and friend, to assist me. She agreed.

The date was set so that I wouldn't miss my suramin treatment on Mondays. Suramin was a new drug targeted at HIV (human immunodeficiency virus, which can lead to AIDS), and I was patient number one on this first antiviral drug trial. I was surprised but thrilled the producer sent me first-class tickets. As I thought about it, with Jim and Tammy's well-known extravagant lifestyle, they probably thought first class was only to be expected.

That next Tuesday, Nancy arrived to pick me up for the airport. As we were about to head out the door, Tammy Faye's producer called again. "Tammy's sick, and we're canceling the interview. Please send back the tickets." I had a hunch that was not all there was to it, but I simply expressed my disappointment and wished Tammy Faye well. It was a big letdown for both Nancy and me.

The next day, the producer called again, and said, "Tammy's feeling better, and we've decided we'd like to do the interview after all, but by satellite. This will be historic for PTL, not only because Tammy will be the first televangelist to interview a gay man with AIDS, but because it will be the first time a satellite interview will ever be done on the PTL network."

On Friday, November 15, Nancy drove me to a TV station in Ontario, California. It happened to be my young niece Jen's birthday, and I saw that as a good sign.

Tammy's producer met us in the lobby of the TV station. After the social pleasantries, I was shown into a dark studio where I sat by myself. I was given an earpiece so I could hear Tammy. I was told that Tammy could see me, although there was no monitor for me to see her. I would just talk into the camera with a boom mike above me to relay my voice to her in her studio. They tested the satellite hookup, and the next thing I knew I was talking to Tammy Faye Bakker. There were still a few minutes before the live broadcast, so Tammy and I talked.

Somehow it tickled my funny bone to hear her say, "Hi, Steve!" This was really happening! She was charming and expressed a lot of gratitude and pride that this would be the first time any television evangelist had ever interviewed a gay man with AIDS. "*Tammy's House Party* is like the *Phil Donahue Show* of PTL," she said. "It's a secular talk show, so we won't talk about Jesus. We'll just talk about the issues." She thanked me and praised my courage for coming on TV to talk about having AIDS. I didn't tell her that I'd been doing that for almost two years, both locally and on CNN. I just said, "It's my pleasure."

As the interview began, we were both having problems with our earpieces staying in place. She asked, "Is this the first time for you, too, Steve?"

"Yes!"

"It is for me, too."

Of course, she was referring to the satellite hookup, but the double entendre was not lost on me and apparently, from her giggles, was not lost on her either.

"I'm lucky because I'm a girl, and I can hook mine around my earring." We both giggled.

I wondered how she'd react if I joked that I'd left my earrings at home. I decided not to go there, at least not yet.

For the next twenty-four minutes, I answered all her questions as best I could, starting with when I first knew I was "different." I quickly introduced the word "gay" to avoid using the word "different" as a euphemism for it, and she followed by saying "homosexual."

"Did you not just feel really good around girls? Did girls make you nervous, Steve? Did you feel put down by women?"

"Oh, quite the contrary, Tammy, I love women. I've always had a lot of girlfriends." If she only knew how often I've called my gay male friends "girlfriend"! But it was true: I'd always had a lot of women friends.

"What did your parents say?"

"My mother cried, and my father held my hand, and he told me I'm his son and he loved me no matter what. My mother has said much the same thing." I kept it to myself that Mom thought my sexuality was all her fault and how disappointed she had been that I would never give her grandchildren.

"Thank God for a mom and dad who will stand with a young person. . . . Jesus loves us through anything. That's the wonderful thing about Jesus."

Apparently, we were going to talk about Jesus after all. "Absolutely. Jesus loves me just the way I am. I really believe that. Jesus loves the way I love." Where did that come from? I couldn't believe I had just said it!

"Listen, Steve. This is an emotional interview for me. . . . I want to put my arms right around Steve."

"Aw, my arms go right around you!"

She plunged into my sex life: "Steve, have you ever had a sexual relationship with a woman?" Gee, she really turned that corner abruptly. How do you jump from "I want to put my arms right around him" to "Have you ever had a sexual experience with a woman?" in the next breath?

"Did you not feel you'd given women a fair try?"

"No, my orientation is towards men."

"What did you feel when you were kissing a woman? Did you not feel anything? Was there nothing there at all?"

"No, I felt that it was disrespectful of the woman." That answer really came out of nowhere. I had never said it that way before.

"I have something else to ask you, Steve. What made you think that you were a homosexual? Was it, did you feel feminine inside? Or did you? A lot of times the gay community—some men look homosexual, other men do not. You do not! You do not. You do not look like, uh, you do not look effeminate at all. . . ." Really? Obviously, she hadn't seen me dance or prance about. Future LGBTQ audiences would laugh uproariously when she said I didn't look gay!

"What made you feel that there was no hope for you to be straight?" No hope? I let go of that kind of hopelessness after I came out. Now, I loved being gay and I wouldn't want to be straight for anything! I felt flummoxed for a moment and decided the way forward was to talk about coming out through the Metropolitan Community Church.

"Well, I discovered the gay community when I was twenty-three. I was very lonely just out of college . . . and I finally found God when I met my gay brothers and lesbian sisters at MCC. I knew that I was finally home."

I couldn't believe some of the questions she asked, but I kept reminding myself they were the right questions for her audience.

Somehow, I was able to answer all her questions. She talked to me about being gay for the first half of the interview and then moved into asking what it was like for me to have AIDS.

"Has it changed the gay community?"

I decided to take it in a positive direction. "Yes, it has. I believe it's made us prouder of ourselves. It's taught us to love each other and care for each other in a way that we never knew how to before."

She brought up Rock Hudson, who had died the previous month. She also referenced the film *An Early Frost*, which she and her husband had watched the other night, as I had. That prompted her to do a little preaching on "how sad it was that we as Christians are afraid to put our arms around an AIDS patient." She assured me, that if it had been at all possible, she would have had me sitting there right beside her and there would be plenty of Christians there "who wouldn't be afraid to put our arms around you and show you that we care." The audience applauded! I wondered if the applause was canned. Years later, I learned it wasn't. There was a live studio audience.

Tammy Faye said the only reason I wasn't in her studio was because "I was afraid the trip would be too hard on him, and he had to get back to his chemotherapy." I didn't say anything, though I was surprised. I suspected (correctly as it turned out) the real reason had more to do with PTL than my chemo.

When I tried to talk about my near-death experience two weeks before, she cut me off and asked if people were afraid to be in the same room with me.

I gave some examples of how I'd been treated by fearful people and concluded with a quote from Mark 5: "Do not be afraid. Just have faith."

She began to preach after that, "We get a disease, we get cancer, that doesn't change us. We're still the same person. I'm still Tammy Bakker. You're still Steve Pieters." That tickled me somehow. It made me feel she understood I was still a whole person, not a disease.

Toward the end of the interview, she asked me, "Are you afraid to die, should that happen to you?" Should it happen? Did she really think I was going to get out of here alive?

"I was afraid until this experience two weeks ago. And I am confident now that there is nothing to be scared of in death. I believe in the Resurrection of Jesus Christ and that means that God is greater than death. God showed us, through Jesus, that we need not fear death. And I believe that."

"That's right. When we know Jesus Christ as our personal savior, we do not need to fear death. Thank God."

I raised my hand as I said, "Hallelujah!" I felt uncomfortable, because neither the raised hand nor the "Hallelujah" was anything I'd ever really said or done before, but I thought, "When in Rome..." I worried for years that I didn't look authentic in that moment, but she seemed pleased and a bit surprised.

"That's wonderful. Only a Christian can know that peace. And only someone who loves Jesus can know that assurance in their hearts, you know." I believe that was the moment when she suddenly realized that this gay pastor with AIDS really was a Christian. It clicked for her, and she got it.

She graciously asked, "What can we do to make it easier for you?"

"You can educate people, Tammy. You have a wonderful forum to teach people, 'Do not fear AIDS. Just have faith you can help people with AIDS.'"

She ended by saying, "God bless you. We want you to beat this disease."

"I will, with Jesus' help." And eventually I did, with the help of Jesus and my doctor, Alexandra M. Levine, MD, MACP.

"God bless you, Steve, and thank you very much for a very eye-opening interview."

After the interview, I met the producer and Nancy in the lobby. They were ecstatic about how well it had gone. I didn't think I'd done a very good job, but they all assured me I had. I couldn't stop thinking about how I should have said this and how I could have put that better. Nevertheless, Nancy and I practically flew home. Her excitement about what had just transpired on the PTL network was infectious, and for the moment, I was pleased, too.

Nancy told me the producer had said they didn't have us come out to Charlotte because they were afraid that I would not be treated well by the hotel staff and, more to the point, that the TV crew might not work if I was in the studio. I had suspected as much, given how often I'd been seated outdoors for TV interviews, my interviewers in "safely" distant studios.

When we got back to my place, I got a call from Rev. Jo Crisco, a friend and the pastor of a Metropolitan Community Church in Texas, who said she'd seen the whole thing and thought it was "fantastic." She said she'd videotaped it on her VCR, and she volunteered to send it to me.

Of course, I said, "Yes, please!" That was the only videotape I ever received, and that was the source of the YouTube post that has now been viewed hundreds of thousands of times.

Jo told me that right after my interview, Tammy came back to do a segment on "women in wheelchairs," but she interrupted herself to talk about my interview. Tammy said how moved she was by it and how important it was that Christians develop compassion and understanding for "gay people and people with AIDS."

At the time, I thought the interview would only be seen by her live TV audience, and that would be it. After I got home, I laughed about the whole thing with my friend, Lucia. I told her I was grateful no one I knew would ever see it.

When the PTL scandal broke in early 1987, I was at the Playboy Mansion visiting my longtime friend Christie Hefner, who was in Los Angeles for business. Christie had been one of the most supportive friends I could have asked for throughout my illness. This evening, Christie, her father, Hugh Hefner, and I were at the dining room table chatting, and the subject of Jim Bakker's fall from grace came up. Christie told her dad that I had been interviewed by Tammy Faye in 1985, about being a gay pastor with AIDS. After discussing that for a bit, Mr. Hefner asked me, "Do you think Jim Bakker is gay?"

I said, "Some of my friends and I have talked about that, and the question always comes up, 'What self-respecting homosexual would ever let his wife wear makeup like Tammy Faye's?'"

Mr. Hefner replied, "That's just the point: he's not a self-respecting homosexual."

Troy Perry, the founder and moderator of the Metropolitan Community Churches denomination, showed my interview with Tammy Faye at the opening of the international General Conference of the Metropolitan Community Churches in Miami in 1987. At first, I squirmed with embarrassment, but I was stunned at the intensity of the audience reactions throughout the video. They gave the interview a standing ovation that seemed to go on forever.

After that, wherever I traveled for speaking and preaching engagements, people wanted to watch the interview—and to watch me watching it with them. People always started off giggling at Tammy Faye, but by the end, many were crying, and everyone always stood up and cheered. A well-respected, gay lobbyist in Washington, D.C., told me the interview should be called The Radicalization of Tammy Faye Bakker.

Troy himself told me he knew the interview was inspired by the Holy Spirit when I said it would be "disrespectful of the woman" after she asked, "Maybe you haven't given women a fair try?" He said that kind of language was perfect for her audience. I remember thinking at the time that I'd never put it like that before. It just seemed right.

When Reverend Crisco sent me the videotape and I watched the interview for the first time, I was struck by how odd it was that I ended up this gay pastor with AIDS talking to the most famous female televangelist in the country, when all I had wanted while growing up was to become a famous song and dance man on Broadway.

Chapter One

Out at Last and Called by God

When I was growing up, I thought being a famous actor would solve all my problems. It would show the bullies who had plagued me throughout my childhood. It would make me popular. It would make me immortal. So I worked hard learning to act, sing, and dance at Interlochen Arts Camp, in summer stock, and at Northwestern University. A drinking problem threatened to derail that plan, and I got into recovery at the age of twenty-three.

If I were to stay sober, I knew I had to get honest about being gay. So I came out in April 1976, but it took me a while to figure out exactly how to do it. As a newly sober person, I knew that going to the gay bars would not be a good idea.

I was attending church at Alice Millar Chapel at Northwestern, and I decided to go to Rev. Jim Avery, the gay-friendly pastor there to talk with him about how I could come out without going to gay bars. He suggested there might be a gay recovery group in Chicago. I asked around at the meetings I was going to in Rogers Park, and a new friend, Fred, took me to my first gay meeting.

There was only one gay recovery group each week in Chicago in 1976. I became a regular. Soon, one more gay meeting started, and then I found a bunch of mostly gay meetings in New Town, the gay "ghetto."

Fred suggested I go with him to the largely lesbian and gay Good Shepherd Parish Metropolitan Community Church (GSPMCC) as another way of meeting gay men and lesbians without going to the bars.

They were having a "Spiritual Renewal" weekend, and Rev. Troy Perry had been brought in to preach.

At first, this church felt comfortably familiar, but when Troy Perry preached his sermon, I became distressed and afraid. He was from an Assemblies of God background and had a loud, energetic, Southern preaching style, the likes of which I'd never heard before. During the sermon, he told us the story of the fire in the New Orleans gay bar not quite three years before, that had killed thirty-two people, including the pastor of MCC New Orleans and a number of his congregants.

I was terrified. I was certain that someone would set fire to this church, and we would all die. Or perhaps someone would come in with a machine gun and kill us all. I wanted to run screaming from the church, but Fred kept a steady hand on me and reassured me we were safe. I wasn't so sure he was right. I was so insecure in being out to begin with that hearing the story of the New Orleans fire triggered every fear and insecurity I had about being out in this "gay" church.

Afterward, I told Fred I never wanted to go back to GSPMCC, but he told me the pastor of the church, Rev. Ken Martin, was a wonderful preacher and a warm, caring pastor. He urged me to come back with him the next week to hear him preach. I did return, and I felt immediately comfortable when Ken preached his sermon. I had found my new church home.

I loved the way they did Communion, with everyone coming forward to receive it either as an individual, as a couple, or as a group of friends. We were fed a piece of bread dipped in juice, and then the server held us in an embrace and prayed. It felt so warm, so loving, so intimate and hospitable. I'd never experienced anything quite like it. I kept coming back, week after week.

I joined the church and volunteered for the choir, and the rewards were immediate. I was warmly welcomed into the choir, with my trained baritone voice. I suddenly had a circle of gay, lesbian, and straight women friends, most of whom were in the choir. I was invited to their parties, and there I met many other members of the church in a social setting. Soon, I was singing solos, and then the whole congregation knew me.

I was still so afraid of my parents finding out I was gay I didn't attend the lesbian and gay pride parade in Chicago that year. Looking back, I now realize how silly I was. The chances of my being photographed or filmed and then being seen by my parents were slim to none. I later learned the saying, "You're not that special," but in June of 1976, my fears still dominated my decision making.

My friend Christie Hefner had just gone to work for her father at Playboy Enterprises, and one of her first projects was to open a store, Playtique, on the ground floor of the Playboy building. It featured women's clothing and record albums. She generously gave me a job selling records. It was fun working there, and I was grateful for the opportunity.

The first anniversary of my sobriety, October 17, 1976, fell on a Sunday. Rev. Ken Martin preached a sermon about the story of the woman at the well and her encounter with Jesus, from the Gospel of John. He described how this woman, rejected by her community because of her many husbands, was so amazed by her experience with Jesus that she left her heavy water pots behind, went back into her community, and shared news of meeting Jesus. She asked her neighbors, "Can this be the Christ?"

Ken suggested that we were called to leave our water pots behind: all those things that burdened us, anything that kept us from being who we were called to be. We were to re-enter our communities, share our experience of Jesus, and ask our neighbors, friends, and family, "Could this be the Christ?"

I was deeply moved. During the prayer time before Communion, I suddenly knew, with the most amazing clarity, that I was to leave behind my dreams of being an actor and become a minister with MCC. It was such a clear, powerful experience of God's call to the ministry, that I had no doubts and no qualms about pursuing it.

A week or two before this, I had heard about another friend, who had also been a theater major at Northwestern, who suddenly changed course and entered seminary to become a minister. I remembered thinking, "How sad. Something terrible must have happened to make her leave behind a career in theater to become a minister." And yet, here I was making the same decision and feeling happy and empowered in a way I had never experienced before.

Whereas my acting career had resulted in nothing but doors slamming shut, as I pursued my call to the ministry, all the doors flew open. I told Ken Martin about my call, and he said, "I've been wondering when you would realize that." I told Jim Avery, the pastor at Alice Millar Chapel, about my decision, and after a few questions, he gave me his blessing.

I told Mom and Dad about my new calling, although I left out the lesbian and gay part. I told them I was applying to McCormick Theological Seminary, and Dad told me that was where his father had received his degree to become a Presbyterian minister. It was another sign I was making the right decision. Dad advised me to apply to more than one seminary. I couldn't tell him that at that time McCormick was the only mainstream seminary that accepted lesbians and gay men.

My pastors at Alice Millar and Good Shepherd Parish wrote letters of recommendation for me, as did Christie Hefner. The director of admissions at McCormick later told me it was the only time they had ever received a letter of recommendation on Playboy stationery, from Christie Hefner no less, and everyone on the admissions committee was delighted and impressed.

I was promptly accepted to be in the class of 1979 that had begun that past fall. I started attending classes in January 1977. At first, I was overwhelmed with all the new words I was hearing: eschatology, ontology, theodicy, exegesis—it was a whole new language. My adviser told me to write down any words I didn't understand and either ask someone the definitions or look them up myself (just like in *Auntie Mame!*). My vocabulary began to grow, as did my theology.

I loved being in seminary. A few years out in the world beyond the ivy-covered walls of academia had made me a better student. I loved the stimulating discussions in and out of classes. I particularly relished the time I spent in the cafeteria with fellow students, arguing scriptures, theology, and current events. Although I was friendly with many other students in my classes, I made a lifelong friend in Donna Weddle, a career Army chaplain who ended up as the chaplain to the chairman of the Joint Chiefs of Staff.

The housing for students at McCormick Seminary was run by the Lutheran School of Theology. Unfortunately, the Lutherans would not allow "homosexuals" to live in seminary housing, so I commuted to Hyde Park from my apartment on the North Side. That was great in good weather: It was a beautiful drive down Chicago's Lake Shore Drive. However, in the winter, when my car was buried under the snow, I took the "L," transferring to a bus on the South Side. It was a long, cold commute, but it was worth it. I was fascinated with everything I was learning, and I thoroughly enjoyed my classmates and professors.

Meanwhile, my life as a gay man continued to unfold, as I continued to come out on various levels. Not only was I learning how to argue gay issues with conservative seminary students (surprisingly, the professors were more progressive than some of the students), but I was learning about gay life and politics from my friends at Good Shepherd Parish MCC and my gay AA groups.

The seventies were a great time to be gay. It was after Stonewall and before AIDS. Gay men and lesbians were coming out in huge numbers, and the party was on! Harvey Milk and many other LGBT leaders, including MCC pastors like Troy Perry and Ken Martin, inspired us to fight for our rights and fight against those, like Anita Bryant, a former beauty pageant winner and Florida orange juice spokesperson who waged a battle to take away our rights first in Dade County, Florida, and then other places where we had had equal rights granted to us.

I loved living in the "gay ghetto" of Chicago, which at the time was in New Town, the area around Belmont Avenue and Broadway. I danced at the gay discos with my church crowd, as well as with members of my recovery groups. I dined in the gay restaurants and shopped in the gay stores. Grocery shopping in "cruisy" supermarkets was always fun, although I wasn't very good at cruising. What school do you attend to learn that?

So, a big part of coming out, at least for me, was learning about gay relationships and sex. I desperately wanted a boyfriend. Guys I knew who had boyfriends told me how they met their boyfriends at a disco, bar, or bathhouse. I was not ready to venture into a bathhouse, but I cruised the discos and bars near my apartment, usually going with friends from AA or from the church. I always came home alone.

I had been out, living in the heart of the gay community, busily involved with a gay-identified church, going out to bars and discos for about nine months without ever having the sex I desperately wanted. I just couldn't figure out how to get laid. Ken Martin suggested it may have had something to do with other guys sensing how desperate I was. That frustrated me because I couldn't figure out how to turn off my desperation.

So, I was surprised that my first week in seminary, I had my first sexual experience since coming out. He was a senior who was in my preaching class. We had to introduce ourselves in the first class, and I, of course, told the class I was studying for ministry in the Metropolitan Community Churches, the "gay-identified church." He approached me after the class and invited me back to his apartment for lunch. It didn't occur to me that he wanted to have sex with me. I naively followed him, thinking we were going to have lunch.

Once we were in his apartment, he didn't have to work hard at seducing me. He was a good-looking man, a wonderful lover, and I thoroughly enjoyed this first foray into sex as an out and proud gay man. It was much different from the few drunken efforts at sex with men I'd had prior to coming out, none of which were gratifying.

Unfortunately, this man was not out and proud. He swore me to secrecy, rightly pointing out that if he came out, he would lose his seminary housing, and he would never be ordained in the Presbyterian Church. I questioned him about whether he could continue indefinitely living in the closet, unable to be himself. He said, "I have to, because I have a call."

He avoided me on campus. He didn't want to be associated with the gay student because people might think he was gay. There were others I pegged as gay who ignored me, too. I started telling my friends that you could tell who was gay by who avoided me.

At least, I had finally had sex, even if we couldn't be boyfriends. We had one more encounter, when he arrived unexpectedly at my apartment one evening. He had been drinking, but I couldn't resist his advances, even though something told me it was a mistake. Later, in an ethics class, I was astounded when he argued against the ordination of lesbians and gay men. I argued with him, of course, but somehow did not succumb to the great temptation to "out" him.

During my first spring break from seminary, I flew out to visit Mom and Dad in Eugene, Oregon, where Dad was now teaching at the University of Oregon.

Mom and Dad were eager to hear about seminary, and we quickly settled into a routine. Every morning, we watched *The Phil Donahue Show* after breakfast. One day, he had Anita Bryant as his guest to talk about her campaign to repeal the gay rights ordinance in Dade County, Florida. When she started spewing her hateful rhetoric, I couldn't help but make some angry comments, without self-identifying.

That evening, as we finished dinner, Dad made his usual appeal to me to write more often, with more than just my usual requests for money. I said, "There's so much about me you don't know, that I just can't share with you."

Dad asked, "Steve, do you think you might be a homosexual?"

I was stunned. At first, I responded with a nervous laugh, and then I said, "Yes, I'm gay." Mom started to cry. Dad reached across the table, took my hand, and said, "Steve, you're my son, and I love you. Nothing can change that. I hope now that you've told us, you'll be able to be more open with us and will write and call us more often."

Dad said Mom and they had discussed the possibility that I was gay when the pastor and a few members of the Metropolitan Community Church in Eugene came to their Presbyterian church to discuss the ordination of homosexuals, a major issue in the Presbyterian denomination at the time. I had been telling my parents that I was involved with an ecumenical church, with people from many different backgrounds. They had guessed that my church was an MCC.

Mom tearfully confessed that she had thought homosexuality died out with the ancient Greeks, until she found a letter in my nightstand drawer from my first big crush, Mike Kenna, a fellow student at Phillips Andover. He had come out in college and urged me to, as well. She had been so upset about it that she went to a psychiatrist. He told her there had been many mothers who had sat in that same chair saying the same thing. She asked him if she should confront me about it or tell me she knew, but he told her to let me tell her in my own time.

The next morning, we did what we always did when confronted with a big issue: We went to a bookstore. I suggested half a dozen books, including *Society and the Healthy Homosexual*, the landmark book by George Weinberg PhD that coined the term "homophobia"; as well as *Loving Someone Gay* by Don Clark PhD; and *Consenting Adult*, by Laura Z. Hobson, a novel about a mother coming to terms with her son being gay. They bought them all, and I took great comfort in that. Dad immediately started reading *Loving Someone Gay*, and Mom started with *Consenting Adult*.

After I returned to Chicago, Dad sent me a beautiful, handwritten letter. He always typed his weekly letters, but in this one, he wrote long-hand what he'd told me the night I came out to them. "I love you, Steve, and nothing can change that. I don't understand homosexuality, but that doesn't change the fact that I love you more deeply than ever." I felt such joy and relief.

That summer, Dad and Mom came to visit me in Chicago, and they attended MCC with me. They loved Rev. Ken Martin and told me they knew I was in good hands with him as my supervising pastor. One evening, Dad dropped Mom off at church before he found parking on the crowded Chicago streets. He told me that walking back to church, he saw a man dressed as a woman. He asked whether that was very common among gay men. I told him that a man dressing as a woman didn't mean that man was gay, and I tried to educate him about drag queens and what we then called "transsexuals," although quite honestly, I didn't know much about the issues myself.

Shortly after I came out to them, Mom and Dad shared my coming out with the whole family and many of their friends in a mimeographed letter, much like their Christmas letter. But they didn't wait for Christmas for this one. I had mixed feelings about this: anger that they took this step without consulting me, but delight that they expressed their support to all their friends and family.

Soon, I got a letter from my godfather, Lawrie Root. He was married to my mother's favorite cousin, my godmother, Lucia. He wrote that now he understood why I was always his favorite. He explained he was gay and had married Lucia in 1955 because he was an elementary school principal, and he needed a "beard." Lucia had always known he was gay, and they had a wonderful marriage. None of the family knew, and he asked me not to tell anyone out of respect for Lucia. It was a secret I kept until after they'd both died.

Before they were married, she hung out with his whole circle of gay male friends when they partied in New York, Fire Island, and Provincetown. I flashed on Mom telling us, "Lucia was always surrounded by the best-looking men." Lawrie had a lover in Washington, D.C., and he and Lucia visited him regularly. Lucia was content to sleep in the second bedroom. She was Lawrie's best friend, and she remained so for the duration of their lives together.

After he came out to me, I spent a lot of time with Lucia and Lawrie over the years. He and I had a voluminous correspondence, first by letter and then by email. I loved hearing his colorful stories about gay life in the forties and fifties. I learned so much from him about the gay community before Stonewall. He didn't really get the whole "gay pride" concept that I was into, but I always knew he was proud of me, and he loved me like the son he'd never had. I loved him as the gay father I'd never had.

He strongly suspected that I would be gay the first time he met me, when I was three. Lucia and he came to visit us right after their honeymoon. He said he was taken with me right away and sensed my future identity because of how very expressive and joyful I was for a three-year-old.

He wrote that my mother looked guilty whenever she looked at me, as if it were her fault that I was born with birth defects. Lawrie said that in his time as a school principal, every mother of a child who had had birth defects looked guilty when she looked at her child. Now, my mother felt it was her fault that I was gay, as if that were a birth defect.

Not long after I came out to Mom and Dad, my brother, Rick, came to Chicago for a conference. As I drove him up Lake Shore Drive one day, he told me I was very lucky our parents accepted me "as a homosexual," but that I should expect them to have problems with any lover I chose. "After all," he said, "everyone knows that homosexual relationships always have one member who's masculine, and one who's feminine. Obviously, Mom and Dad will have trouble accepting your effeminate lover." I laughed to myself at his stereotype of gay relationships. And to think he thought I would be the butch one! I didn't say anything. I just hoped that any future relationships I had would teach him differently.

My last year in seminary, I finally had a boyfriend. He was the pastor of the Metropolitan Community Church in Cincinnati, Ohio. We spent a lot of time on the phone between visits. It was great to have a boyfriend. I thoroughly enjoyed my time with him in Cincinnati, a city I came to love. We enjoyed traveling together, too. Once, we met Lucia and Lawrie in Washington, D.C., and it meant so much to me to "double date" with them!

Around this time, I started smoking marijuana despite continuing to attend AA meetings. At first, it was just casual use at parties. But when I was with my boyfriend in Cincinnati, I began feeling desperate for it. When he would run out of it, I pushed him to find more, which was not always easy to do. I would pout until he found some. I didn't yet see smoking marijuana as a problem, although I kept it a secret from my friends in recovery. I rationalized that if I didn't drink, getting stoned from time to time wouldn't be an issue.

As my senior year continued, I began looking for a job as a pastor. My boyfriend wanted me to move to Cincinnati to be his associate pastor. He said I would eventually become co-pastor after the congregation got to know me.

By this time, we had a new pastor at our church in Chicago, Rev. Jay Deacon. He urged me to candidate for the pulpit at the Metropolitan Community Church of Hartford, where he'd been the founding pastor. He thought it might be a perfect fit for me and for them. I applied, and they invited me to come and candidate for the pulpit. I enjoyed my two weeks in Hartford. I liked the people, and they seemed to like me, both personally and professionally.

While I was a candidate there, I attended my first funeral. My sister-in-law, Pam, had died a couple of months before from complications of injuries she'd sustained in a car crash during college. Her funeral was in Norfolk, Connecticut, in the same white-steepled church where she and Rick had been married only eight years before. My parents picked me up in Hartford, and we drove to Norfolk for the funeral.

I'd never seen Rick so emotional before. He grieved deeply, sitting in front of the coffin of his young wife, the mother of his two-year-old daughter. Dad didn't do anything to try to comfort him. So, I put my arm around Rick's shoulders. That seemed to set him off even more. All the Pieters men had difficulty with emotion, and I was not yet accustomed to taking on the role of grief counselor.

At the end of the service, when Pam's coffin was wheeled down the aisle, we sang "O God, Our Help in Ages Past." One verse hit me hard: "Time like an ever-rolling stream bears all of us away . . . ." The very concrete reality of death struck me that day as never before.

It hit me again when, the next day, Rick wanted to go to the cemetery to say one final goodbye to Pam. Mom, Dad, and I went with him. Watching him now at the fresh grave, I was moved by the depth of his grief. This was the first time I had confronted the death of a young person and the first time I had witnessed, up close, the horrible, earth-shaking grief that such a death can cause.

Mom and Dad drove me back to Hartford, and I preached for the MCC congregation that evening. The board of directors offered me the job, and so I had a decision in front of me. Was my call to be the senior pastor at our church in Hartford or to be an associate pastor at our church in Cincinnati with my boyfriend as pastor? I didn't have to think too long about it. I knew I was more in love with being in love than I was in love with him. Furthermore, I didn't think it would work very well to work for him. All the arrows pointed to Hartford, and so I accepted their call.

I was awarded my Master of Divinity degree in June 1979, and I preached my last sermon at Good Shepherd Parish Metropolitan Community Church. They gave me a tearful, warm farewell. I packed up my belongings in my Plymouth Gold Duster and drove to Hartford.

On the way to Hartford, I stopped in Bloomsburg, Pennsylvania, to see Alvina Krause, my last acting teacher. Lucy, her housemate, answered the door and told me I could find her in her rose garden. Miss Krause looked up as she heard me approach. I told her that I had changed course and decided to become a minister with the largely lesbian and gay Metropolitan Community Churches, and I was on my way to take my first pulpit in Hartford. She looked deeply into my eyes, smiled, and said, "You were always different from the others." She wished me well, and I left feeling deeply gratified she'd given me her blessing.

Chapter Two

But Do I Have AIDS?

I ARRIVED IN HARTFORD AS THE NEW FULL-TIME PASTOR OF THE MET-
ropolitan Community Church of Hartford, ready to change the world.
It was June 1979, and I was twenty-seven years old. I had come out less
than a year before starting seminary, so I didn't have much experience
as a gay activist when I arrived in Hartford. Now, as the pastor of the
Metropolitan Community Church there, I was one of the only publicly
gay leaders.

On one of my first Sundays as pastor, I led the contingent from my
church to the New York City Lesbian and Gay Pride Parade. We gathered with the other Metropolitan Community Churches near Washington Square. It was the tenth anniversary of the Stonewall Uprising, and
it was a huge event, unlike any other I'd ever attended. The *New York
Times* estimated the crowd size between fifty thousand and one hundred
thousand.

At one point as we marched up Fifth Avenue, we reached the top of
a hill near the Empire State Building. Someone told me to turn around
and look behind me. Tens of thousands of lesbians and gay men and their
supporters filled the broad avenue behind us all the way to Washington
Square. The sight brought tears of joy to my eyes. Through much of my
childhood and adolescence, I had thought I was the only homosexual in
the world. Now, in this moment, I finally knew deep in my soul what
gay pride really meant. I was so proud to be a part of this huge wave of
lesbians and gay men celebrating our freedom. Proud that after Harvey
Milk had been assassinated the previous November, we were living out

his legacy of being out and proud. I felt taller and stronger than I'd ever been before.

I was formally installed as pastor in October. Rev. Ken Martin, my first MCC pastor and my mentor, flew in from Chicago. It was wonderful to have him preach an inspiring sermon at my installation service. In the sermon, he warned me about becoming a star. I didn't think there was much danger of that in Hartford, but I understood it as a call to humility.

That first year in Hartford, I worked out of my apartment. When I wanted to take time off at home, I was in my workplace. The church phone as well as the Gay Switchboard for the capitol region were in my living room. So, if the phone rang, or if there was a knock on my door, then suddenly I was back at work. I was never sure if I was on duty or off. My marijuana habit did not help. I was free to smoke grass any time I liked, and that led to some stoned conversations with parishioners or on the Gay Switchboard.

I knew being the pastor of a primarily LGBT congregation would be challenging, but it was a lot harder than I'd expected. The first year I was there, there were three suicides in the congregation of forty-five. Two of them were middle-aged men: one whose lover had died and the second a victim of his own internalized homophobia.

The third was a young man about twenty years old, whose parents had institutionalized him a couple of times to change him into a heterosexual. His father was a strict military man, and this was his only son. He called me to check out what kind of church his son was going to. It was an awkward conversation, but when he asked, I was honest with him about it being a church where lesbians and gay men were welcome. Not long after, he told his son that he was going to put him in the psych ward again, "to straighten him out." That night, his son wrote letters to his parents and to me, went into their garage, and turned on the car. He was dead by morning.

In April 1980, Fidel Castro decided to deport people from Cuba whom he considered "undesirable," including many homosexuals. The Metropolitan Community Churches got involved right away. Troy Perry sent out word that we needed to raise a lot of money fast, to help settle some of the more than one hundred thousand refugees on the "Mariel boat-lift."

I appealed to my congregation that Sunday, made a few phone calls, and managed to raise a large amount of money, which I sent right off to denominational headquarters in Los Angeles. Troy Perry sent out a letter to all the churches, using my fundraising as a model for what he expected of other churches.

The next week, I had a visit from the director of the federal immigration authority in Hartford. First, he grilled me to confirm I was legitimate. Then, he asked me for assistance in dealing with all these gay Cuban immigrants they were sending to the Hartford area. I agreed, and we helped settle them. Many of these gay men had spent years imprisoned by Castro simply for being gay. They were ecstatic to be free, but some ended up in trouble with the law in this country, mostly for drug offenses.

As the publicly gay pastor in town, I did a lot of interviews throughout my years in Hartford, both for print and television. Each time, I received hate mail from individuals as well as conservative religious groups. Envelopes filled with photos of aborted fetuses and drawings of souls burning in hell arrived in the church mail. The hate mail scared me. I worried for my safety and my life. I prayed for protection and courage and found some comfort and peace.

When a local gay man was brutally murdered in his apartment, I went to the police, dressed in my collar, to offer my help with the investigation. The police showed me gruesome photographs of the crime scene and questioned me about what I observed. "Were there any gay fetishes that would account for the way he was mutilated?"

I was horrified, but I said, "The only thing that I can see is a horrible attack on a gay man by someone who had probably become enraged when the victim came on to him."

This was not the only homophobic violence I witnessed in Hartford. A sweet, middle-aged man in my parish was beaten to a pulp by someone he'd brought home. He was lucky to survive. He told the police, and me, that he had met an attractive man in a park and invited him back to his home. He thought they would have a sexual encounter. But when my parishioner suggested it, this thug not only beat him but robbed him of his money and jewelry as well.

When I went to see him in the hospital, his whole head was purple and swollen beyond recognition. I could barely see my friend in there, but when he spoke, and when I looked in his eyes, it was clearly him. I paid close attention to him as he began his slow recovery.

There were many gay men in the Hartford area who lived secretive lives, informed mostly by fear and shame. It was said that any lesbians or gay men who grew up in the Hartford area with any amount of LGBT pride soon left for New York, Boston, or some other major city. I thought that was unfair to some of the LGBT folks who stayed in Hartford and fought the good fight. Also, there were out and proud LGBT people who moved to the Hartford area because of a job. Still, there were a lot of LGBT folks there who had mental health issues due to their internalized homophobia.

Another murder of a gay man, in which the victim was found strangled and stabbed on the banks of the Connecticut River, went unsolved for a time, and the police questioned me again, this time wondering whether this could have been inspired by the Al Pacino movie *Cruising*.

There were things I enjoyed about being the pastor of MCC Hartford. Thanks to my predecessor, Jay Deacon, I inherited a seat on the boards of the Capitol Region Conference of Churches, Center City Churches, and the Sexual Minorities Task Force. So I was constantly attending meetings of one sort or another. My colleagues offered welcome support and understanding.

I particularly enjoyed doing pastoral care and counseling. I liked the way people shared their lives with me. I heard so many different stories of growing up lesbian, gay, and transgender. I always seemed to learn something, and hopefully, I was able to give hope, inspiration, or comfort to those who turned to me.

My friends in and out of the church kept me going through all this mayhem. Soon after my arrival in Hartford, I found a best friend in John Andy, the manager of the Club Baths in East Hartford. Some of my parishioners were scandalized that their pastor hung out with the manager of the only gay sex club in the area, but one member of the church reminded them that Jesus hung out with Mary Magdalene, and that made John's and my friendship okay. John and I loved to play backgammon and listen to music. He introduced me to cocaine as well as Quaaludes, and we would stay up all night smoking grass, doing lines of cocaine, and swallowing chips of Quaaludes as we played endless games of backgammon. I felt guilty about my drug use, but not guilty enough to stop. John also took me out dancing every weekend. He drove like a demon as he introduced me to gay nightlife from New York City to Boston. I was heartbroken when he decided to move back to Miami, where he had lived most of his life.

Another friend, Sally, was with me when my cat, Lance, died of feline leukemia on my kitchen floor. She found my next kitten, Preshy, by rescuing a mother cat and her whole litter. I picked Preshy out when she was just a few weeks old, and Sally trained her to be a lap cat before she came to live with me.

Sally and I became so close that it became an issue for some. They felt she had too much influence on me. There were times I felt they were right, and so I tried to back off and not be as available to her, but I enjoyed her company. There wasn't anything I couldn't tell her. We were also quite codependent. She made sure that I always had plenty of marijuana and cigarettes. She shielded me from some of my worst critics and fought a few fights for me that I was only peripherally aware of.

Then there was Adam, who served for a long time as the church treasurer. He made sure I was paid, even when we didn't collect enough in the Sunday offering. There were a few wealthy members of the church, and Adam wasn't afraid to ask them to write a check to cover my salary. Unfortunately, he went to the well a few too many times, and in my third year there, the church had to stop paying me. So I got a job at a new gay disco, the Lost and Found, where I worked as a doorman. It bothered a few members of my church that I was doing this, but I told them I had to find a second job because they weren't paying me anymore, and this job worked with my schedule as their pastor. If they were able to start paying me again, I would gladly quit this job. That silenced the objections, at least to my face.

After a couple of years of holding our services at the Unitarian Church, Center City Churches offered us the chance to rent the large chapel in St. Elizabeth's, their newly acquired building near downtown Hartford. It had been a convent, but Center City Churches made it a ministry center to serve the homeless.

There was plenty of parking, I could have my office there, and we would have our own space to hold meetings and worship services. So, I took board members on a tour of the facility. The chapel was painted lavender, which we saw as a sign that it was meant for us. The board approved the move, and that was where we gathered for the last year I was in Hartford.

There were some who felt that the folks who were comfortable attending MCC at the Unitarian Church in a well-to-do neighborhood would never come to church in the "inner city." They felt it was dangerous, not just due to the "inner city" neighborhood, but because of the homeless shelter and food bank in the same facility. Nonetheless, most, if not all, of the current regulars continued to attend.

In the fall of 1981, I enrolled in the Clinical Pastoral Education program at Hartford Hospital. This was a formal program to train people as hospital chaplains. Hospital chaplaincy was not something I was particularly interested in, but colleagues had been encouraging me to do it, so I signed up.

It turned out to be a great decision. The training not only helped me professionally, by learning to minister to hospital patients, but it also helped me personally because the training involved a deep look into our own souls.

Right away, I made a couple of good friends whom I loved seeing every time our class met. We ended up hanging out together a lot. A few of the other students were not as friendly. They disapproved of my lifestyle and my theology, and they didn't think I could be a real Christian as a gay man. One accused me of "playing church with other homosexuals," trying to compensate for our "deeply sinful lifestyle." At first, I thought I might be able to soften them up and even change their minds, but that was not to be. Nonetheless, I was grateful to learn a lot about discussing LGBT issues with homophobic clergy.

I learned a lot from listening to my patients. One patient told me about dying and being brought back to life. When she talked about the other side, it was so real that it seemed as if she was describing her living room. The steadiness of her eyes, the peace she exuded, and the compassion she had for others enthralled me. It was as if she understood something I couldn't yet grasp.

The entire time I was in this program, I continued all my duties as pastor, including my interfaith work where I occasionally met closeted gay clergy. At least a couple of them were in a closet with a window: They never self-identified, nor, God forbid, were they activists in any outward sense, but they would quietly support my work at the Metropolitan Community Church and sometimes even voice support for lesbian and gay rights from their pulpits. I was only invited to preach in one other church. It was an Episcopal parish whose rector eventually came out when he moved to a Los Angeles church.

A Roman Catholic priest reached out to me and confided he was gay. He invited me to a party one Friday evening and told me it would be filled with gay priests like him. He said that a group of priests from all over Connecticut and western Massachusetts rented this big house in Hartford so they could have somewhere to party on Friday evenings. Of course, I was intrigued, so I went with him.

It was wild. All kinds of drinks and recreational drugs were available, and there was sex going on all over the house. I saw one priest whom I had debated on TV about gay rights. On TV he was antigay. Nevertheless, here he was having his way with some other man. There were several priests there I knew, but I hadn't known they were gay, although I had my suspicions. There they were, flirting outrageously with other men and then following through within the confines of that house.

When I asked one man about his vow of celibacy, he told me, "Celibacy doesn't mean no sex. It means no committed relationships." Oh.

A couple of months into 1982, I noticed a light green, cracked coating on my tongue. It struck terror in my heart. A few months before, I had read about this new deadly disease that was attacking previously healthy gay men. I had a flash of fear that I had contracted this fatal disease, which at the time was called GRID: Gay-Related Immune

Deficiency. I quickly banished the thought. I did see a doctor, who said the coating on my tongue was thrush, or candidiasis. He said it meant I had "some kind of virus on board," and the stress I was under was exacerbating the condition. He gave me something to swish in my mouth and told me not to worry.

Shortly after discovering the thrush in my mouth, I attended a clergy retreat. The retreat facilitator gave us a stress test that listed fifty events that could cause stress. We were to check all the ones that we had experienced in the past year. Each event carried a point value, and the more stressful the event was considered, the higher the point value. Most of the other pastors had thirty-five to fifty points. I had more than one hundred. There it was in black and white: I was stressed way beyond tolerable levels. I began to think seriously about resigning as pastor of my church.

Here was proof that being a pastor in the Metropolitan Community Churches was more stressful than being a pastor in a mainstream denomination. Our pastors were shepherding flocks of people, like ourselves, who suffered from the psychological damage of internalized homophobia. This often resulted in low self-esteem and self-destructive behaviors.

I knew there was a disproportionate incidence of addiction issues among LGBT people. I had personal experience with that. I had recognized my alcoholism eighteen months after graduating from college. I was sober and clean for four years, but when I got to Hartford, I stopped seeking support for my sobriety. I wanted to smoke marijuana, and I thought if I didn't drink, marijuana wouldn't hurt me.

Soon I was smoking a lot of marijuana and cigarettes and occasionally bingeing on cocaine and Quaaludes. Drugs seemed to help for a while, but I knew they were becoming a problem. I began considering a geographic solution.

I decided to fly out to Los Angeles and visit Ken Martin, his partner, Tom, and all the other folks I knew in Los Angeles. I had a great time. I had always loved Southern California and dreamed of living there. Ken was now the pastor of the Metropolitan Community Church in North Hollywood, and hearing him preach and lead worship again felt as if I were swimming in a warm, comfortable pool of love.

A new friend told me about Body Builders Gym, an all-gay male gym, within walking distance of Ken and Tom's. Working out was an important part of my self-care. I'd always been attracted to muscular men, and shortly after I came out in 1975, I read that you should work at becoming the kind of man you'd like to find as a life partner. So I set to work on sculpting my body. It did a great deal to improve my self-confidence.

Body Builders Gym didn't have any real bodybuilders, but it was a friendly neighborhood gym in Silverlake, Los Angeles's "other gay ghetto." Its membership was almost all gay men. From the moment I walked in, I loved the wall-to-wall mirrors where all these very good-looking men were watching themselves and each other work out in skimpy shorts and tank tops. I reveled in the gay male sexual energy of it all.

There was nothing like this gym back in Hartford. The whole gay scene in Los Angeles was something I yearned to be a part of. The sunshine and warm weather of Southern California didn't hurt either.

Back in Hartford, things did not go well. I was fatigued almost all the time. My motivation for doing the job had decreased considerably, and I began to think more and more about resigning and moving to Los Angeles.

I had little preparation when John Andy called from Miami to tell me his former apartment mate, Bill, was admitted to Hartford Hospital with what was suspected to be tertiary syphilis. John told me Bill was gravely ill and might even die from this. "Really?" I thought. "How could that be?" I'd never heard of anyone having tertiary syphilis. And why would he die from it? Couldn't that be treated?

Bill was a healthy gay man in his twenties who, like me, took great care of himself. He was a flight attendant, a fun-loving guy, handsome and self-assured. He might party occasionally, but he didn't indulge in alcohol, cigarettes, or drugs the way John and I had. It seemed so strange that Bill, of all people, got so sick and so quickly.

When I visited him at Hartford Hospital, he was in bright spirits. He downplayed the seriousness of his condition, but it scared me to see him so thin.

Bill died later that summer, reportedly from pneumonia, not syphilis. I didn't hear about his death until weeks later. I felt guilty that I hadn't paid closer attention to him. After all, I had finished my training to be a chaplain at the very hospital where Bill spent his last months. I felt I should have visited him more often, and I should have been there when he died. At least I prayed with Bill when I visited him there in the spring. I prayed for his healing. I wanted God to make him all better. But he died.

I was a pastor, but at twenty-nine, I remained a distant bystander to death. I had not had any experience of officiating at funerals. I had only been to that one funeral in my life. The people who attended the Metropolitan Community Church of Hartford were all young and healthy, as was largely true throughout the denomination, so death and dying, memorials and funerals were not common for many of our clergy.

Of course, there were those three suicides my first year in Hartford, but I did not perform their funerals since their families called on their own pastors.

As the spring and summer went on, I found myself getting more and more fatigued and depressed. After graduating Clinical Pastoral Education, I wasn't quite as busy, and I found myself napping every day. I couldn't focus on my work and struggled to get things done. I was clearly burning out working two jobs.

Doing drugs was not helping either. I was smoking more and more marijuana and occasionally indulging in heavy cocaine binges. The next morning, I would crash, unable to stop sobbing. I had lost touch with any joy I might have had. I treated my depression with more marijuana, but I was still careful not to drink alcohol.

More and more, I felt I wasn't very good at being a pastor, that I was in the wrong job, in the wrong place, and I began to regret my decision in 1976 to abandon an acting career to pursue my call to the ministry.

As if I didn't have enough else to do, I had taken on the job of the Metropolitan Community Churches Northeast District Co-Coordinator, along with my friend, Rev. Shelley Hamilton. One of my tasks was to mediate between church boards and their pastors when conflicts arose. One Sunday morning, I drove a couple of hours to attend that kind of mediation. I managed to help them resolve it, but it was a gut-wrenching meeting.

As was my habit after a stressful event like that, I lit up a joint as I drove back to Hartford. I thought I would get stoned, then take a nap back home before going to lead worship that evening. Unfortunately, I couldn't sleep when I lay down for my nap. When it came time for worship, everything went fine until I got up to preach. I was still stoned, and I just couldn't seem to speak clearly or even make sense of the notes I preached from. And so, finally admitting I was burned out, I quit my job as pastor of the Metropolitan Community Church of Hartford.

My final service in August 1982 was well attended. My parents came from Providence. Some former regulars also came to the service. In my more paranoid moments, I thought the former members came to make sure that I was really going to leave.

My final sermon was defensive. I threw blame for my departure in many directions and took very little responsibility myself for the downturn the church had taken, particularly in the last year. As in my first sermon as their pastor, I talked about the priesthood of all believers, hoping they would step up and make sure the congregation survived.

I packed up my car and my cats, who were lovingly cared for during my many absences, and drove away from Hartford in a defiant cloud of marijuana, cocaine, and cigarettes. I was glad to see Hartford disappear in my rearview mirror, although I would miss my friends there.

My first stop was with my cousins, Lucia and Lawrie, in Rochester, New York. It was always good to be with them, and now it was particularly wonderful, although I'm sure they could tell I was in an altered state from all that marijuana and cocaine I'd done on the way there. I stayed with them a couple of nights and reveled in their loving kindness.

We were in the kitchen the second evening, as we prepared dinner together. I've never been very good around the kitchen, so they assigned me simple tasks. Lucia asked me to open the little baggie of shredded parmesan we would be using later. I struggled with the little black tape around the top of the baggie. I just could not undo it. Grabbing a pair of scissors, Lucia snipped off the top of the baggie and muttered, "Life is too short."

When I arrived in Los Angeles, my friend, Rev. Lucia Chappelle, told me the cottage across from hers was available for rent. I moved in right away, without realizing that the main railroad tracks from downtown LA were right across the street. When trains went by, the whole house shook. Somehow I got used to it. It didn't hurt that I was smoking a lot of marijuana.

Soon after I arrived, I got sick. I went to see Dr. Joel Weisman, a doctor with a large gay practice. He was one of the first to recognize a new disease among gay men. After a battery of blood tests, he told me I had Gay-Related Immune Deficiency, or GRID.

I drove to the Metropolitan Community Church in the Valley where my mentor, Ken Martin, was the pastor. I told him my news and casually threw my keys up in the air as if that could somehow express my anguish.

There was nothing I could do but continue with my daily life, serving as an associate pastor, and teaching at Samaritan College.

On Valentine's Day 1983, I was teaching the Psalms at Samaritan, when I started to feel feverish. I broke out in a sweat in front of the class, but laughed it off, not wanting to alarm my students. I don't know how I drove home, feeling as awful as I did, but when I got home, I somehow knew that I wouldn't be going anywhere but the doctor's office for a good, long time.

I was jaundiced, and Dr. Weisman diagnosed me with active hepatitis and pneumonia and told me I had been exposed at some time to mononucleosis and cytomegalovirus. The term GRID was no longer being used. There was a new name, acquired immuno-deficiency syndrome (AIDS), but you had to have one of these specific conditions to be diagnosed with AIDS:

- Opportunistic infection
- Malignancy (Kaposi's sarcoma, high grade B cell lymphoma, or cervical cancer)
- Wasting syndrome
- AIDS dementia syndrome

As time went on, the following were added to the list:

- Recurrent bacterial pneumonia
- Tuberculosis
- Immunologic AIDS where the CD4 (T-helper cells) count was under 200/dl

I hadn't been diagnosed with any of them, so my diagnosis was AIDS-related complex. Sometimes it was called pre-AIDS. No matter what you called it, I was sicker than I'd ever been. Because my immune system was still severely deficient, he suggested I do everything I could to prevent any further infections, including pouring boiling water over all my dishes after washing them.

In addition to hepatitis and pneumonia, I started having terrible genital herpes attacks. Each attack lasted about ten days. Then I would get a day or two off, before another attack happened. These herpes attacks were among the most painful things I'd ever experienced. There was a topical treatment, but I found it did not help much. All I could do was suffer through the excruciating sores on my penis. They would not stop itching.

I was so sick, all I wanted to do was get out of my body. I couldn't help but wonder when I would be diagnosed with AIDS. There was no test for HIV antibodies then. They hadn't even discovered the virus. The doctors knew so little. All I knew was that I was sicker than I'd ever been. There seemed to be no escape except the final death sentence of full-blown AIDS. I fell into a deep depression.

I found that some people didn't believe I was sick at all. I heard later that some of the denomination's leadership thought I was "faking it" to get attention, as the latest member of the clergy to land in Los Angeles. None of those who thought I was pretending ever came to see me or call me during this period. If they had, they would have seen how sick I was. It left me feeling angry, bitter, and abandoned once again.

I was too sick to go to church, but I missed the community. I missed taking Communion, a tangible sign of being included in the community. So, I began looking for someone at my church to bring me Communion at home. Communion would be a great comfort, but it took three months to find someone who would bring it to me. There was such fear about how AIDS might be transmitted.

Finally, a deacon from my church agreed to bring me Communion. Jeri was a wonderful person, with a warm, compassionate heart. She came to my little cottage and carried her traveling Communion kit into my living room. She consecrated the elements, but she insisted that I serve myself. It was clear she was afraid of putting the wafer on my tongue. Without touching me, she prayed with me and for me. I deeply appreciated her courage in coming into my house when she was so obviously frightened.

I was grateful for my women friends. They were the first to step up and take care of me. If it hadn't been for my neighbor Lucia, I don't know what I would have done. She enlisted other women who would visit me regularly. We would get stoned, laugh, and talk about everything and anything.

They told me the body has its rhythms, and they helped me become aware of mine. They taught me to ride the waves of illness, knowing the waves would crest and fall and finally wash up on the shore of health. Or so we all hoped.

Lucia brought me groceries and kept me company almost every day. She spent countless hours with me watching TV. We loved watching televangelists Jan and Paul Crouch and Jim and Tammy Faye Bakker. We watched them because they made us laugh hysterically. We had a great time watching movies, recorded off the Z channel with my new "toy," a videocassette recorder.

Lucia and the other women couldn't keep me company all the time, and as I settled into my shut-in existence, I developed a ritual of TV shows, including *The Today Show*, *The Waltons*, now in syndication, and, of course, *I Love Lucy*. The people on these shows became dependable companions in my daily life. Jane Pauley, John-Boy Walton, and—God knows—Lucille Ball were special to me.

Most of the time during those months, I suffered through my illnesses. My whole body ached, I ran fevers all the time, and when I wasn't burning up and sweating, I had horrible chills. My coughing seemed to be incessant. Food tasted awful, I had no energy, sleep was fitful at best, and when I did sleep, I was plagued with nightmares. Then, of course, there were the near constant herpes attacks. I lost a lot of weight, and I didn't have a lot of weight to lose, so I looked gaunt. I tried to "ride the waves," but sometimes I just got depressed.

Then, one day, as I crawled from my bed to the bathroom, feeling as sick as I'd ever been, I had a clear and transcendent moment. I became certain that I would be healthy again one day, and my current suffering would help others. It was as unmistakable as my call to the ministry had been in 1976. I felt as if God were telling me to take notes, because this agonizing experience would be the basis of a whole new ministry. Somehow, this relieved me and gave me hope. I felt a new sense of purpose, although I continued to be ill for several years.

At one point, I developed large red spots in the middle of my palms, with matching red spots in the center of each foot. I kidded with Lucia about these being stigmata, but I felt kind of spooked about them, too. Was I being warned about an impending prognosis of terminal cancer or AIDS? Was this another sign that I had a calling beyond GRID or AIDS? Or were they just red spots?

Lucia knew I missed seeing other gay men, so she introduced me to Garry Lane, one of the best-looking gay men I'd ever met. He was as sweet and caring as he was handsome. I later learned he was the tall, good-looking Montana cowboy who had been Troy Perry's first love. Troy was the future founder of the Metropolitan Community Churches, the denomination I served. When Garry told him he wanted to leave, Troy was so overwhelmed with grief that he tried to commit suicide. Fortunately their roommate, Willie, saved his life. Soon thereafter, Troy held the first service of the first Metropolitan Community Church. Now I saw Garry as a true angel of mercy. He drove me over to his beautiful house occasionally, and in his presence, I felt the spiritual healing of good gay energy.

While I was grateful for these friendships, I missed having a boyfriend. Before I was sick, my hair stylist, Dan, seemed interested in me. During one haircut, he told me he was a bodybuilder. I was into the gym scene, but I couldn't believe he was a bodybuilder, because he was so overweight. But he was sweet.

I didn't see him for a few months when I was housebound. When I finally felt a little better, I called him for a haircut and explained my situation. He told me he'd been going to the gym and had gotten back in shape. I invited him over, and much to my surprise, he accepted. I was thrilled when he appeared at my door looking incredibly hot, and we proceeded to have the first of many good, safe times together. We limited ourselves to mutual masturbation, enhanced by some creative role-playing.

My dates with Dan were an affirmation that I was still able to be sexual, albeit from a distance. We dated off and on for over a year, and these times filled a great emptiness that for a while I thought would never be satisfied again. I was only thirty years old, and even though I was ill, I still wanted to be sexual.

By mid-May, I was feeling better. I asked Dr. Weisman if I could start back to the gym. He said, "Yes, but take it very slow and easy, and don't try to lift the kinds of weights you once did."

I headed back to Body Builders Gym. I was surprised at how tired I was after only a light workout, but I was so happy to be back in this gay gym environment. To see these gay men working on their bodies felt incredibly good. I had spent so many years in the closet, feeling ashamed of my attraction to muscular men. Now, I was free to enjoy it, and I did.

After that first workout, I started into the gym shower. With my right foot, I stepped into a pool of murky, standing water about two inches deep. Obviously, there was something wrong with the drainage. I backed out, washed off in the other shower, and then headed home.

The next morning, the bottom of my right foot itched horribly. Soon, huge blisters bubbled up all over the bottom of my foot. For the next nine months, these blisters grew until they popped, spraying fluid everywhere. I couldn't wear a shoe on that foot since the blisters were so large and painful.

Dr. Weisman sent me to a dermatologist, the first of five or six I saw about my foot. One told me it was a fungal infection he had seen only once before, when he was serving as a medic in the South Pacific during

World War II. He told me it was caused by walking barefoot in sheep dung, something I had never done. I was sure the murky water in the gym shower was to blame.

Each dermatologist offered a different treatment, and nothing worked. One recommended that I soak my foot in ice for fifteen minutes, five times a day. At first, Lucia would literally have to hold my hands to keep my foot in the ice. I couldn't stand the pain, but I gradually got used to it since I knew the ice would numb the painful blisters after five minutes. Despite doing this for months, it didn't stop the blisters.

The fungal infection on my foot took a heavy toll on my general health. I was sick again by the time I drove to Sun City, Arizona, to spend Christmas 1983 with my parents. I had lost a lot of weight, and I became exhausted with the least bit of exertion. The blisters continued to bubble and pop. My foot looked like it was beginning to rot with painful, secondary infections. I felt depressed and resigned to my fate. I could see my parents' anguish.

Mom and Dad gave me crutches for Christmas. I needed them, but it felt like a slap in the face. I knew my parents felt helpless and afraid, and this was their effort to do something to help. We saw news reports about this fatal disease among gay men. I was terrified this rare fungal infection on my foot would lead to a diagnosis of Kaposi's sarcoma and full-blown AIDS. The fear centered in my gut, and I could not let it go.

I drove home to Los Angeles a few days after Christmas, with my new crutches leaning up against the passenger seat. I felt faint and weak most of the drive, but I smoked a couple joints along the way, and somehow, I got back to my cottage.

The six-hour drive depleted me of all vitality. I tried watching TV, but I had no energy even for that, and I was in too much pain to sleep. It seemed my disease was giving my soul an eviction notice. As the night wore on, I felt my soul detaching from my body. My essence hovered above my body, flirting with death and the afterlife.

I fell asleep. When I woke up, I had enough energy to get breakfast. With the new day, it felt good to be back in my cottage across from the railroad tracks, with Lucia right next door.

I stayed stoned all the time. Marijuana comforted me, and it certainly helped me bear all the painful suffering of this "pre-AIDS" period of severe illnesses. It kept me mellow, and it kept me eating, although there were times when even marijuana couldn't make me hungry.

For New Year's Eve, I dropped acid with a friend. We watched movies all night long. The next morning, I crashed. Everything looked hopeless. I felt a deep, aching loneliness that seemed as incurable as my constant illnesses. I wanted to cry, but I just couldn't. I grieved my lost future. I tried smoking a joint, but it did nothing to pull me out of my despair.

I felt guilty about my drug use. I knew it couldn't be helping my pre-AIDS condition, and I knew I was addicted to altering my mood. Nevertheless, I wanted to be at peace and happy again, or even just content, and I kept trying to achieve that through drugs.

Later in January, a friend of my parents suggested I see his dermatologist for my foot. This doctor had me soak my foot in a potassium solution, and it worked. After nine months of those painful blisters, they finally cleared up. All that was left were some purple scars. I was deeply relieved and grateful. I could hardly contain my joy.

When I saw Dr. Weisman again, he was also delighted the blisters had cleared up. As I stood to leave the exam room, he put his hand on the back of my neck. Thinking he was being affectionate, I put my arm around his waist. He said, "No, I'm feeling your lymph glands. They're badly swollen." He then told me he had to refer me to Los Angeles County–University of Southern California (LAC–USC) Medical Center, the hospital of last resort for those without health insurance, The church in Hartford had stopped paying my health insurance not long after I resigned, and Dr. Weisman had only been charging me for my lab tests.

There was no AIDS clinic at LAC–USC at that time. I was seen in the Pediatric building at the Contagious Disease clinic. When I showed up for my appointment on a warm day in February, I was told to wait on a wooden bench in the corridor outside the clinic. Also waiting were two extremely thin men with blankets around their shoulders and over their hair. They clutched at them, as if they were suffering from chills. Their faces were partly covered with what looked like white warts. I guessed these were men with AIDS, and I wondered if I was looking at my future. I was terrified.

In a large exam room, I changed into a hospital gown. Dr. Alexandra Levine entered and introduced herself. I was struck by her youthful beauty and her charm. She did a physical exam, particularly focusing on my swollen lymph glands, as well as inspecting the sole of my right foot with its purple scars.

She sat down on the side of my bed, rubbed my shoulder with the back of her fingers, and smiled as she started to talk to me. I could feel how much she cared. She eventually said, "I'm not really sure what's going on here, so we'll need to get a biopsy to figure it out." I knew I had found the right doctor. She was intelligent, friendly, and caring, and I knew I could trust her.

I asked her if all this was happening because I was smoking so much marijuana. To my surprise, she laughed and said, "Absolutely not!" She had a reassuring, bright spirit about her. I left feeling hopeful. It had been months since I'd felt that way.

After thinking about it, I told her I wanted to wait for the biopsy until after the denominational Clergy Conference in early March. Despite that burst of hope on first meeting her, I feared the final AIDS diagnosis was around the corner. I didn't want to go there. Not yet.

The Clergy Conference was held at the Metropolitan Community Church of Kansas City. It was good to see so many great friends there. I was quite open about my upcoming biopsy but played it light. I didn't want my colleagues' fears to drag me down. Nevertheless, I allowed one of our charismatic preachers to lay hands on me. Some of the other clergy joined him. I was embarrassed, since we were in the church social hall with many other clergy, and laying on hands was not part of my background. But it did feel good to have my colleagues lovingly lay hands on me and pray for the best possible outcome, especially after the way some of the leadership in Los Angeles had insisted I was making it all up.

At the Friday night worship service, Rev. Karen Ziegler, the pastor of our church in New York, consecrated Communion. She dedicated it to Rev. Michael Collins, who, she said, was dying from AIDS/Kaposi's sarcoma. I was stunned. At that moment, I intuitively knew I had AIDS, because I had had my first anal sex with Michael, and I had bled, leaving me vulnerable to the virus that caused AIDS.

During my first fall in Hartford, I had met Michael in New York City at an LGBT Seminarians Conference. He was the keynote speaker, a Methodist minister who had dared to come out. He gave a great speech, and I went up to speak with him afterward. I thought he was sexy, and he liked me, too. We arranged to meet for dinner near his home in Chelsea.

After dinner Michael showed me the village. We walked to the docks, where we stopped and kissed. He explained how exciting it was for him to be a "sexual outlaw," having sex with three or four men a night, almost every night. All he had to do was walk around his neighborhood to connect with countless men. Now he wanted to connect with me. We headed back to his place and had sex.

That all flashed through my mind at the Clergy Conference, and I knew. The certain death sentence hit me like a body blow. I became over-whelmed with paralyzing fear and deep grief, for Michael, and for myself.

I needed some comic relief, even if I had to provide it myself. At the worship service the next morning, I sang my new lyrics to the show tune, "Everything's Up to Date in Kansas City." Everybody laughed as I sang a recap of the whole conference, including a satire of the alphabet soup of all the denominational structures and committees.

Everyone stood up and cheered. As we said goodbye at the end of the conference, one of my colleagues told me he suspected that I would soon be the first member of the MCC clergy to be diagnosed with AIDS. I had a terrible fear he was right.

When I returned from Kansas City, I decided to go ahead with the lymph gland biopsy. I wanted to know, once and for all, if the past two years were the precursor to a full-blown AIDS diagnosis.

At the conference, I had talked with Rev. Nancy Radclyffe, who was just starting her ministry as chaplain to our denomination's clergy. Nancy was aware, because of her own crises, that there were no resources for our clergy going through tough times. So, she started a ministry focused on that.

By this time, I had learned that it was important to have someone with me at medical appointments, both to make sure I had a second set of ears to listen to the doctors and to provide comfort if I needed it. So, when Nancy offered to take me to my medical appointments, I eagerly took her up on it. In late March, she took me to the hospital for my biopsy, an outpatient procedure.

She dropped me off at the surgical ward where I got into a hospital gown and lay on a gurney. An orderly wheeled me into a corridor outside the operating room. The head nurse for people with AIDS, Scott, started an IV, and to soothe my frayed nerves, he gave me a good dose of valium through the IV. It did the trick, and I enjoyed counting the dots in the ceiling.

I waited and waited. I was learning why we were called "patients." I waited for so long, I fell fast asleep. When I awoke, it felt like the valium had left my system. I was neither stoned nor calm anymore. I was nervous and scared.

The surgeon was to remove one of the swollen lymph glands from my neck, and one from my left armpit. Having someone slice open my neck made me nervous, never mind how worried I was about the results of the biopsy. I continued to wait. Someone told me the surgical team had now gone to lunch. Eventually, an orderly wheeled me into the operating room and helped me squirm off the gurney and onto the operating table.

Another long wait.

Finally, the surgical team came back and prepped me. They put big bandages over my eyes and strapped my head down on its right side. When I asked for more valium, the anesthesiologist said I couldn't possibly have come out of the previous dose. I knew I had. I needed something more to relieve the panic I was feeling.

They numbed the area, but I certainly wasn't asleep when the surgeon cut into my neck. He started pulling on my lymph gland and cutting it to get it out. I wasn't in any pain, but I wanted to yell at him that I could feel and hear everything he was doing. It was freaking me out, but I didn't dare speak or move because I was so scared the surgeon would cut something he shouldn't.

Finally he was done, and I was wheeled into recovery. After a couple of hours, I was ready to go home. I had a large bandage over the wound in my neck and one in my armpit. Nancy was waiting for me outside the surgical ward, and she got me home, where I took a long nap.

A week later, I went back to the outpatient clinic at County Hospital for an appointment with the surgeon. Nancy wasn't available. This time, a friend from church, Lennie, accompanied me. His lover, Robert, was the friend who introduced me to Body Builders Gym. I paid the modest flat fee for my outpatient visit, based on my ability to pay, and then went upstairs to the clinic.

After waiting more than three hours on a long, wooden bench in a windowless corridor, I was finally called in to see the surgeon. He took a quick look at my neck, and said, "The wound looks fine." He got up to leave.

I quickly said, "But what did the biopsy show?"

"I don't know. I'm just the surgeon."

I was dumbfounded. "How am I supposed to find out the results of the biopsy? I don't have any further appointments."

"Let me see what I can find out."

He left the exam room, and I waited, becoming more and more anxious. I kept reassuring myself that he was going to say, "It was benign." I told myself that this long wait was because there was nothing to report, and he had simply forgotten about me.

Finally, he came back in, sat down, and said, "You have lymphoma: cancer of the lymph glands."

"Does this mean I have AIDS?"

"I don't know."

"What's the prognosis?"

"It's terminal."

I was stunned. As scared as I had been, I had hoped that this was going to be something benign. Not cancer. Not terminal. I knew I probably had AIDS, but I didn't truly "know" it. This was a punch to my gut, to put it mildly.

When I walked out of the exam room my head was spinning. I was weak-kneed, but still walking. Lennie stood up.

"I have lymphoma. It's terminal."

Looking stricken, he grabbed me in a tight hug. After a minute, I pulled away and said, "Let's go." I didn't trust myself to speak any further, and Lennie obviously didn't know what to say. We walked out of the building to my car. He offered to drive, but I said, "No. I need to drive." I wanted to stay in control of something.

When we got home, I called Nancy and told her. She said she'd come right over. Lennie called his partner, Robert. He said he'd come soon. I called the number I had for Dr. Levine's office to try to get some more information. I left a message, and a doctor on her staff, Dr. Gill, called me back.

"We haven't worked you up yet, so we can't be sure." He told me with this kind of lymphoma, even if left untreated, I could survive ten years or more, but somehow, I thought I heard him say this kind of lymphoma usually gives a person three years to live.

Three years. In three years, I'd be thirty-four.

"Does this mean I have AIDS?"

"No. AIDS is defined by having one of several specific diseases. This lymphoma isn't one of those. We'll have to stage the lymphoma and determine if there are any other complicating factors."

I hung up and dialed more friends. I kept reaching people's answering machines. "Hi. I just found out I have cancer. It's terminal. Please come over."

First to arrive was Nancy. More friends started to show up. Lucia was at a seminary class, but she always came to see me after she got home.

Pretty soon, I had seven friends around me. Nancy stood near me as I started to cry. I was terrified as I stared at my death. The dream of a life partner died. The dream of children died. My future died. I closed my eyes and sobbed.

I cried out, "I'm so scared!"

In that moment before anyone could say anything, I wanted and expected Nancy to say, "Don't be scared. Everything is going to be all right." But she didn't.

She said, "You're right to be scared." That pushed me off the edge into that abyss of my deepest fears of an imminent death.

I felt myself falling, still sobbing. Then, suddenly, I felt God catch me and fill me with love. Immanuel—God with us. God with me, even as I faced death.

I felt Nancy's hand on my back, over my heart, as if she was transferring God's love from her heart to mine. I stopped crying. I looked up and saw my circle of loving friends. I rubbed my eyes and laughed. "I'm so glad you're all here!" There was nervous laughter. I took a deep breath, gave a big sigh, and managed a smile.

I was ready to tell the other important people in my life. When Nancy offered to call my parents, I hesitated, but then figured it would be better coming from her. I dialed and gave the phone to her. She made sure both were on the line. She told them. I could hear my mother let out a howl of grief. After Nancy talked to them in her calming way, she gave the phone to me. I apologized for bringing them so much pain with this news. Dad said, "Oh, no, Steve. There's no reason to apologize. We love you, and we just wish there were more we could do for you."

Nancy then called Rev. Ken Martin and gave him the news. When she gave me the phone, I was surprised that he was crying and couldn't seem to stop. I found myself comforting him. He collected himself enough to invite me to dinner the next evening. I loved spending time with Ken and Tom, and Ken's cooking was always inspired. At least I had that to look forward to.

We needed some comic relief. I put in my video of the "Vitameatavegamin" episode of *I Love Lucy* and hit "play." I fast-forwarded to the rehearsal sequence when Lucy proceeds to get drunk on this "health tonic." We laughed hysterically at Lucy's hilarious routine, rewinding the scene, and watching it again and again, exploding in laughter each time.

I had first seen *I Love Lucy* when I was about four, and I loved it right away. Mom would hold me as we lay on the couch together watching Lucy. We loved to laugh at her antics. *I Love Lucy* became comfort viewing for me throughout my life.

My friends and I decided we were hungry for pizza. We had a spirited discussion about what kind of pizzas to order. When they finally arrived, we dove right in. After the pizza, I had fun serving big bowls of ice cream, and we all settled in to watch the movie *Poltergeist*. I hoped it would give me a fun scare and pull me out of my own fear and despair. It was a great escape. The horror of the news I received that day subsided as we watched the film.

After the movie, people began to say goodnight. Each one gave me a big hug. A lot was said simply through eye contact. I asked Nancy if she would spend the night on the fold-out bed in my living room. We sat up for a while, just talking. When we went to bed, I fell right asleep. I was exhausted. It felt great to escape into sleep.

The next morning, I awoke crying. My terminal prognosis enveloped me immediately. I went out to the living room and woke up Nancy. She looked a bit disoriented, but she saw that I was crying, and she got up immediately.

Over the first cup of coffee, I asked her if she could teach me "Because He Lives," a hymn I'd heard many times in denominational General Conferences and local churches' worship services. We sang it directly to Jesus, changing "Because He Lives" to "Because You Live." The words of the chorus gave me hope, courage, reassurance, and joy:

> *Because You live, I can face tomorrow.*
> *Because You live all fear is gone!*
> *Because I know You hold the future,*
> *And life is worth the living just because You live.*

Nancy also taught me the verses, and we sang it all again. "This will help me face my cancer treatment and my death." I was telling myself as much as I was telling Nancy.

Nancy said, "I don't believe this will kill you. I think you're going to survive. You're not getting out of this life that easily."

I didn't say anything, but I thought, "Dear Nancy, you're clearly in denial." I tried to smile for her.

I shared a psalm that had meant so much to me in difficult times. Psalm 13 starts with a lament but ends with praising God anyway: "And yet I will praise Thy holy Name." Yes.

After breakfast, I felt good enough emotionally to go to the gym. I worked out like a maniac, bargaining for my life with every rep.

I went to the grocery store. As I was picking out an orange, I was suddenly overwhelmed with the enormity of the diagnosis. I froze. I dropped the orange back in the pile. I left my shopping basket on the floor and left. I knew I had to get home.

As I drove over the high curve of the interchange between two freeways, it occurred to me that I could simply drive through the guardrail and crash onto the busy freeway below. I thought it would bring death quickly and free me from all the suffering to come. But then it occurred to me that it might make me into a living vegetable. I thought about the pain my suicide would bring my parents and my friends. I turned the steering wheel to follow the curve of the interchange, and I got home safe and sound.

I called Ken Martin and told him I didn't trust myself to drive, so he came over and drove me back to his and Tom's home, where Ken had made an amazing jambalaya. Over dinner, I told Ken and Tom, "People have been so incredibly cheerful when they call. I'm grieving, and I want to know other people feel sad about what's happening to me, too. But everyone is so damned chipper and upbeat. I resent it when some friends act as if happy talk would somehow make it all better. And everyone has a surefire way to fix this. It seems to me they're all just trying to make themselves feel better."

"Steve, you have to allow each person their reaction to your news."

As we finished dinner, Ken said, "I'd like you to preach the Easter sermon at MCC in the Valley the Sunday after next."

I wasn't sure I'd heard him right. "You mean Good Friday, don't you? I mean, I'm dying."

"No, you need to preach Easter."

It turned out to be one of the best gifts anyone has ever given me. I spent much of the next ten days in prayer and meditation, focusing on what faith in the Resurrection might mean in the face of my terminal prognosis.

One of the other things Ken told me that evening was, "You can't tap-dance your way through this one, Steve."

I didn't say anything, but I thought to myself, "Just watch me."

I usually preached from notes, but this time I wanted to make sure I got it just right, and so the notes for my Easter sermon came close to being a manuscript I could read to the congregation if I got overly emotional or nervous in delivering it.

Easter Sunday arrived. Many in the congregation had seen Ken pray over me the Sunday before, a few days after my diagnosis. The rest heard about my illness through the grapevine, so I imagined they were as nervous as I was about what I could possibly say in an Easter sermon. I stood at the pulpit and started to read my notes out loud, but I didn't get very far. With that same clarity I had experienced before, I knew what I had to do.

I threw my notes in the air, looked directly at the folks in front of me, and said, "I don't need these. I know exactly what I want to say." People laughed, and the tension was released.

With more conviction than I had ever preached before, I shouted, "Jesus Christ is risen today! Hallelujah!" I shared my lymphoma diagnosis and prognosis with the congregation. Even though I was not yet diagnosed with AIDS, several people had told me they were afraid that was coming for me. The fear of AIDS had such a powerful grip on so many people. So, I preached, "If God is greater than the death of Jesus on the cross, then God is greater than AIDS." The congregation gasped, but then I could see many people start to understand.

I continued, "Our Easter faith tells me that even though they told me the worst news they could possibly tell me, I can still dance!" And I did a tap dance right there in front of the altar. The congregation cheered. "It means I can still laugh, I can still enjoy my friends, I can still be fully alive, even in the face of death!" When I finished the sermon, the congregation rose, applauding and cheering.

When it came time for Communion, I didn't think people would come to receive it from me because of the fear I might have AIDS. But many did come. It was extraordinarily meaningful to me that these folks were not afraid to have me put the wafer on their tongue. I couldn't help but remember Jeri, the deacon who, just the year before, was too frightened to place the wafer on my tongue herself.

After the service, I got a lot of hugs. A few people held back, one bluntly telling me he was afraid to shake my hand. I was riding so high on my own Easter joy that it didn't upset me. That Easter was a day of grace that empowered me to be fully alive even as I faced the very real possibility of an imminent death.

CHAPTER THREE

Creating Conditions for Healing

A FEW DAYS AFTER EASTER, CHRISTIE CALLED TO SAY SHE WAS GOING to be in Los Angeles and wanted to come see me. The evening arrived, and she was late. Not a big surprise, with all the demands on her as the president of Playboy. When she finally arrived, she told me she had been knocking on doors up and down my street. I could only imagine what Playboy security would think if they'd known that.

After we hugged and sat down, I started to make small talk. She suddenly reached for my hand with tears in her eyes, and we sat there holding hands without talking. I was so touched that she had come to see me and was so moved at the depth of caring she showed me that evening with that simple gesture of reaching for my hand with no need for talking.

Over the next few weeks, Dr. Levine's staff worked up my case, doing all kinds of tests, including a bone marrow biopsy. I was surprised that Dr. Levine performed it herself. Nancy came with me, as she now did to almost every appointment I had.

I leaned over an exam table for the biopsy. While Dr. Levine drilled into my hip bone to extract the marrow, Nancy distracted me by describing the new Electrical Parade at Disneyland. It helped, along with the lidocaine, to numb the spot. I marveled at how calm Nancy was while she watched Dr. Levine bear down on the big needle.

The results of the bone marrow biopsy showed that the lymphoma had spread to my bone marrow, as well as being in my neck, armpit, and groin. Dr. Levine explained to me that this meant I had stage 4 lymphoma.

She also sent me to have a biopsy of a lesion on my right foot. I saw no reason for it, but Nancy persuaded me to agree to it. I had hoped the lesion was just a scar from the fungal infection that had bubbled away on my foot for almost a year. Although I respected Dr. Levine's wish, I was angry about it as they cut into my foot. Nancy came with me to that appointment, too. She tried to keep me distracted, but it was painful despite the lidocaine they used on the lesion. I was relieved when it was over.

When I came back to my next appointment, the dermatologist told me that the lesion was Kaposi's sarcoma (KS). He didn't know whether that meant I had full-blown AIDS but said I should ask Dr. Levine or someone on her staff.

Nancy and I walked over to General Hospital for lunch. We ran into Dr. Gill, from Dr. Levine's staff. I stopped him. "The dermatologist just told me the lesion on my foot is Kaposi's sarcoma. Does that mean I have AIDS?"

With compassion, Dr. Gill said, "Yes, it does."

It was odd: I experienced relief to have my AIDS diagnosis finally confirmed. They couldn't tell me anything worse. There was a certain freedom in that. At the same time, I felt terrified.

At our next appointment, Dr. Levine told me, "Even though we have no specific therapy for AIDS, I am convinced that this treatment will become available, and when it is, you will have it right away. In the meantime, your mission, should you choose to accept it, is to stay alive long enough for us to find a way to manage this." She added, "There are no 100 percents in medicine. Not everyone will die from AIDS. If there is a one in a million chance of surviving this, why not believe that you will be that one in a million?" She added that there were many things I could do to create conditions for a treatment to work once they found one.

Dr. Levine didn't have to remind me there were no treatments for AIDS. One doctor had told me, "You in the church have more to offer people with AIDS than medicine does."

About this time, I was delighted to get a call from Patti McKenny, a friend from my old college crowd. She was so genuinely upbeat that when she offered to correspond with me, I immediately took her up on it.

She began sending me twenty-page typewritten letters, filled with stories about her adventures with the Chicago Renaissance Faire. She referred to herself as a "party girl tramp" and told me any number of stories to back that up. I loved her letters and read and reread them. I wrote back to her, of course, and regaled her with stories of my experiences with AIDS.

Paula Schoenwether, the editor of the MCC denomination's magazine, *Journey*, asked me to write a monthly article about my experiences living with AIDS. I jumped at the opportunity. Some questioned the wisdom of going public about having AIDS, but I had been public about being gay for so long that this seemed like a logical next step. So, over the next year, I wrote nine articles for *Journey*.

I found my voice as a writer by first writing each article as a letter to Patti. When I imagined her reading my letters, it kept me upbeat and positive about all these new experiences I was having. Through Patti I rediscovered the power that language has on our thoughts. I started thinking of myself as *living* with AIDS, not dying from AIDS. I began looking at challenging events as *adventures*. And I began to insist on changing "terminal" to "life-threatening."

I decided it would be wise to explore my options. I'd heard they had drug trials for Kaposi's sarcoma at City of Hope, so I made an appointment. The physician I saw said he had an experimental chemotherapy for Kaposi's sarcoma, but it had some severe side effects.

I was impressed with how I was treated at City of Hope. Back at County, I was struggling with the culture shock of going from Dr. Weisman's comfortable, suburban office to a crowded hospital for people with little or no health insurance. As privileged as I had been in receiving medical care, I found it challenging now at County how first they told me I was terminal, and then they had me waiting for hours on hard wooden benches in windowless corridors. The medical staff at County were undeniably superb, and I had to marvel at how they attended to so many patients at any given moment. But it was still difficult for me to deal with the long waits in crowded corridors. So, I deeply appreciated the prompt attention I received at City of Hope. Plus I found hope that they offered something I could do for the Kaposi's sarcoma.

My friend, Julie, a registered nurse, brought me a steak dinner that evening. I told her about being so well treated at City of Hope and how they were offering me an experimental treatment. The next day, she called to ask me to see a friend of hers, a nurse on Dr. Levine's staff.

Julie's friend told me, "I've read your chart, and with two kinds of terminal cancer and full-blown AIDS, you won't live to see 1985." She urged me not to go to City of Hope. She said I stood a much better chance of getting on a successful drug trial right there at County Hospital. Dr. Levine was one of the best doctors there was, and she would be at the forefront of drug trials for AIDS. Julie backed her up when I talked to her later. So, I decided to stay on at County, with the hope that something would come along soon to treat my lymphoma, Kaposi's sarcoma, and AIDS.

I took it seriously when Dr. Levine told me about creating conditions in my body for a treatment to work when one came along. I developed my own wellness plan. There were no books or articles about recovering from AIDS, but I read books about people surviving supposedly "terminal" cancers.

Singing was a big part of my healing work. Sometimes I drove around the freeways, just to sing at the top of my lungs. I sang along with Maggie in *A Chorus Line* as I paraphrased her lyrics: "I really need this life! Oh God, I need this life! I've got to save my life!" And I sang along with Judy Garland. If I could just hold that last note in *Swanee* as long as she did, then I knew I could beat AIDS!

I got back to the gym and worked out with renewed vigor and purpose. My workouts before diagnosis had been primarily about vanity. Now they were all about my health: ensuring my body was strong for whatever treatment might come along.

I studied nutrition. I loved salads and all kinds of fruit, because I could visualize them making me strong, giving me energy, and helping me stay healthy. There was a lot of peer pressure among people with AIDS back then to go on a macrobiotic diet. I decided against it because macrobiotics made people too thin. AIDS tended to "waste" us away, so it seemed more important to keep my weight up.

Believing in the power of prayer, I asked everyone I knew to pray for me. My parents put out word to their church and all their friends as well as the family on both sides to pray. I asked the entire MCC denomination to pray for me. Of course, I prayed, too, for everyone living with AIDS.

I started meditating, using guided meditations on tape. Dr. Levine told me I should do it every day, three times a day, as if it was a pill. I found that when I listened to these meditations, I soon began to achieve "the alpha state," an altered consciousness where I could feel myself rising out of my body.

When meditating, I visualized my body looking and feeling the way I wanted it: muscular and healthy. I visualized my T-cells as bodybuilders getting stronger and multiplying like crazy. I visualized my cancer cells dissolving. I saw my swollen lymph glands as knots, loosening and untying. I visualized my KS lesions being erased. It was as if I was brainwashing myself into believing that I was getting better, that my immune system was getting strong, and that my cancers were disappearing.

Following the advice of Norman Cousins in his book *Anatomy of an Illness*, I started a vitamin regimen that included large amounts of buffered vitamin C. For a long period of time, I took one thousand milligrams of buffered vitamin C every hour that I was awake. If it wasn't buffered, that high dose would have wreaked havoc on my stomach.

Also following Norman Cousins' advice, I started laughing all I could. It just made sense to me since I'd always loved to laugh. Again Dr. Levine told me to use laughter therapy as if it was a medication that I had to take every day, two or three times a day. So, I watched *I Love Lucy*, *Cheers*, or *M*A*S*H* three times a day. When I was laughing, I couldn't be depressed or scared. I knew the endorphins released when I laughed had a direct and positive influence on my health.

I had been a pack-a-day smoker up to this point, but I knew it was time to quit. I also knew I couldn't stop on my own. I'd tried and failed any number of times. Friends referred me to a low-cost acupuncture school in downtown Los Angeles. The acupuncturist put tacks in my right ear. Any time I felt the urge to smoke, I would press on the tacks, and the urge would go away. I was finally able to stop smoking.

I started psychotherapy sessions with Barbara Bailey, a former hospice nurse, to help me deal with whatever was blocking me from taking the best care of myself. She also helped me face my mortality and grieve the possible loss of my future.

Barbara referred me to a bodyworker, Linda. I'd never heard of bodywork. Our sessions would open with me talking about whatever was going on that week. Then she would have me lie face-down on her massage table. Over the next ten to fifteen minutes, she would hold her hands lightly on my body, sweeping clean the bad energy and feeling what was going on for me emotionally in various parts of my body. Then we would sit back down, and she would tell me what she felt in my body. She would often tell me something that contradicted what I'd reported earlier, and she would invariably be correct.

Linda told Barbara what she discovered in my bodywork, so Barbara could work with me on it. It seemed to speed up therapy. One week, Barbara told me that Linda saw a Divine Being appear at my head during bodywork. Linda reported knowing something special was going on with me. She'd never had that experience before, and it seemed as if I was particularly blessed. I tucked that away to ponder.

Linda gave me a book she thought would help me: *Who Dies?* by Stephen Levine. I dove right in, thinking this would be the book that tells me who lives and who dies. Of course, the answer to "Who dies?" is "Everyone." It was also a deeper question about what part of us is it that dies? The book taught me about both conscious dying and conscious living. When Levine and his wife, Ondrea, came to Los Angeles to do a workshop for people with AIDS, I jumped at the opportunity. It was a huge help in learning more about meditation and, of course, about both dying and living consciously.

AIDS Project Los Angeles (APLA) was only a year old when I registered as a client. I had delayed registering because that would confirm once and for all that I really had AIDS. However, being told I wouldn't live to see 1985 gave me a new urgency about getting help. So, I called APLA and made an appointment for an intake interview.

Coleen Johnson was the first and, back then, the only social worker at APLA. She was a young, vibrant woman, obviously smart, and with an upbeat attitude. I liked her right away. She did a needs assessment and immediately referred me to the Buddy Program, to a support group, and to an attorney to do my will.

Knowing that I was a clergyman, she put me to work as a volunteer "phone buddy" for other clients. There were so few people with AIDS in Los Angeles County back then that I could call half of them within two hours. I would ask how they were doing and if they needed anything from APLA. It helped to hear how others were coping with AIDS, and it felt so good to be of service after wondering if I was through as a pastor.

Because I had experience being interviewed by the media, I quickly became the client AIDS Project Los Angeles called on for interviews. However, in those days, camera crews refused to work if I came into a studio. They wouldn't even enter the APLA building and certainly not my home. So, I was often interviewed while sitting on a chair in an alley outside APLA, with an earpiece and a lapel microphone. When the interview was over, I would start to hand back the earpiece and mike, but invariably, the sound engineer would step back with hands in the air, saying, "You keep them." I would learn later that this wasn't just my experience, but that of the APLA staff, too.

When the director of the buddy program at APLA, Jerry Clark, interviewed me about what I would like in a buddy, I said, "Someone I could go dancing with." Apparently, I was the only client who ever asked for that. Jerry assigned me an experienced buddy named Beau. Beau's first client had died not long after they had become buddies. So, Jerry felt Beau needed a more upbeat experience for his next buddy. Beau was a sweet, serious, soft-spoken man. I enjoyed making him laugh. We went out to dinner often, and of course, we went dancing, too.

One of the things I remember most clearly about Beau was his great capacity to listen. He was easy to talk to, and I shared any number of secret feelings, fears, and longings during our times together.

Coleen referred me to one of the attorneys who were volunteering to help clients write their wills. Richard Berger had a fancy office in the mid-Wilshire district. He drew up my will and all my other end-of-life documents. The thing I remember most clearly from my visits with him was how he told me, "Plan for the worst, and hope for the best." Yes.

I was attending a support group set up by APLA, run by a psychologist. The group was filled with gay men with AIDS, of course. Most would disappear after a few months in the group. Each week, the psychologist announced who'd died, and we always spent time processing that. Of course, it affected us deeply, as each man who died had died of what we all had.

Somehow, the AIDS Project Los Angeles staff found out about all my experience on boards in Hartford, and it wasn't long before I was asked to be on their board of directors. Seeing it as another chance to be of service, I said, "Yes."

The agency grew quickly, perhaps too quickly. When I began on the board in late 1984, AIDS Project Los Angeles had an annual budget of around $70,000. Soon, the budget expanded to more than $700,000. Then in the summer of 1985, after Rock Hudson's AIDS diagnosis increased our ability to raise money, the budget expanded to $7 million.

Within the first year after my diagnosis, I also became an executive committee member of the Los Angeles City / County AIDS Task Force and a founding board member of the AIDS Interfaith Council of Los Angeles, co-chaired by then Archbishop Roger Mahoney; Alan Freehling, the president of the Board of Rabbis; and Oliver Garver, Suffragan Bishop of the Episcopal Diocese.

Most important, I became friends with a group of people who had nothing to do with the church but were all connected to AIDS Project Los Angeles. Nancy Cole, Max Drew, and Matt Redman had been three of the cofounders. Steven Kant, Max's partner, was the facilitator of the agency's spiritual support group and soon became my best friend. They were all impossibly good-looking, and all but Matt lived together in a mansion at the top of Beverly Hills, among the homes of the stars.

The mansion belonged to my new friend, Nancy, whose father had been in oil. I had a few Nancys in my life at this point. This Nancy was a fixture of the West Hollywood gay scene, as well as a star of the summer Fire Island gay scene. She was a heterosexual woman who preferred the company of gay men, because she told me they made much better lovers in their considerate approach to her as a woman, their sensitivity to her needs, and their sexual skill and adventurousness. Not long after I met her, she married a handsome man, Lou Sawaya, and soon, they adopted a baby girl.

When I first met them, Nancy and I were hanging out, and I mentioned I was getting hungry. Nancy and I went to the kitchen, where she started making me a sandwich. I felt uncomfortable, and I said, "Nancy, I can do that. I'm sure you have more important things to do." She stopped, looked at me for what seemed to be a full minute, then silently handed me the knife and took off for another part of the house. I thought I had offended her somehow, but later when we knew each other better, she told me, "That's when I knew you were someone special."

Max was just beginning to get sick with AIDS, but the rest of the gang were all healthy.

The autumn following my terminal prognosis, I decided to take a trip to Chicago and Boston. I told my friends and family I just wanted to see them all, but in my heart, I wondered if it might be my farewell tour.

My first stop was Chicago, where I stayed with Christie Hefner. I loved spending time with her. She had always been such a good friend. She graciously offered to host a dinner party for eight of my friends from Northwestern, Good Shepherd Parish MCC, and McCormick Seminary. I was excited about seeing them all for the first time since my diagnosis. It was particularly good to see Patti, my faithful correspondent. We had a great time that evening. The dinner Christie cooked was delicious, the conversation was great, and we had fun singing show tunes around the piano after dinner. It was a real celebration of life!

The next evening, Patti hosted a party so that I could see many of my Northwestern friends. I had a blast reconnecting with my college crowd. One friend, I learned, couldn't handle seeing me in person. I was surprised there weren't more who felt that way. It did feel as if everyone was being cheerful to a fault, but I joined right in. The hard work of grieving could wait.

Sunday morning, Bill Mueller picked me up at Christie's. He was another friend from Northwestern, and we had shared a lakeside cottage in summer stock in 1972. We headed up to Evanston where we met his wife, Jill, my first good friend from college. I adored Jill, and I might have pursued her if I had been straight. Jill and Bill took me to church at Northwestern's Alice Millar Chapel, where I had been a member for a few years after college.

The Chapel had been an important part of my recovery from alcoholism and my coming out. I started drinking right after graduating from Phillips Academy Andover in 1970, when I did summer stock on Cape Cod. From that first drink, I loved the feeling. Alcohol filled a hole in my soul I didn't even know was there. Drinking gave me back the joy that had all but disappeared in my painful closet. I began drinking every night after each performance. I felt such joy when I was high.

I drank all through my four years at Northwestern. I was the one who always said, "Let's go out for pizza and beer." I got blazing drunk at every party. Somehow it didn't prevent me from playing leading roles all through college. Drinking hadn't gotten me into trouble . . . yet.

My first eighteen months out of college, my alcoholism took off. I drank every day, often all day. During that time I tried geographic cures, moving around the country from Chicago to St. Louis to Los Angeles to Bloomsburg, Pennsylvania (where friends were studying with Alvina Krause, a great acting teacher) to Andover and back to Chicago. Somehow I kept thinking I wouldn't have to drink so much if I lived in the next place. But nothing stopped me from drinking. I knew I was in trouble, but I didn't want to give it up for anything.

By the fall of 1975, now back in Chicago, I was drinking a quart of whiskey every day. I didn't want anyone to know how much I was drinking, so I sat in my apartment and drank straight out of the bottle. I isolated myself from all my friends. I lay there on my bed, watching TV all day and night, while I fantasized about men and cried. One drunken night, I pounded my face until I had black eyes.

After a while, I started vomiting blood. That scared me enough that I finally reached out and got help. I was afraid of going to any kind of recovery group, but I was more frightened of continuing to drink. So, I called Michael Vodde, who was always a kind and loving friend, and asked him to go with me. He agreed and starting then, I got sober, one day at a time.

I started reading again, which I hadn't been able to do while I was drinking. One of the books I read, *The Front Runner* by Patricia Nell Warren, was so compelling, I read it twice. It was the love story of a championship runner and his coach. I was totally amazed that two athletes could have such a committed, loving relationship. I wanted that. More to the point, I realized that if I was to stay sober, I had to get honest about being gay. I had to come out.

When I decided to come out, I started going to Northwestern's Alice Millar Chapel for services. The counsel of the pastor, Rev. Jim Avery, was crucial as I ventured out into the gay world for the first time and throughout my years in seminary.

So, it held a great deal of meaning for me to return to Alice Millar Chapel in 1984. While Bill looked after their three toddlers, Matt, Abby, and Jessie, in the chapel nursery, Jill and I went into the beautiful sanctuary for worship. It was all so familiar, and yet everything felt so different now. Here I was back in the church where I had had a spiritual awakening when I first got sober, and where I came to Rev. Jim Avery for guidance in coming out. He had given me such great support and guidance through that time. Now, I had AIDS.

I started to cry with heaving sobs when I saw Rev. Jim during the processional hymn, and I couldn't sing. Jill was lovingly attentive and had trouble singing herself. As the service continued, I knew others in the congregation were looking at us, but I could not stop crying. Jill kept her arm around my shoulders or her hand on my arm through the whole service, and fortunately, she brought lots of tissues.

I couldn't stop thinking that if I'd never come out and if I'd never had sex, I wouldn't have AIDS, and I wouldn't be facing an early death. Of course, I reasoned with myself, if I'd never come out, I'd have probably died an early death from alcoholism. Or maybe I'd have killed myself in my shame-filled, lonely closet. But here I was, back in the place where I'd decided to come out, where my adult life began just a few years before, and now I was going to die. Soon.

Jim prayed for me in his pastoral prayer, and his tender words touched my heart. My tears stopped for the moment, but when we stood to sing the closing hymn, I started weeping again. Jill was so loving. I could not have asked for a better friend in that service. She was already a dear friend, but she forged a special place in my heart after showing me such loving kindness that morning.

It was hard to say goodbye to Jill, Bill, Christie, Patti, and all my Chicago friends, not knowing if I would ever see them again. But I put one foot in front of the other and got on the plane to Boston, as I had planned. My childhood friend, Tripp Royce, picked me up at the airport and drove me to his home on Cape Cod. Tripp and I became friends at age four when his family moved next door to mine, and we were best friends all through our childhood. We'd lost track of each other for a time, but we'd reconnected shortly before my diagnosis. It felt so good to be with him again, and I enjoyed meeting his wife, Lisa. I felt safe and comfortable in this house Tripp had built. It was as if nothing could harm me.

My cousins, Lucia and Lawrie, joined us on the Cape. It meant the world to me that they had driven out from Rochester to spend time with me for what looked to be the final time. Tripp, Lucia, Lawrie, and I took a long walk on the beach on that gray November morning. I was filled with so many feelings as we talked, so much anguish, certainly, and at the same time so much joy and gratitude because I had such a deep connection with each of them. We drove up to Provincetown for lunch and then had dinner in Barnstable, where they treated me to a lobster dinner.

The next day, I said a difficult goodbye to Lawrie and Lucia. Tripp drove me to my brother's home outside Boston, where Tripp and I said our emotional farewell. I spent a couple nights with my brother and his wife, while we celebrated the birthday of my young niece, Jen.

My next stop was my hometown, Andover. I rushed around, saying hi to my friends on the faculty and staff. Of course, I had to see Tripp's mom who had been a second mother to me. I found her at her job at the Phillips Academy audiovisual department. She greeted me with a bright smile and said, "I hate the way you're doing this." Then she gave me a warm hug. I was sorry I hadn't scheduled more time with her, but I didn't want to be in Andover for long. It seemed too painful.

My final stop was back in Boston, where I stayed with my friend and MCC colleague, Rev. Shelley Hamilton. We went for walks along the Charles River and talked into the night. She cooked, baked bread, and fed me with great love.

I had been so worried that I was going to die without ever having a life partner. But in reflecting on my time with all these wonderful friends and family, I realized they collectively loved me in the way a single life partner would love me. It was as if I had a partner in mosaic. I felt loved and not so alone.

Back in Los Angeles Dr. Levine and her staff continued to see me regularly. A couple of times a month, I went to see the AIDS nurse, Scott, at his small office in County Hospital. Scott routinely saw people with AIDS there to assess their condition. There weren't many chairs, so sometimes I sat on the floor in the corridor as we waited to see him. He'd take our vitals, draw our blood, and do a short "interview" to see how we were coping. I always told him I was doing everything I could to create the conditions for healing and that I considered surviving AIDS to be my full-time job. With my volunteer work, as well as being a client, a board member, and a patient, I had become totally immersed in the world of AIDS.

In a letter to Patti, I'd mentioned how I'd always wanted to fly somewhere just for a party. Since it was apparent that I was indeed going to live to see 1985 after all, Patti invited me to Chicago for their New Year's Eve party.

It was a terrific party, packed with fun people. When midnight arrived, of course, everybody started kissing. I felt sad that I didn't have anyone to kiss. There weren't any people who wanted to kiss a person with AIDS. My friend, Dusty, noticed I was alone, and she gave me a warm hug.

Then Patti proposed a toast to her friend who wasn't supposed to live to see 1985. "Here he stands, just as alive as could be." Everyone raised their glasses to me with a huge cheer. I was embarrassed but pleased. In May, I had been told I wouldn't live to see 1985. And here I was, alive and in relatively good shape, celebrating the dawn of 1985 with great friends in Chicago. It was a joyful triumph.

Chapter Four

A Drug Trial and a Partner

I FLEW HOME TO LOS ANGELES ON NEW YEAR'S DAY, JUST ONE DAY after flying to Chicago. I could now cross off flying somewhere just to attend a party from my bucket list. I felt quite smug about having outlived my prognosis by a whole day, but at thirty-two, I wondered if I would live to see another New Year. I decided I always had to give myself at least a year to live. That way, I would never feel this was my last Fourth of July or Christmas.

At my first medical appointment in 1985, I was surprised that Dr. Levine herself came into the exam room in the Hematology Clinic, which served as the AIDS clinic at the University of Southern California / Los Angeles County Hospital at that time. Usually, one of her staff doctors would see me, but this time, it was Dr. Levine.

She told me that they were going to begin a trial of the first antiviral to be used to fight HIV. The drug was called suramin, a treatment for African sleeping sickness. Researchers had discovered that in a test tube it inhibited the replication of HIV. So they wanted to do a trial with people with AIDS.

I would be asked to sign an "informed consent" document, even though Dr. Levine said she couldn't inform me of all that might happen since they had never used suramin on HIV and certainly not for long periods of time. It could prove ineffective, and there could be side effects that might harm me physically. "But," she emphasized, "if this does work as we hope it will, then you would be the first to benefit from it and get well."

Next, on paper from the roll on the exam table, she drew pictures of how they expected suramin to work. It would, she explained, inhibit the replication of HIV and block it from killing more T-cells. Then, hopefully, my immune system would kick back in and put my lymphoma and Kaposi's sarcoma in remission.

I wanted to say "Yes, I'll do it" right away, but she urged me to talk to as many of my friends and family as possible before I decided. Then, she said, I should close my eyes and listen to my heart for the answer.

I asked a lot of different people for their advice. Some said, "No! You mustn't do it!" A few even said, "They're trying to kill all the gays, and this could very well kill you." Other people said, "Yes! This could be the cure, and you'd be getting it first!" One longtime friend who knew me well offered, "You've always been a living-on-the-edge kind of guy, Steve, so I'd say go for it!"

I still wasn't sure what I would say when I next saw Dr. Levine. As I waited to see her at clinic, I closed my eyes and said a prayer asking for guidance, and then I listened to my heart.

I was ushered into an exam room where Dr. Levine was waiting for me. She asked me what I'd decided. I told her, "After talking to my friends and family, I listened to my heart. My heart said, 'Yes.'"

She beamed, and said, "You've made the right decision. I'm so glad, just so delighted that you've decided to do it. I have the feeling that it might be able to work for you." Pulling out the "informed consent" document for me to sign, she warned me again that she couldn't inform me of everything that might happen with either results or side effects. I said I understood, and then I signed the document that listed a myriad of potential toxicities and side effects.

"We still have to get the approval of the hospital's Institutional Research Committee (IRC) that must approve every drug trial," she said, and she added that it could take a couple of months, but then they would get the suramin trials under way. She told me I would be "patient number one" on the trial.

I was starting to feel as if the lymphoma was advancing. My energy was declining, and I felt weaker. My neck seemed to be buzzing with activity, and my lymph glands were consistently swollen. I was getting impatient to start the suramin trials.

I decided I needed to move to get away from the railroad tracks across the street and to be closer to Silverlake where my gym was and where I shopped. Silverlake was sometimes called "the San Francisco of LA" or simply "The Swish Alps," given the hilly terrain and the largely lesbian and gay population.

My therapist, Barbara, told me her friend, Micheline, had an apartment to rent on the lower floor of her house in Silverlake. The house, built in 1926, had character and style. It was on a hill, with the apartment one flight down from the street. The front of the apartment was one flight above the big backyard, with a huge cypress tree in the middle. The apartment had a balcony on the front, which would be wonderful for sitting outside and reading or visiting, with a view of Silverlake Hill and all the amazing houses there. I moved in at the end of January.

In February a boyfriend from Hartford, David Templeton, announced that he would like to move in with me and be my lover. He now lived in Santa Fe, where I had visited him on my way out to California. He told me he'd prefer being called Temp now, after always being known as David.

I asked Temp if he was moving in to take care of a dying friend or to be my lover. He answered, "To be your lover." I was overjoyed. When I was first diagnosed, I thought I would die without ever having had a lover. Some of my friends were skeptical about Temp moving in with me, but I was determined to have a life partner before I died.

To celebrate his arrival, I had a combination housewarming/Temp-welcoming party for my friends to meet him. After everyone had left, we stood holding each other in the living room. We kissed. I looked into his eyes and said, "I love you." He said, "Thank you." Clue.

One afternoon, he got in bed with me to have sex before my nap. One of my cats jumped up to be with us. He threw the cat at the wall. I was horrified. The cat was fine, and Temp scoffed at my reaction. I was so angry with him that sex was out of the question, at least for that day. Another clue.

It became apparent to me that he was expecting me to support the two of us in exchange for him cleaning and cooking. Unfortunately, I didn't have the resources to support two people, so soon I insisted he find a job. He found one as an executive assistant. He didn't have a car, so I would drive him to work and back some days. Many days, I let him have my car because I just didn't feel well enough to drive, let alone leave the apartment.

Despite the clues, I was happy to have a live-in lover. We watched TV in each other's arms on the couch. We played board games. We resumed our usual great time with sex, albeit safe sex. We smoked a lot of marijuana together, and I smoked a lot of it alone when he was at work.

I was eager to get the suramin treatments started. The IRB Research Committee finally gave their approval for the suramin trial at the end of March. So, I was given a test dose on Good Friday, April 5, about a year after my initial diagnosis of AIDS. There were no side effects, and I celebrated Easter that Sunday with hope, excited that the suramin might work.

The first full dose was on April 8, the day after Easter. I was to be hospitalized overnight. So I checked in to LAC–USC, with Temp accompanying me. It seemed to me that he was more nervous about it all than I was. Another AIDS patient, George, "patient number 2," was in the other bed. Scott, our nurse, was there with us throughout. Scott had a warm, compassionate demeanor, he was extraordinarily skillful, and I always felt that I could trust him with my life, which, in fact, I was doing.

Dr. Levine came in and gave each of us a physical exam as required by the research protocol. "Do you have any questions?"

"In case we do get sick tonight, I think you should know that I tend to get depressed when I feel sick."

She smiled and said, "You just told me you're a human being." I felt relieved and cared for.

Scott started the suramin through an IV drip in my forearm. When I didn't have any immediate side effects, he started the suramin drip for George. Scott took our vitals every fifteen minutes. Nothing happened. Occasionally doctors would poke their heads in to look at George and me. Scott said they were all curious about what might happen with that first big dose of suramin. Nothing continued to happen.

There were no TVs, radios, or phones in our room, so George and I started singing show tunes like "Everything's Coming Up Roses!" After a while, Scott wrote in our charts, "The only side effect with suramin is singing like Ethel Merman."

We spent the night, with Scott keeping a close eye on us and Temp sleeping in the chair next to my bed. The next morning, with no adverse reactions in either George or me, we were discharged. I was glad to get home and take a hot bath.

Over the next nine months, I checked in to the newly designated County AIDS clinic, "5P21," every Monday morning, Rev. Nancy Radclyffe usually accompanied me, and George was there each week as well. When we got there, we had to wait in a long line to register and pay for the clinic visit, based on our ability to pay. Then we had to wait in line to have fourteen or fifteen vials of blood drawn. Next, we had to wait for several hours outside 5P21 on those long wooden benches in windowless corridors, while we waited for the blood test results to come in. If the tests indicated that it was safe to proceed, we would then enter the chemo room and sit in recliners. Scott would start our IVs, and George and I, and soon a few other patients, would receive the suramin infusion over the next hour. The drug made me tired, so I would go home and take a long nap.

As the suramin built up in our systems over the next weeks, I became increasingly fatigued. It felt like I was on the bottom of a bowl of Jell-O. It was hard to move through the air, and I was just so tired. The fatigue let up after a couple of days.

The glands in my neck started hurting, but Dr. Gill suggested, "Maybe that's because they're getting better. Healing can hurt, like when you've cut your finger."

After six weekly infusions, Dr. Levine arranged for another lymph gland biopsy. This time, with Scott scrubbing in, all went well. She also wanted another bone marrow test. Once again, Dr. Levine extracted the bone marrow while Nancy kept me distracted, describing the newly remodeled Alice in Wonderland ride at Disneyland.

A dermatologist then took another biopsy of that original KS lesion on my foot. The difference this time was that my KS lesions had disappeared, so he was doing a biopsy of the scar from the original lesion.

On May 26, 1985, Dr. Levine called me and said, "I've got terrific news: Both your Kaposi's sarcoma and lymphoma are gone; the biopsies of your foot and the bone marrow show no cancer; you are in complete remission." I was stunned. This was the best news possible. Suramin worked! Dr. Levine had given me back my life.

I wanted to call friends in the news media right away, but Dr. Levine said, "Please don't. First, we must replicate this result in other patients, and then we must see if there are long-term side effects." Of course, I agreed. It was her news to present to the world when the time was right.

I hung up the phone. I still didn't quite believe it when I turned to Temp with the good news. After kissing me with tears in his eyes, he suggested that we walk up to the top of the hill and shout it to the Hollywood Hills. The fact that it was easy for me to climb that steep hill was yet another sign of how the suramin had done its job.

Dr. Levine said it was okay to tell my family and friends. It was interesting to see how people responded. Most were thrilled. Others couldn't quite believe it. Despite how much better I felt, I found myself not quite believing it and wondering if I could really trust it.

After my cancers went into remission, things really fell apart between Temp and me. Even our once hot sexual chemistry was not working for us. The disease process, and then the suramin treatments, had dampened my sexual desire considerably, and he wanted rougher sex than I did. So we stopped having sex altogether.

He was seeing a therapist, Jack, whom I had suggested. I knew Jack from the AIDS Project's board of directors. He asked Temp and me to join the couples' support group that he and my friend and APLA cofounder Nancy Cole ran every Monday evening. Even though I received the suramin treatments on Mondays, I agreed to go. There we met other couples, some of whom became my close friends in their last years of life.

Not long after I went into remission, the more rugged side effects of suramin began to grab hold of me: profound fatigue, decreasing appetite, and deep depression. Temp stopped taking care of me almost completely, just when I needed him most. We each became easily angered by the other. To make matters worse, when he had my car, he frequently came home from work late at night, drunk.

He complained to the couples' support group that it was difficult for him to handle what the suramin treatments were doing to me. He told them I was exhausted and depressed for days at a time. He said I began to get some energy back by Friday, but then on Sunday, I would withdraw again, with the anxiety mounting about the suramin treatment the next day. So I just wasn't much fun anymore.

The straw that broke the relationship's back occurred during a visit from my parents. They wanted to take Temp and me to dinner one evening. My parents had never met Temp, but he turned the invitation down flat. That upset me, of course, but there was no persuading him.

I was not in a good mood during dinner, but my parents understood. I was touched they came to see me during the suramin trials, but I couldn't muster much joyful talk for them. After we ate, I dropped them off at their motel and went home.

I found Temp having sex on our couch with the man I thought was just a friend from New Mexico. They told me that they had been lovers all along and that Temp was simply "on loan" to me, a dying friend, and he had every intention of returning to this man after I died.

Temp admitted he had hoped that when I died he would be able to return to this lover with all the money he expected to inherit from me. He wanted it to buy land where the two of them could build a house. When my cancers went into remission, he grew increasingly antsy to get out of there. I couldn't believe he hadn't figured out that I didn't have any money to leave him.

The next morning I told him, "I want you to leave. Life is too short for us to continue to be this miserable." He agreed to leave as soon as his lover could drive back to LA to pick him up.

That last morning Temp and I lay in bed, and I started to cry. Then Temp started to cry, and we wept together, grieving the relationship and all it had meant to each of us. I had feared that I would die without ever having a relationship. Now I'd had one, but it was a miserable, short-lived failure. When I next saw my bodyworker, Linda, she told me I should have found someone named Perm.

To avoid having his lover come to my home again, we agreed I would drop Temp off at the Plummer Park parking lot, across the street from APLA. He transferred his luggage, got in the car with his real lover, and drove away. I couldn't cry, despite my pain. I started over to APLA to see if I could find someone I could talk to.

I poured out my heart to one of the social workers. I told her how abandoned I felt and how deep and old that wound was. I was born with a cleft lip. In the early 1950s, it would have been conventional medical practice for me to have the surgery on my nose and lip almost immediately after birth, but I developed terrible allergies, and the doctors had to delay the surgery until they cleared up.

Mom and Dad brought me home for a few months to allow my allergies to subside before they did the corrective surgery on my lip and nose. When I was three months old, I was finally deemed healthy enough to have the surgery. My parents left me at Boston Children's Hospital, where the operation was performed.

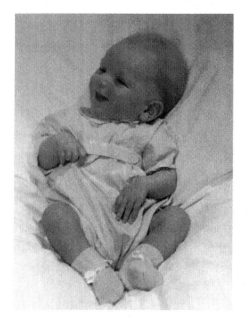

The author at about four months old, December 1952. Full of joy even then! COURTESY OF REVEREND PIETERS'S PERSONAL COLLECTION.

In those days, parents were not allowed to see their babies for three weeks following the operation, as they feared that it would upset the parents to see their babies bound in the straitjacket designed to keep them from touching their lips and noses. Nor did they want parents to see their babies with clamps on their faces to keep them stable while they healed. While most babies had the surgery soon after birth, I had spent three months bonding with my parents at home before the hospitalization and surgery. Suddenly I was alone, in a straitjacket, and with my face clamped so that I couldn't even smile. In the hospital, I had no parents to love me.

This began my long struggle with abandonment issues. As a baby, of course, I had no idea why I was left by my parents in this strange world of the hospital. I had no idea that this would ever end. I still feel the hurt in my stomach when I think about the agony I must have felt as a baby in that hospital. Even after my parents brought me home, they kept me in that straitjacket for three months.

When I was growing up, my parents loved to travel, and they usually left my brother and me in a boarding camp or in boarding school. Every time they dropped me off and drove away, that old sense of abandonment overwhelmed me. I didn't see other little boys, nor my brother, react so emotionally. What was wrong with me?

So, when Temp left, my heart sank, and once again, I felt alone and abandoned. Watching him drive off with his real lover, I thought he was the last chance I would ever have at a love relationship. Even after my cancers went into remission, I thought AIDS would still cut my life short.

I told my therapist about being in a straitjacket as a baby, and she had me pantomime taking off my straitjacket. With that simple exercise, I felt a new freedom, and I rarely struggled with feeling abandoned after that.

As they say, timing is everything. Right after my now ex-lover drove away from me that day in the Plummer Park parking lot, a car pulled up beside me. It was Peter Scott, the handsome chairman of the APLA board of directors. I'd been a member of the board for quite a while at that point. Peter asked how I was and, my voice breaking, I told him, "My lover just left me."

He said, "I'm sorry." After a pause, he continued, "Would you be willing to serve as secretary of the board? You'd be on the Executive Committee, of course."

They had realized they needed a client on the Executive Committee, and at the time, I was the only client on the board. I agreed to serve as secretary. That immediately doubled the number of meetings I would have to attend each month. By this time, I was also serving on the Executive Committee of the Los Angeles City / County AIDS Task Force, as well as the board of the AIDS Interfaith Council of Southern California. Plus, I was on the AIDS Project Los Angeles Spiritual Advisory Committee, and I was doing a lot of interviews on television news and talk shows, usually from that chair in the alley next to the AIDS Project Los Angeles offices.

I didn't particularly enjoy board and committee meetings, but I found myself attending more and more of them. I often didn't know what to say. When other members of these boards and committees began commenting on this, I grew increasingly uncomfortable and even more tongue-tied. And yet I kept getting asked to serve on this, that, and the other board, task force, and committee. I was a well-educated person with AIDS, whose title of Reverend looked good on any letterhead, and I had had plenty of board experience in Hartford. I kept getting recruited, and I kept saying, "Yes," despite my illness and the suramin trials. I felt obligated to attend every meeting, but I was miserable during most of them, knowing I was just not very good at participating, especially now that suramin was taking so much out of me.

Finally, one AIDS Project board member took it upon herself to help me. Jackie Goldberg was a prominent member of the Los Angeles Unified School District Board of Education. She was a powerful figure and certainly knew how to navigate and participate in board meetings. So, at her invitation, I went down to her office, and she gave me very specific instructions. She told me to read every report, every page of material that was mailed to us each month. I was to underline everything I had a question about, or wished to address, and then make notes. I did just that and became more of a vocal participant on all those boards and committees, thanks to Jackie Goldberg.

Meanwhile, I continued going to the couples' support group a few more times after Temp left. I was reluctant to let go of that support, but Jack insisted that I stop attending, since it was a couples' group, and I was now single again. It saddened me greatly when other members of the group agreed. It was just as well, as it was getting harder and harder to muster the energy to drive over to West Hollywood on Monday nights after the infusion of suramin earlier in the day, but it was still hard to say goodbye. Even though I was the one who was leaving, I felt the deep pain of abandonment again.

In June, Bill Misenhimer, AIDS Project Los Angeles's executive director, asked me to identify four people living with AIDS, including myself if I liked, who would ride in the car at the head of the AIDS Project's contingent in the Christopher Street West Parade, West Hollywood's LGBT Pride parade. I asked two of my suramin buddies, George and Floyd, and they were delighted and excited. None of the other suramin patients at County Hospital wanted to do it, and it was understandable. AIDS was still a stigmatized disease, and many people did not want to be publicly identified.

I asked Mace, a friend from a support group I'd attended in the first year after my AIDS diagnosis in 1984. We'd hit it off right away and talked regularly. I knew from our lunches together over the months that his Kaposi's sarcoma was advancing rapidly. His face and body were covered with the purple lesions, and he had taken to wearing a wide-brimmed hat with a veil over his face.

He had been a member of a gay motorcycle club called "The Cycle Sluts" but was no longer able to participate. Mace was known for having challenged a well-known West Hollywood coffee shop where, when he was healthy, he'd eaten almost every day. When his purple lesions started becoming obvious, he was asked not to come back to the restaurant. Word spread throughout the LGBT community, and a strike against them hastened their demise.

As his disease progressed, Mace became depressed. He told me it felt as if people were killing him off before he died. Some people didn't want to watch him suffer and die, so they said goodbye not long after he was diagnosed. This kind of rejection was common among people with AIDS. It had happened to me with a couple of former friends.

The day of the Christopher Street West Parade, the three of us suramin patients found the convertible at the head of the APLA contingent and climbed in. George, Floyd, and I climbed up on top of the back seat. We were each wearing T-shirts that Scott had had made for us, with "Suramin AIDS-Busters" on the back and a big red circle with a red slash through the word "AIDS" on the front. This was the month after my lymphoma and Kaposi's sarcoma had gone into remission, and at that point, we were expecting great results with the other suramin patients. We liked being identified as the "Suramin AIDS-Busters."

Mace arrived dressed all in white, with a white hat and a veil covering his face. I offered to let him ride on the top of the back seat while I took the passenger seat, but he said he didn't feel strong enough for that, and he wanted the support of the front seat. I asked him if he was going to wear the veil for the parade itself. He said yes, so I reminded him of a passage from *The Color Purple*, in which Alice Walker writes, "I think it pisses God off if you walk by the color purple in a field somewhere and don't notice it."

As the parade got started, Mace took off his hat and veil and showed his face with its purple lesions to the crowds. I was moved beyond words to witness his willingness to show people what advanced Kaposi's sarcoma could really look like, with such large, purple lesions covering and even distorting many of his facial features.

Most of the crowd cheered for us, and we cheered and waved right back. Many in the throngs of people along the parade route were clearly cheering for Mace, with some folks running out into the street to shake his hand, to commend him for his courage, or to just cheer him on and offer their best wishes.

A few people here and there reacted with looks of disgust or looked away. I noticed one handsome man along the route turn his rather frail companion away before he could see Mace. It upset me to see that happen, even though Mace seemed only to hear the cheers.

A few years later, I read Paul Monette's *Borrowed Time*. At one point, he described how horrified he was by seeing this man covered with

Kaposi's sarcoma lesions in the AIDS Project LA car at the Christopher Street West Parade in 1985 and how he had to turn his lover, Roger, away so that he wouldn't see the horror of that man with his purple lesions. It made me so angry when I read that, to think that this brilliant author could not see what a triumph it was for Mace. It taught me something about the way people can see the same event so differently.

I could see Mace was buoyed by all the cheers. At the end of the parade, as he got out of the car, he was beaming with joy. The experience of the parade had lifted his spirits in a way that probably nothing else could have. He had such a great energy about him as we embraced and said goodbye. Mace died a couple of weeks later, but I was so glad and grateful that he'd had those joyful moments of shining pride and self-confidence that he had been sorely lacking for quite a long time.

That summer, the biennial General Conference of the Metropolitan Community Churches was held in Sacramento. Almost all the churches from around the world sent delegates, and almost all the clergy were there, as well as many observers. This was the conference where the business of the denomination was taken care of.

At the opening press conference, Rev. Elder Troy Perry, the founder and moderator of the denomination, told the press that the first member of the denomination's clergy to be diagnosed with AIDS had gone into complete remission on an experimental drug and was cured. I had to correct him in front of the media, telling Troy and the press that this was Dr. Levine's news to tell, that it wasn't considered a "cure," and that they didn't know if it would work for others, nor if there would be long-term side effects.

Nevertheless, word of mouth at the conference spread that I was in complete remission, and many in the denomination interpreted that to mean I was "healed" or even "cured." I spent a lot of time that week correcting people. Some of those people helped me to begin to see that I had indeed experienced a healing, in that my cancers were in remission, even if it wasn't a cure.

I was a high-profile person at the conference, since the whole denomination had been reading my articles in *Journey Magazine* about my life with AIDS. I had lots of strangers introducing themselves and telling me how AIDS had affected them, although there were not many people living with AIDS there.

One afternoon of the conference was devoted to AIDS, but it was the one day in the week when there was no business meeting. So, a lot of people went out sightseeing instead of attending the AIDS plenary session. For the faithful remnant, I had helped plan an afternoon of AIDS education covering everything from a medical update to suggestions for AIDS ministry in local churches. Troy opened the plenary, and in his speech, he said, "We all know that Rev. Steve Pieters is, well, vanilla. So, if he can get AIDS, then we're all at risk." Funny, I didn't think of myself as vanilla, but Troy did have a point about people's risk factors.

Throughout the spring and summer, the weekly suramin infusions continued. Nancy Radclyffe continued to accompany me to almost all of these treatments. By this time, there were twelve of us receiving suramin at County Hospital and around ninety people around the country. We still had to wait two to three hours for our lab work to be done, but at least we could wait on recliners in the chemo room now.

Reverend Nancy, sensing the need for entertainment, had us answer Trivial Pursuit questions. Our attempts at answering had us roaring in laughter, with cheers and applause scattered in among the hilarity. At first, doctors and nurses would stick their heads into the chemo room to see what was causing all this raucous laughter, an unusual occurrence in the chemo room, to be sure. We were delighted to surprise them with our good spirits, and then we would giggle among ourselves after they left.

When we got our lab results, those who were well enough received the suramin. The drug felt cold as it dripped into our veins. The laughter dwindled. We all became quiet with the immediate effects of the treatment. The suramin pushed us down to where movement was difficult and our energy was gone.

One of the members of what we were calling the Suramin for Brunch Bunch was Linda, a sweet-spirited young woman who looked skeletal and frail when we met. She had been infected by her bisexual husband, who had died leaving her with three young children. She had remarried before she herself was diagnosed. The suramin treatments did not seem to be helping her, but she kept coming, and we were glad to have her with us.

At the time, there were very few women diagnosed with AIDS for a variety of reasons. For one, many physicians weren't looking for AIDS in women. Also, AIDS tended to present differently in women. So by the time they figured out a woman had AIDS, she was usually quite sick, and as a result, many women did not live long after their diagnoses. Indeed, Linda was the first of our suramin group to die.

In late July 1985, AIDS Project Los Angeles held the world's first AIDS Walk. We had expected the Walk would raise $100,000, but a few days before the event, Rock Hudson disclosed that he had AIDS. The world was shocked not only to discover that Rock Hudson had AIDS, but that he was gay. Fellow board member Paula Van Ness told me she did between thirty and forty interviews with the media after his announcement. Our executive director, Bill Misenhimer, told me he did forty or fifty interviews. I did quite a few myself. I had mixed feelings about Hudson's diagnosis. I was sad for him but pleased that a movie star's diagnosis would bring much-needed attention to AIDS.

With the world's focus now on AIDS, a surge of close to forty-five hundred people signed up to walk and raise money.

With the increasing side effects of the suramin treatments, I wouldn't be able to walk the ten kilometers, but as a board member, I attended the Walk. All the board members were asked to thank walkers as they returned to the starting point just inside the famous gates of Paramount Studios.

I didn't want to miss a moment. My heart raced with excitement just walking through those famous gates. There was a program before the Walk began, in the Paramount "tank" where they had filmed Charlton Heston parting the Red Sea in *The Ten Commandments*. The program featured many speakers, each cheering on the walkers and wishing Rock Hudson the best.

Oddly enough, there were no people with AIDS speaking. After the walk began, I raised the issue with the Walk organizers. Embarrassed at their oversight, they asked me if I would speak at the closing ceremony. I said, "Of course," and immediately began to worry about what I would say. I had a good long time to worry, since the walk would take several hours before all the walkers were back for the closing.

As they started to come back in, we cheered for them, shook their hands, and asked them to be sure and sign the huge "Get Well" card for Rock Hudson. It was four feet tall and twenty-five feet long, and I signed it along with many of the nearly five thousand walkers and over a hundred volunteers.

I don't remember what I said at the closing ceremony, beyond "Thank you on behalf of all the AIDS Project's clients," but I got lots of backslapping and handshakes from people, thanking me for my courage in being so public about having AIDS, both here and in my media appearances.

The Walk ended up raising $673,000 for the AIDS Project. The board of directors meeting after the Walk was spirited, with people excited for the huge amount raised. The discussion about the organizers' fee was spirited, too. The contract we had signed gave the organizers a certain percentage of the funds raised, but when it turned out to be such a large amount, some board members wanted to break the contract and pay them a flat fee. The organizers won that battle, but this conflict impacted all future contract negotiations. It left a bad taste in many of our mouths after what many considered a huge success.

As the suramin treatments continued, I had to stop going to the gym. I was exhausted all the time. I managed to summon enough energy to drive to the AIDS Project board meetings, but I began missing other meetings.

As September began, I was losing interest in food. I lost a lot of weight even though I didn't have much weight to lose. When I had hepatitis in 1983, I was devastated that I'd lost the musculature I had built up in previous years. I worked hard at rebuilding my body after the infections and illnesses of 1983. Now, once again, I grieved for the muscular body I lost, this time due to suramin.

I was sleeping a lot, taking an hour-long nap in the morning and two- or three-hour naps in the afternoon. Many nights, I couldn't sleep. I couldn't get comfortable. I ached all over. At least my lymphoma and Kaposi's sarcoma were still in remission, but I was once again seriously ill.

When I couldn't sleep, I ached for someone to hold me and comfort me. After a few nights of praying about my loneliness, I remembered my grandfather's seminary class hymn, "Jesus, Lover of My Soul." So, I invited Jesus into my bed. I pictured Him strong and handsome, with beautiful, long, dark hair. I felt Him holding me in His strong arms, blessing me, and giving me comfort and reassurance, as a lover would. This got me through many lonely nights.

With Rock Hudson hospitalized at the University of California–Los Angeles hospital, Bill Misenhimer, our executive director, decided it was time to appeal to the entertainment industry to raise money for AIDS Project Los Angeles. He was able to enlist Rock Hudson's close friend Elizabeth Taylor to chair the event, called "Commitment to Life." She told Bill and the banquet's committee that she didn't want to be called a chairwoman, chairperson, or chair. "If a man can be a chairman," she told them, "then I can be a chairman."

Elizabeth, Bill, and the organizing committee planned a star-studded banquet with speeches and entertainment at a hotel in Century City, but it quickly became necessary to find a bigger venue. Everyone wanted a ticket, and many people were turned away, even in the much larger ball-room of the Bonaventure Hotel. Elizabeth would give former first lady Betty Ford the first "Commitment to Life" award, and stars of film and TV would entertain. Even so, since AIDS was still such a controversial issue, Elizabeth had to strong-arm some of the major players in Hollywood to attend.

As plans took shape, I realized there were no people living with AIDS who would be speaking. I brought it up with my therapist, Barbara, and she told me I should offer to be that person. I wasn't at all sure I would be the best choice, as thin and frail as I was, and frankly, I didn't have the nerve to promote myself like that, although deep in my heart I wanted to do it.

The next time I was at the agency, I suggested to Bill that there be at least one client addressing the crowd, and Bill immediately asked me to be that client. I was, after all, the client representative on the board of directors, and he knew that as a minister, I had a lot of public speaking experience. I said yes and was immediately swamped with self-doubts and fear.

Two weeks before the event, Bruce Vilanch, a comedy writer who was becoming quite well known in Hollywood, called to say he would be writing the Commitment to Life event. He asked what I wanted to say when I spoke. I gave him my ideas. He told me Shirley MacLaine was going to introduce me, so he wanted some biographical material as well to write an introduction about me for her. "Oh my God," I thought. "Shirley MacLaine!" I'd read all her books and always enjoyed her performances on film.

A couple days later, I received my script in the mail, with a note from Bruce saying that I could edit it however I like, but I could use this as a guide. It was practically perfect. I did my best to memorize it, but there were a few phrases that didn't sound like me, so I changed them to suit my style, with Bruce's approval.

One night, as I was trying to get to sleep, I got the idea that I should close my speech with a little soft shoe to show I was still alive and kicking, just as I did in my Easter sermon right after my diagnosis. Could I get away with it as the client representative on the board? Would I really have the nerve to tap-dance in front of all of Hollywood? I mean, Gene Kelly might be there! Nevertheless, the more I thought about it, the more it seemed like a good idea. I was initially worried that I would embarrass myself, or the agency, but then, I thought, it would certainly show that as a person with AIDS I was indeed still dancing and still living.

There was a rehearsal the night before the actual event. Joe Layton, a Tony and Emmy Award winner, was directing the show, and I knew some celebrity participants would be there, too. I was nervous.

The only time I'd ever met any movie stars or TV celebrities was in 1974, when Dad arranged for me to meet his former student Oscar winner Jack Lemmon. That in no way prepared me for all the encounters I knew I was about to have. I dressed up for the Bonaventure rehearsal in a two-toned gray outfit a friend from the couples' group had helped me pick out from a store on Hollywood Boulevard. I should have worn a suit.

The rehearsal began in a suite at the Bonaventure. I was shown in and introduced to Joe Layton. I felt awkward and self-conscious as I found a seat. Phil Donahue (in a suit) and Marlo Thomas were on my left. Morgan Fairchild was talking with them. On my right was Helen Kushnick, a talent agent who eventually became the controversial, first producer of the Jay Leno *Tonight Show*. Her three-year-old son had died of AIDS in 1983 as the result of a blood transfusion, and she was speaking at the event as well.

It was amazing and somewhat nerve-wracking to be among all these famous people. I was still stunned that I would be sharing the stage with Elizabeth Taylor, Betty Ford, Shirley MacLaine, plus an array of entertainers like Carol Burnett, Sammy Davis Jr., and Cher.

In the rehearsal suite, there was one old man who didn't seem to fit in at all. He was quite disheveled, with a few long wisps of gray hair growing out of his bald head and long, out-of-control eyebrows. He was dressed in a threadbare, plaid shirt and faded coveralls. Then he spoke. There was no mistaking that voice. This rumpled old man was Oscar winner Burt Lancaster. For the event, he was going to read a letter from his friend Rock Hudson. He turned out to be quite friendly, and I was delighted to have a chat with him as we headed downstairs to the banquet hall for the rest of the rehearsal.

The banquet hall was huge. Joe Layton gave general directions to all of us before giving his attention to the various stars who would speak. There were three stages, each one an island among the tables. I was to speak on the center stage, where Shirley MacLaine would introduce me. There was a platform behind the center stage where the Peter Matz orchestra would play and where the podium stood for Elizabeth Taylor and Betty Ford to make their remarks.

Joe Layton began to give me directions on how I was to get on stage. He kept calling me "Reverend Steve," and I said, "Please, just call me Steve." He paused for a moment, as if he wasn't sure what to say, but then continued with my staging. When he was done, Helen Kushnick took me aside and sternly told me, "You must never, ever correct the director like that." The way she said it with such authority left me shaking with embarrassment.

The next evening, Bill Misenhimer drove me to the hotel, which I deeply appreciated, as nervous as I was. We were told to head down to the press area. We were shown into a long, wide corridor. Off this hallway, there were three large rooms: one for photographers, one for the print media, and one for television news and entertainment shows.

Bill disappeared to consult with some publicist, and at another publicist's request, I joined the long line of movie and TV stars, as well as a few political figures, all of whom were waiting to be ushered into each of the three rooms. I found myself standing next to Diahann Carroll, who was strikingly tall and statuesque. Betty Ford was there, with her secret service detail standing close by. She was the first to be whisked into the photographers' room.

I couldn't believe I was standing in that hallway with Carol Burnett, Shirley MacLaine, Cher, Linda Evans, and Mayor Tom Bradley as well as many other celebrities. I felt totally incapable of speaking to any of them. Fortunately, my "old friend" Burt Lancaster was there, now well groomed, with his toupee and tuxedo and looking exactly like Burt Lancaster. Again he was friendly and down-to-earth, and I was delighted to have his company.

After most of the stars had taken their turns in front of the photographers, I was finally ushered into their room. I was introduced as the APLA client and board member who would speak at the event. As I faced them, flashbulbs started going off all across the bank of photographers in front of me. It wasn't difficult to smile. It was a thrill to have so many photographers taking my picture, as if I was a celebrity.

Next I was shown to the other end of the corridor, where I was introduced to the print media. I spelled my name, as instructed, and spoke briefly about what I would say that evening as the APLA client representative. I answered a few questions and exited back into the hallway.

As I waited outside the TV reporters' room, I watched Betty Ford, Diahann Carroll, and then Shirley MacLaine each give brief remarks, followed by any number of questions from the media journalists in that room.

After Shirley MacLaine was done, I was ushered into the same room and introduced. I was dismayed that many of the video cameras stopped

Steve Pieters poses for the bank of photographers at the first Commitment to Life, the film and television industry's fundraiser for AIDS Project Los Angeles, September 1985. COURTESY OF APLA HEALTH.

or never even started. After I was introduced, I made a few opening comments. Silence. Finally, Rona Barrett, the Hollywood gossip columnist, asked me a question: "What do you hope this evening's event will do to dispel the real fear of AIDS in this country?" I answered, "I am very hopeful that the turnout of stars and celebrities will really help people across the country realize there is nothing to fear in being in the same room as a person with AIDS, in embracing a person with AIDS, in being present to a person with AIDS." She gave me a polite smile, and after some more silence, I was shown out of the room. I was relieved my three moments in front of the media were over.

My speech at the dinner was yet to happen, so I was still nervous. I was shown upstairs to the ballroom, which had come alive with over 2,500 people in attendance. It reassured me to see some familiar faces, not just the estimated 250 celebrities, but the friendly faces of people I knew from APLA. All the staff were there (there weren't that many of them in 1985), as well as my fellow board members and many of my fellow clients. My good friends, APLA cofounders Matt Redman, Nancy Cole Sawaya, and Max Drew were there, along with Max's partner, Steven Kant, and Nancy's husband, Lou.

I was shown to my table, right next to the center stage, down front. I was seated next to Helen Kushnick and her husband. The feminist politician and social activist Bella Abzug was also at my table, along with Renée Taylor, an Oscar-nominated writer and actress. In her loud voice, Bella complained to anyone who stopped by that she and Renée were upset that they were seated at a table with no other celebrities.

I was amazed to see Cher, with braces on her teeth, appear at the table to chat with Bella Abzug. As I looked around, I noticed that Rod Stewart and Cyndi Lauper were at the table next to me. Everywhere I looked there were famous faces, like Angie Dickinson, Burt Reynolds, and members of the casts of *Dynasty* and *Dallas*. I felt star-struck, and I panicked that I would never be able to speak in front of all these celebrities.

I was given last-minute instructions by the stage manager. Bruce Vilanch sat down with me for a moment to make sure I was ready with my speech. I told him about my idea of tap dancing at the end of my speech to show them I was living with AIDS, not dying. He laughed and said, "Do it!"

Elizabeth Taylor made her entrance in the glare of a spotlight. She looked gorgeous with that hourglass figure and that exquisitely beautiful face. After her welcoming remarks, she sat down at the table across the stage from me, with Betty Ford, Burt Reynolds, Mayor Tom Bradley, and my friends Nancy Cole Sawaya, Lou Sawaya, Bill Misenhimer, and APLA board chair Peter Scott.

After the main course, the program finally started. When Shirley MacLaine was introduced, I started doing some deep breathing to calm myself, but my nervousness remained.

Shirley MacLaine went on with her speech for what seemed like an eternity but was a little less than ten minutes. She said that AIDS was aptly named, as it was "aiding" the world in so many ways, to learn so many lessons. While she spoke, a volunteer came, gave me my mike, and ushered me to the stairs up to the stage where Shirley was speaking.

She finished her speech to great applause and began to exit. Then, seeing me, she turned back and said, "And now, another person who chose love over fear, and who's a constant and continuing reminder of this evening's theme, being a 'Commitment to Life,' the Reverend Stephen A. Pieters."

"Yikes," I thought. "She got my name wrong, but I'm ON! Please, God, don't let me fall climbing these stairs." Funny what goes through your head at such moments.

I stepped up to the stage, and she greeted me with the words, "Don't be nervous, Reverend. Just speak your truth!" I couldn't quite believe I was being greeted by THE Shirley MacLaine. Up close, she looked just like Shirley MacLaine, which somehow surprised me. I was so full of nervous energy that I felt as if my heart would burst and my head would explode. She gave me a long, tight hug, and when we pulled back from the hug, she gave me a smile and left the stage.

I launched into my speech, telling them how I preached the Easter sermon two weeks after my AIDS diagnosis. I told them, "They told me the worst thing they could possibly tell me, and I could still dance!" The audience applauded. I looked down, and there were Elizabeth Taylor, Burt Reynolds, and Betty Ford applauding me. Oh my God.

I somehow continued, "The point I want to make this evening, is that I am still alive."

Shirley MacLaine shouted, "Bravo!" and the audience applauded again.

I said, "There are quite a few of us who have AIDS who are here with us tonight." Silence. "On behalf of people with AIDS everywhere, I would like to thank you all ... for the love and the support that you are showing us tonight, because that love and support is giving us life. I really hope that the world learns an important lesson from all of you. God bless you all ... and keep on dancing!" I did my shuffle off to Buffalo step over to the stairs where I would exit. I raised my hand with the mike in the air in triumph, and the audience applauded and cheered. I came down off the stage, and the spotlight caught Shirley MacLaine giving me another big hug. Her mike was live, and she said, "Bravo, Reverend." The applause continued and continued.

I returned to my table, and Bella Abzug made eye contact and applauded me. Renée Taylor threw me a kiss. Helen Kushnick hugged my arm and said, "Well done." I've always been nervous after a speech, and this evening was no exception. Despite the positive feedback I was getting, I began questioning everything I'd said, wondering if I'd said too much, or not said enough, or put it wrong. Maybe I shouldn't have tap-danced in front of everyone. I worried my soft-shoe was leaden. But deep down, I felt a lot of joy and self-satisfaction.

Linda Evans, one of the stars of *Dynasty*, got up to speak after me. There had been many rumors about her being angry with Rock Hudson for kissing her on the show, with the fear that he might have given her AIDS. She dispelled all that in her remarks, talking about her continuing friendship with Rock and how she had learned that there was no reason for her to be afraid about his having kissed her on *Dynasty*.

She then introduced Burt Lancaster, who read a letter from Rock Hudson, now hospitalized at UCLA. Hudson's letter spoke of being proud of his friend, Elizabeth Taylor, as well as all the folks from his industry that showed up that evening. He wrote he hated having AIDS, but he was grateful that his celebrity had brought needed attention to the disease. It was a gracious, well-worded letter, and of course, Lancaster read it beautifully. There was a momentary silence, and then a surge of applause as Lancaster left the stage, with people standing and cheering. Hudson died less than two weeks later.

The entertainment portion of the evening began. Carol Burnett and Sammy Davis Jr. sang "a medley of every song ever written," or so they joked. Diahann Carroll, accompanied by Richard Carpenter, sang "You've Got a Friend" and "We've Only Just Begun," joined by the Gay Men's Chorus of Los Angeles. Then Cher spoke, substituting for Bette Midler, who, Cher said, "was waylaid." She paused for the laugh, then added, "in Italy." She then introduced Sam Harris, who sang the rousing finale to the evening, "You Gotta Have Friends," also accompanied by the Gay Men's Chorus.

As soon as the program was over, many people rushed over to me to thank me for my speech. Bill Misenhimer congratulated me and invited me to an after-party upstairs for the participating celebrities, as well as for APLA board members and major donors.

When I was able to break free of all the people wanting to talk with me, I headed to the elevator, and I was excited to see that Shirley MacLaine was right in front of me, also waiting for the elevator, with a familiar-looking man talking to her. As we got on, she turned around to face the elevator doors and saw me right in front of her.

She gave me a big smile and another hug and said, "I loved what you said."

I thanked her, and then she introduced me to Stevie Wonder. He put out his hand, and I took it, saying what an honor it was to meet him. He said, "I recognize your beautiful voice. I loved what you said, too." Stevie Wonder thought I had a beautiful voice! And he "loved" what I said! I thanked him, just as we arrived at the floor where the party was. There was an amazing buffet of food and drink, but I couldn't eat, because I was just too excited by the whole evening, let alone being with all these stars.

One of the moments that meant the most to me was when one APLA board member who had always been gruff with me, rushed up to me with a big smile on her face. She gave me a hug and said, "You said all the right things. You gave us all hope. You were perfect!"

I left the party after many others had left. I just didn't want to miss a moment, and I didn't want to let this evening go. Bill Misenhimer left earlier, so I took a taxi home. After this evening, I felt justified in splurging on a cab ride, just like Eliza Doolittle.

When I got home, I had to smoke a joint to try to come down from this most exciting night of my life. I was still smoking marijuana every day at this point, but I hadn't on this day because of speaking at the big event. So, now I lay back on my couch, with my cats on top of me. I watched some of the local TV news reports about the event as I got stoned. I thought back over the evening. Despite all the compliments I'd gotten from so many people, I began second-guessing everything I had said. I replayed every moment of the whole evening in my head. I simply could not believe I had met and mingled with so many stars.

I went to bed and tried to sleep, but I couldn't. I was still way too excited. I got up and smoked another joint, but that didn't help. I went back to bed and dozed off here and there, but my heart would not stop racing, and my brain would not stop replaying the evening.

The next morning, I could feel something in my body had shifted. It was as if a switch had been flipped. I suddenly felt I was on the bottom of a bowl of gelatin all the time, and I had no appetite. I started to get sicker and weaker every day.

As sick as I was, joy filled my heart because no one could take away the memories of my evening among the stars.

CHAPTER FIVE

A Renewed Commitment to Life

AFTER THE COMMITMENT TO LIFE EVENT, I BEGAN SLEEPING TWENTY to twenty-two hours a day. I had no appetite, and I continued to lose weight until I was not much more than a skeleton with skin. Even my heart seemed to be beating more slowly.

My body was failing me, and I couldn't help but think about dying. I was eighteen months out from my terminal prognosis, and that was the life expectancy for people with AIDS. My body was deteriorating rapidly, and the doctors could not figure out why, since my lymphoma and Kaposi's sarcoma were still in remission.

I was frightened of dying, particularly of dying alone. I felt my faith in the Resurrection was supposed to give me courage in facing my mortality, but now I was fearful that dying would be a horrible experience. The thought of not having anyone with me who loved me and cared for me made dying even more terrifying. My pain and suffering seemed to be a preparation for dying. It was as if God was allowing this suffering to happen to make me willing, even eager, to leave my body behind. And yet, I was scared. I desperately wanted loved ones with me, to share in my terror and pain. I did not want to die alone.

I forced myself to eat a little bit every day. Barbara said that it sometimes worked to bribe your appetite with favorite foods from your childhood. So, I had my APLA Buddy, Beau, buy me Trix cereal, rainbow sherbet, and Fig Newton cookies. I was able to eat some of each, but nothing seemed very appetizing.

Of course, the suramin for brunch bunch kept meeting every Monday. Reverend Nancy continued to drive me there each week, and she tried to perk us all up with more Trivial Pursuit. None of us had the energy to play. Nancy kept trying, but we were all frail and weak. While they ran lab tests on each of us, we waited quietly for the suramin drip.

I was deteriorating rapidly. The few hours I was awake each day, I was so weak that I could barely get to the bathroom. It always lifted my spirits to see Beau, Reverend Nancy, or Steven Kant. All three of them were a great comfort to me. For their sakes, I tried eating the scrambled eggs Beau or Reverend Nancy would make for me, along with a single section of an orange, but I could only manage a bite or two. After they left, I'd smoke part of a joint, but even that didn't help my appetite.

Somehow, I flew to Chicago in this condition. I had been invited to preach at the weekend-long celebration of the church's fifteenth anniversary. I stayed with Roger "Rebel" Goodman, the first openly gay man I had ever met. I was desperately weak and in so much pain, but it meant so much to me to stay with him.

We had first met right after I graduated from Phillips Academy Andover, on my first day with the College Light Opera Company. When my parents dropped me off, the manager of the company asked me if I had a dance belt. I had no idea what a dance belt was, but he told me all the men in the company were required to wear one in each performance. He sent me upstairs to see the company choreographer, Roger "Rebel" Goodman, about ordering dance belts. I marched upstairs and knocked on Rebel's door.

A tall white man with an Afro, wearing an African print kaftan opened the door, and the pungent smells of marijuana and patchouli billowed out. I glanced around the room, which was painted black with photos of naked boys on the walls, and nervously told him that I needed to order some dance belts. With an amused leer, he asked, "What size?" I worried he'd want me to take my pants off to determine that. But he didn't, thank God. I told him "medium," and he said, "No, small," and he laughed in falsetto. This experience shocked and scared me. Was this how I would have to be if I came out?

Now, staying with him in Chicago, Rebel and I became intimately acquainted. I was too weak to bathe or shower, so he got in the shower with me and held me up while he washed me. He held me close as we slept together. I was so appreciative of his loving kindness. I felt so safe and comfortable with him, far from my experience with the same gay man who'd frightened me on my first day in summer stock. I wished I had him to sleep with me back home. I hoped I would have him or someone holding me close in my deathbed.

Christie and her mom, Millie, took me to lunch at the Drake Hotel the first day I was back in Chicago. It was right across the street from the Playboy building. The restaurant was up a long, wide flight of stairs. I was so weak that Christie and Millie had to stand on either side of me and push me up the stairs.

I had never been to the large, beautiful restaurant at the Drake. I had no appetite, but Millie and Christie encouraged me to eat something. The fruit salad sounded all right, but I could only nibble at it. I was delighted to bask in their loving, cheerful, and compassionate presence and tried hard to stay engaged in conversation, but I lost focus and drifted several times. I could see Christie and Millie were alarmed at my condition, but I felt powerless to perk up and engage with them, much as I'd have liked.

On Saturday, the *Windy City Times* interviewed me about having AIDS, as well as about my experience at Good Shepherd Parish Metropolitan Community Church when I did my clergy internship there. I told the reporter about "The Golden Age of Good Shepherd Parish" when Rev. Ken Martin was the pastor, and there were around a dozen people on staff. We routinely had a packed congregation each Sunday evening. We were a loving, vibrant community of faith.

Saturday night, I preached at the second service of the MCC Anniversary weekend. Christie came to hear me, which was a great surprise. I did the same message I had delivered at that first Easter service right after receiving my terminal prognosis. When I said, "I can still dance," I tried to do a tap step. I thought I was about to fall over. It felt jarring and sluggish to me, but the congregation applauded supportively.

It felt good to be back among the people in the church where I had come out, received my call, and done my student clergy work. I couldn't muster the energy to meet and greet everyone as they left the sanctuary. I felt bad about that, but at least I knew that limit.

On Sunday Christie picked me up to take me to the airport. She had a new recording of *West Side Story* she knew I'd enjoy on the drive, since I was not up for conversation. At the airport, she got me a wheelchair and took me to the VIP lounge. There, she had me lie on a couch with my head in her lap, as she stroked my hair.

When the flight was called, she took me to the gate in the wheelchair and then accompanied me onto the plane, supporting me all the way. She pushed aside the flight attendants to make sure I was seated comfortably in the front row of economy, next to the window, so I could lean up against it. I thought I detected tears in her eyes as she said goodbye to me. She could not have been more loving.

Beau met me at the airport to drive me home. I was so weak and in such pain that I knew I couldn't sit up for that long drive. Beau put the passenger seat all the way back, and I lay there motionless. He got me settled back at home but later told me he should have taken me right to the hospital.

On Monday, October 21, I was denied the suramin treatment for the first time because my lab tests showed that I was just too sick. That was not a big surprise. Nancy took me home, scrambled an egg for me, and then had to leave. I smoked part of a joint and fell asleep on the couch. I woke up hours later and turned on a rerun of *M*A*S*H*. Partway through an episode, one of Dr. Levine's staff doctors, Jeannie Hawkins, called. She told me they finally figured out that the suramin had caused my adrenal glands to fail. She insisted I come into the hospital right away so they could give me hydrocortisone to replace the cortisol that my adrenal glands had not been producing for weeks. I asked her, "Can't it wait until morning? I'm just so tired, and I'm about to go to bed."

She replied, "No, you could even die from this by morning. You've got to come in now."

That scared me. I remembered hearing the great preacher William Sloane Coffin saying, "We can be scared to death, or we can be scared to life." I could be paralyzed by my fear, or I could take action. I called Mitch, my landlady upstairs, and she agreed to drive me. She came downstairs to help me up the stairs to her car. I had no energy for conversation.

Dr. Jeannie had said to come to the emergency room, and she would make sure I was seen right away for the hydrocortisone treatment. When we got there, Mitch told me she was just going to drop me off, because it was nighttime, and she didn't want to have to park and walk in that neighborhood.

I couldn't believe that she was going to drop me at the door to the ER and leave, but I understood her reason, and she drove away. I wished I had someone with me, to advocate for me, and to be there with me, in case I died. But now I was facing this all alone. I was scared.

Neither Dr. Hawkins nor any of the other doctors or nurses I knew were there at that hour. I signed in, and as weak as I was, they put me on a gurney right away in what seemed like the waiting room from hell, filled with gurneys with other patients in severe distress. The fellow on the next gurney had wounds from a stabbing. Another patient close by was vomiting blood. There was horrible suffering all over the room, and the medical staff were busily doing everything they could to help. I was so depleted, I wanted to fall asleep, but I couldn't afford to. I knew I had to stay awake somehow, even if I did have to witness all this suffering.

Finally my gurney was wheeled down to a hallway right outside the "Red Blanket Room," where patients were triaged. As I lay there on my gurney, in severe distress, with no energy and no ability to get up or advocate for myself, I seriously wondered if I would die there in the hallway. Doctors and nurses were scurrying everywhere. I prayed, "Please, God, don't let me die here, alone without any family or friends."

Suddenly, a man attacked one of the patients on a gurney just a few feet away. A loud fight broke out around that patient, but not for long, as security broke them up and escorted the attacker out. An orderly arrived at my gurney and wheeled me into the Red Blanket room where I was put on an exam table between two other patients on exam tables and across from three others. A nurse attached me to wires that would keep track of my vitals.

A resident asked me if I knew why I was there. I said, "Yes, because my adrenal glands have failed, and I'm supposed to get hydrocortisone."

He replied, "You're an AIDS patient, so we have to work you up before we can administer any treatment, to be sure that this is safe." Someone did a chest x-ray right on the gurney.

The nurses and doctors had to attend to the patient on my left. She died, and her body was taken away. Was I next to die? I began to panic that they would not give me the hydrocortisone soon enough. After all, Dr. Hawkins had said I might be dead by morning if I didn't get the treatment.

I could feel that I was dying. I was terrified of dying alone, but here I was, dying alone. I didn't have anyone around me who loved me. No one was there to hold me close as I faced my death.

Then a familiar face arrived. It was Bopper, a young doctor who worked for Dr. Levine. A nurse said, "His blood pressure is 50/30 and dropping."

I was so relieved that Bopper was there. His familiar face and demeanor lifted my spirits. He said, "We're going to draw some blood from that IV in your arm."

I could feel the life leaving my body. It began in my feet. It wasn't that the feeling was disappearing. The life force within me, my very essence, was departing my body, first up my legs, then through my torso, up my arms, and through the top of my head. "Oh God, I'm dying alone."

The nurse tried to draw my blood, but the blood wasn't flowing. She said, "Pump your hand, Steve. Pump your hand."

Suddenly, I was above my body wondering, "Why isn't that guy doing what they're telling him to do?" Then I detached from the scene. I was suddenly experiencing the deepest peace I'd ever known, truly the "peace that passes all understanding." I was without worry, without anxiety. I understood everything I'd never understood about myself and about the world. I was in perfect peace.

I felt surrounded by love. There were loving beings all around me, shadows, but some I could see were relatives who had gone before, some were figures from my early childhood, like the mailman who used to call me Steverino, and some of the people with AIDS I'd known. I realized my fear of dying alone was simply irrelevant, because I wasn't alone, not in any sense. I could even feel the love from my family and friends who were still alive in their bodies.

I found myself in a dark tunnel, surrounded by these moving shadows, pointing to a great light far away. The love that surrounded me was the most joyful thing I had ever felt. I knew then that the most important aspect of life is our relationship to others, the ability to look in each other's eyes, to really see each other's essence, and to love each other. That love is what is eternal.

Then I was back in my body. I was in pain, and I was pissed. To save my life, Bopper had started the hydrocortisone through my IV, but I was no longer in perfect peace.

When I shared this experience in future years, a doctor told me that out-of-body experiences were just chemicals going off in the brain as it shuts down. Maybe, but it helped me at the time. My attitude about death and dying changed from this experience.

I was wheeled upstairs to a six-bed ward and transferred to a hospital bed. Large purple signs announcing "BLOOD PRECAUTIONS" were slapped onto the wall above my bed and at the foot of my bed. I somehow got to sleep.

When I awoke the next morning, I felt hungry, a feeling I hadn't had in weeks. The hospital breakfast tasted good.

I looked at the patients in the other beds. They were each suffering, some loudly. They all spoke Spanish with the nurses and attendants. No one else had a large purple "BLOOD PRECAUTIONS" sign above them or at the foot of their beds.

Tom Reinhart-Marean, a Methodist pastor I worked closely with on the Spiritual Advisory Committee at APLA, walked in, and rushed to my side. Sitting, he held my hand, and I burst into tears. All the stress and distress of the long night just came pouring out of me, and Tom gave me such compassionate, caring attention. It felt so good to purge myself of all that fear and loneliness. The peace and love on the other side of the veil did not come back to me right away. All I could remember was the pain, fear, and suffering I'd been through.

Tom saw the big purple signs above me and on the foot of the bed. He angrily confronted a nurse about them when she came in to attend to another patient. She was blasé about it, noting it was hospital policy. Tom, who was acutely sensitive to the justice issues as well as the stigma associated with AIDS, was not only angry about the words on the signs, but he was affronted by their bright purple color, as if they were especially colored that way to indicate I was gay. I was embarrassed, but secretly pleased, that he was making a fuss.

After a good visit, Tom took off, saying that he was going to address this issue with hospital administration. When a bed became available, I was transferred to a private room. I still had those "BLOOD PRECAU-TIONS" signs on my bed. While I was glad to have my privacy, I became profoundly lonely. I didn't have many visitors, partly because my church friends were all on their way to the regional MCC's District Conference.

There was no radio, TV, or phone in my room, so I read and slept. A good part of my nights was taken up being wheeled around to various tests. They scheduled these tests at night because during the day they were kept busy by outpatients. One night, I was supposed to have a CT scan in the evening, but that time came and went, and I fell asleep until someone came in and woke me up to tell me it was delayed again because of new emergencies. I couldn't sleep after that and was relieved when they finally came and got me in the early morning hours. After the scan, I finally got to sleep.

Later that morning, I was still asleep when a resident came in and started grilling me. "Why are you sleeping so much during the day?"

"It's because you kept me awake for that CT scan until the early morning hours." He didn't know how to reply to that.

While I was hospitalized, my meals were left outside the door to my room a few times. The first time, a visitor spotted the tray in the hallway and brought it in. Other times, a nurse would bring it in. It didn't always happen, and I was extremely grateful when an orderly would bring in my meal tray.

One of those orderlies made conversation with me, for which I was very grateful. One day, she asked, "Why do you have these purple signs?"

"It's because I have AIDS."

She said, "Not a problem. I think I had a touch of the AIDS myself a couple weeks ago."

The day I was to be discharged, Eduardo, a friend from church, came to drive me home. I was so relieved, since Nancy and my friends were at the District Conference. I became embarrassed, though, that he had to wait with me for hours while the nurses took care of my discharge papers.

Dr. Hawkins visited me before I left and taught me exactly how and when to take the hydrocortisone and fludrocortisone that would now replace what my adrenal glands no longer produced. She told me always to take them with food, because otherwise the hydrocortisone would be quite hard on my stomach.

Furthermore, if I were ever sick again or were injured somehow, I was to increase my hydrocortisone dosage. Normally, the adrenal glands would increase the cortisol whenever my body was stressed. She also told me I would need to get a MedicAlert bracelet to wear, and she gave me the MedicAlert pamphlet and paperwork. I was so grateful for how clear and concise her instructions were about my new life without functioning adrenal glands.

I was so happy to get home. I hadn't known if I would ever see my home again or my two cats, Grindel and Preshy. I lay on the couch, with Preshy lying on my legs and Grindel on my chest, both holding me down as if they were not going to let me go anywhere any time soon. I loved my blanket of kitties.

I was feeling better. By the next Monday, they had put all the other suramin patients on hydrocortisone and fludrocortisone. After nearly losing their patient number one, they tested all the patients at USC and found that each one had problems with adrenal gland function as well. Later autopsies in a few showed that the adrenal glands had been replaced by scar tissue. The doctors knew that my adrenals would probably look the same.

As soon as the results for the adrenal tests on all of us came in, the suramin study was officially closed, in terms of receiving any more of the drug, although we continued to be examined in the clinic on a weekly basis.

I was so glad to have an appetite again. Everything tasted great, as if my taste buds were brand new and I was experiencing food for the first time. I hadn't eaten much since before the Elizabeth Taylor benefit for APLA, over a month before.

I was far from being well. I still didn't have the energy to go to the gym. I did start attending board meetings again. The rest of the time, I was at home, smoking marijuana and watching TV; eating salads, fruit, and frozen dinners; and drinking Hansen's grapefruit soda.

I soon recovered the memory of my near-death experience, and it gave me peace. I became more intentional about looking in my friends' eyes and really seeing them. I was no longer afraid of dying, nor of dying alone, because we are never alone. I know now that love is eternal, and that we need not fear death.

My interview on *Tammy's House Party* on the PTL Network came a couple of weeks after my near-death experience. I decided to be as loving and compassionate as I could be with her. It was an amazing experience, and it changed both our lives. It has been argued that it changed the dynamic between conservative Christians and the LGBTQ community.

When the suramin trial was officially stopped, I was scared to go off the drug, but Dr. Levine assured me that if my lymphoma or Kaposi's sarcoma came back, she could treat me with other medicines.

Several months later, most of the other members of my suramin for brunch bunch had all died, each of an opportunistic infection.

As Christmas neared, I was still thin and frail despite coming off the drug completely. I had a couple of big events coming up, and I did my best to put on a little weight and regain some of my old energy, but I was mostly unsuccessful.

At the first AIDS Mass, celebrated by the Episcopal Archdiocese of Los Angeles, I was honored with the Bishop Daniel Corrigan Award, named for the early civil rights activist. Also honored was Louise Hay, the leader of the weekly Hayride in West Hollywood. These Hayrides drew a couple of hundred people with AIDS and many of their loved ones every week. She talked about healing AIDS from a New Age perspective and was a much-loved figure of hope.

I was privileged to be honored with her. When the two of us were introduced, I stood alongside her before the packed congregation and beamed. I knew the long, standing ovation was primarily meant for her, but it sure did feel good after all I'd just been through.

The next event was the Lazarus Award dinner, a fundraiser for the West Hollywood Presbyterian Church's Lazarus Project. My longtime friend Chris Glaser was the director of the Lazarus Project. This was an extraordinary honor for me, particularly because my friend, Rev. Elder Nancy Wilson, had received the award for her work the year before.

My family came in from all over: my parents; cousins Marianne, Pat, and Rick and their spouses; as well as Lucia and Lawrie, who flew in from Rochester, New York. The morning before the awards, I drove Mom, Dad, Lucia, and Lawrie on a tour of the stars' homes, including Elizabeth Taylor's home and the Playboy Mansion where I'd spent time with Christie.

That evening, my cousin Rick and his partner Jack hosted a cocktail party in their beautiful home, but I declined, knowing that I would be too tired to handle the dinner and awards program if I also attended the cocktail party. I did see my family in a hotel room right before the dinner, and it felt wonderful to have them gathered around me. Dad was remarkably quiet, but other than that, everyone seemed to be happy.

Many of my MCC friends were at the dinner, including Rev. Elder Troy Perry, Rev. Elder Nancy Wilson, Rev. Ken Martin, and their spouses. There were a few of my APLA friends as well. At one point, I noticed Mom and Dad go off with Troy. Years later, Troy told me they were planning my funeral.

The dinner began, and Dad continued to be unusually quiet. When I tried to engage him in conversation, he just looked at me. I couldn't figure out what was going on with him, but I had to make a speech, and I couldn't worry about keeping everyone happy, even if it was my beloved Dad.

Years later, my cousin Rick told me his life partner, Jack, had taken great delight in plying Dad with alcohol at the cocktail party. In hindsight, it was funny, and of course, that explained what was going on.

Unaccustomed as Dad was to drinking that much, he chose to stay silent, rather than risk slurring his speech.

After dinner, the Lazarus Project awards were presented to its outstanding volunteers. I was getting tired and was not feeling all that well, which surprised me, since I hadn't had any suramin treatments in well over a month.

Finally, it was my moment. Chris Glaser made a speech about me and then offered others the opportunity to make a speech. I was particularly pleased that both Ken Martin and Troy spoke, although it threw me when Troy told the crowd, "Steve wasn't a very good pastor when he was in Hartford, but he really blossomed and came into his own when he got AIDS." I knew he was right, but it was nonetheless surprising to hear him say it out loud and in front of my family.

Chris presented me with a beautiful crystal bowl. After saying thank you I told the gathering about how surprisingly wonderful my life had been since being diagnosed with AIDS, citing the miracle of my remission and all the amazing friends I'd made in Los Angeles. I talked about how exciting it was to have met so many movie stars at various AIDS events, citing my encounters with Ted Danson, Morgan Fairchild, Phil Donahue, and others. Somebody in the audience interrupted me, jeering, "Those aren't movie stars." I responded, "How about Shirley MacLaine and Elizabeth Taylor?" That silenced him, and the audience applauded appreciatively. I finished my speech with what had become my motto, "God is greater than AIDS."

As the audience applauded, I jumped off the platform, not noticing there were stairs on the side. When I landed, it felt as if every nerve in my body had been painfully jolted. I knew something was very wrong.

After the program, people rushed up to me to offer their congratulations. I was particularly touched that Mom and Dad got to see their alcoholic, homosexual son being celebrated by so many people. I knew they were proud, and I knew they were scared that I might die soon, even though they took some comfort in knowing that my cancers were in remission.

My cousins offered their congratulations and their love. I will never forget how one of them gave me a hug and said, "It was good to know you. Goodbye." It seemed obvious she thought I would be dead soon. I didn't argue with her. Instead, I accepted her well-intentioned final goodbye. The whole evening did feel a little like a retirement dinner for me, or even a preview of my funeral.

The next day I had brunch with Lucia, Lawrie, and my parents. Dad must have been suffering a hangover, but he was talking again. I said my goodbyes and then went home and called Dr. Levine about my increasing difficulty in using my left arm and the painful neuropathy in my feet. She told me to come into the AIDS clinic the next day.

When Dr. Hawkins saw me she ordered my immediate hospitalization. I was put in a ward of County Hospital with five other patients, although this time, they were all AIDS patients. A team of neurologists did a series of horribly painful tests that led me to believe that neurologists were the sadists of the medical world.

The next morning I was scheduled for a lumbar puncture. I'd had a couple of them before for the suramin trial, so I knew what to expect and that didn't help. A couple of doctors showed up shortly before 8:30 a.m. The older doctor said, "The resident will do the spinal tap, and I will be standing by, to assure that it all goes well."

The resident prepped me and proceeded to do the spinal tap, with me on my left side, while I watched the countdown and launch of the space shuttle *Challenger*.

Just as he was finishing the tap, the space shuttle exploded and disintegrated in the air. The resident warned me to keep still, otherwise I would develop a horrendous headache, a fact I knew to be true since it had happened after one of my earlier spinal taps.

The reporters on TV began to talk as if everyone had to have died in the explosion. Cameras were recording the astronauts' families' horrified reactions. I was trying not to move after the spinal tap. The doctor congratulated the resident, and the resident thanked me for my courage in letting him do this lumbar puncture.

In the end, all those painful tests led only to a diagnosis of peripheral neuropathy.

Things continued to get worse throughout February. I was off suramin, but I was wasting away. It became more and more difficult to walk, as every step jangled the nerves in my whole body. I was becoming much weaker. My left arm became useless as the neurological damage took its toll. To top it off, neurological damage to my eyes had caused them to become so inflamed and painful in the light that I wore dark glasses even at night. It wasn't long before I was unable to see much more than shadows.

Dr. Levine had me see an ophthalmologist at the county clinic. After his exam, he asked if I would mind being seen by his students. Of course, I agreed. I was led to a large eye exam room. All the lights were turned off, as light was still extraordinarily painful. A crowd of students came into the room, and then a light came on and focused on me and my painful eyes. Numerous voices asked questions of their professor. Not one word was addressed directly to me. I felt like an object.

I continued to attend board and committee meetings at APLA. As secretary of the board, I took the minutes. At one meeting, I was feverish and sweating so profusely that the minutes I was writing became a mess. No one seemed to notice, or if they did, they didn't say anything. I finally gave up and told them I had to leave. I asked someone else to take over the minutes. I was surprised that no one expressed concern that I was drenched with sweat, nor did anyone offer to take over. I was obviously having a hard time, but nobody noticed.

I became so weak during this period that I could not leave my apartment except for doctors' appointments, and for those, I had Reverend Nancy or another kindhearted volunteer help me up the stairs to the street and then drive me to and from the appointment.

As the second anniversary of my AIDS diagnosis approached, I had wasted away so much that my skin looked like it was painfully stretched over nothing but my bones. In those days, it was rare for a person with AIDS to live more than eighteen months past their diagnosis. Much later, some people told me they assumed I would be dead soon. All the others in the "suramin for brunch bunch" were dead. It was logical to assume I would soon follow.

Paula Van Ness, now the executive director of APLA, arranged for me to have a home health-care nursing assistant. The nurse came to my apartment every day for a few days before she reported to Paula that I had dementia "because Steve told me his cancers were in remission, and that he intended to get well."

Paula had her fired from my case and told her, "You've accused the wrong guy of having dementia. He may be deathly ill, but he is a respected board member." Paula had talked to me the day before this nurse was assigned, and she knew my brain was still working well.

A new nurse was assigned, and she was marvelous. She had attended John Wayne and Henry Fonda in their last months. I loved living in Hollywood, where even when you're dying, you can have a nurse who cared for movie stars before you. She was great company and took good care of me. She bribed my appetite with delicious meals, and she helped me with my bathing and grooming.

During this time, I gave a couple of TV interviews. The first one was on Tom Snyder's new afternoon talk show. Two of us clients from APLA were invited to be on it. I remember feeling strong during the interview, but looking at the video later, I was obviously ill, slow of speech, and short of breath. The other client was much healthier.

When the live show began, Tom Snyder leaned into me and asked, "Did you notice how I shook your hand when you first came in the studio?" He proceeded to pat himself on the back for it, but then continued the discussion with more substantive matters. I noted that things had changed in the two years I'd been doing interviews as a person with AIDS. Now I was allowed inside the studio.

I kept getting weaker, but when an opportunity arose to do another TV interview, as sick as I was, I wanted to do it. This time the interview was with Beau, about APLA's Buddy Program. It was for a local news show in St. Louis where their AIDS Project was just starting a buddy program. Beau's quiet warmth, compassion, and good humor had become very important to me, and doing this interview, as challenging as it might be physically, would give me more time with him.

The interview took place at the apartment of APLA's Buddy Program director, Jerry Clark. Beau picked me up, and when we arrived at

Jerry's, he said, "There's a long staircase up to his apartment. Do you think you can make it?" I was afraid I wouldn't be able to climb it, but Beau and Jerry made it happen, supporting me on both sides, while pushing me up. It reminded me of Christie and Millie supporting me on the stairs to the Drake Hotel restaurant in Chicago.

When we got to the top of the stairs, the camera crew was still setting up equipment in Jerry's living room. Beau asked if it would be okay for me to go back into the bedroom to lie down while we waited. I objected, saying I didn't need to, but Beau and Jerry insisted. They were right. When they helped me onto the bed, I felt such relief that all I could do was sigh and close my eyes. I was able to rest, and that helped when they were finally ready for me.

First, the reporter interviewed me by myself. "What has Beau meant to you as your buddy?"

"I wanted a buddy I could go dancing with, and we've done that. Mostly, he's been an enormous help and comfort." Then Beau joined me, and we talked about each other, and the times we had taught buddy trainees.

On the ride home, I told Beau, "How far we've come. The crew was not afraid of me, not even when I handed the mike back."

After Beau brought me home, I lay right down on my couch, totally worn out. I had to rest for several days afterward. I was resting almost all the time these days. I couldn't do much else. My cats, sensing my fragile condition, lay beside me, rather than on top of me. I loved that they adjusted to how frail I was.

My cousins David and Nancy Pieters came to see me a few days later, but of course, I was much too wasted and fatigued to do anything but visit with them in my apartment. I loved David and Nancy. They were always so helpful and supportive, even before my illness.

They drove on and spent the next night with my parents. Mom and Dad called me not long after they arrived, with Mom in tears. I was touched by Mom and Dad's emotional response. Even though they didn't say that David and Nancy told them I was dying, I could tell they had. There was something about being close to death that heightened my intuition. I tried to reassure them that I would be fine, but I wasn't sure I believed it myself. David later confirmed that he had indeed told them I was dying, and it wouldn't be long now.

I was going in and out of believing that I would get well. I couldn't bring myself to accept that I was dying, but from the way many people around me were acting, I could tell they were certain it wouldn't be long before I left this body. If I were dying, I was getting a hell of an eviction notice.

One night I was so lonely and in such pain, that I invited Jesus to hold me in my bed again. As He held me, I had the now familiar experience of detaching from my body. Once again, I was at peace. Loving beings surrounded me, and everything made sense. I was ready to stay in that place of perfect peace, but I could not. I was back in my body, wracked with neurological pain, unable to see comfortably, with a useless left arm, and painfully fatigued.

Although I wasn't eating much, I became horribly constipated. After a few days, it became extraordinarily painful. Dr. Levine had me try every remedy there was, but it went on for almost a week.

When the constipation was finally resolved, I began to feel better. But there was still one more side effect of suramin: My hair started falling out. At an AIDS Project Los Angeles committee meeting, one of the staff said, "Steve, I love what you're doing with your hair." I responded gently, saying, "Thanks, but it's falling out." Handfuls of my hair were coming off every time I showered or touched my head. Soon I was hairless, on my head, face, and all over my body. I felt like a bald little boy.

Despite my hair loss, my health was improving. The inflammation in my eyes decreased, and I began to be able to tolerate light again. My left arm was still useless, and I couldn't lift my hand much above my waist. Dr. Hawkins gave me a simple exercise: I put my left hand on a wall and crawled up the wall with my fingers "walking" like a spider. At first, I couldn't get my hand to go higher than the middle of my chest. Soon, however, I began going higher and higher.

I wanted to go back to the gym to see if I could start strengthening my left arm with weights. So, I asked the neurologist at the AIDS clinic if it would be okay to start back to the gym. To my surprise, he said, "Absolutely not. You must never lift weights again. If you do, the muscles will break down and get weaker and weaker. You've had too much neurological damage to ever lift weights again."

I saw Dr. Levine that same morning, and I told her what the neurologist had said. She knew how much I loved the gym and how important it had been to my self-care before the suramin treatments, so she said, "If you believe it'll work for you, give it a try. Start off with *very* light weights, move up slowly in the weights, and remember to be patient. Nerves take a long time to heal, and that's normal."

So, I went back to Body Builders Gym and began to do my own physical therapy. The men who owned the gym were happy to see me back after all the time I'd been gone because of suramin. They gave me great support and encouragement, which became the model for how other gym members treated me. I was delighted when everyone started cheering me on. I felt cared for by my fellow gay gym-goers, and that, in and of itself, was healing.

I found the tiniest dumbbell I could find. I put it in my weak left hand, and I made my left arm do a curl or two using my right arm to make it move properly. I very slowly increased the weight, first to two pounds, then five. Even then, I still had to make my left arm work using my right arm.

After a month or so, my left arm began to work on its own. I was careful not to lift any more weight with my right arm than I could handle with my left, but gradually, I could do alternating curls with heavier weights each week. Soon I added other exercises to begin to develop the rest of my body.

There's a saying that "the muscles remember." I found that to be true, and my body responded to my light weightlifting. I was building my body back up again, and soon, my left arm worked as well as my right.

A few months later, I was at my regular checkup with Dr. Levine. As I was waiting, I saw that neurologist coming toward me. I got up and said, "Hi, Doctor! Remember me?" I flexed my now muscular arms and smiled. He looked shocked. Without a word, he turned and walked away from me. I never saw him again.

I continued to hang out with Steven, Max, Nancy, and Lou. My hair began to grow back in, but it was now curly and a mousy gray. Steven, being a hairstylist with a studio right there in the house, suggested dyeing my hair until my own color started coming back in. He dyed it "Swedish crystal," a platinum blond color. When I traveled back east that summer to see my parents and Jenny at the farm, they were glad to see me looking better after all I'd been through, but they were shocked by my Swedish crystal hair. At least I had hair.

Soon after I got back to Los Angeles, Max Drew died, surrounded by Steven, Nancy, and Lou. His funeral drew people from all over. Not only was he one of the four cofounders of APLA, but he was a respected member of the theater community. Plus, there were friends from New York City and their Fire Island crowd, or what was left of them five years into the AIDS epidemic. I led the service, and his father was tearfully grateful. I was honored.

I felt so bad for Steven, but he seemed to handle Max's death with grace. He told me he was relieved in a way, as was true for many men who saw their lovers go through the agony of death by AIDS. I spent more time with Steven, both at the Mulholland house and at my place. I hoped that he and I would become lovers after a decent time of grief had elapsed, but I didn't push.

Steven's housemate, Nancy, was diagnosed with AIDS before Max died. When she was hospitalized, I went to visit her. She greeted me, saying, "Here's my role model! I want to get well like you!"

We visited for a while, but then she began to look tired. She said she wanted to listen to a meditation tape. I asked if it would be okay for me to lie down on the other bed and meditate with her. She said, "Of course." I lay down as she started the tape. She reached her hand across to me. I reached back and we touched hands as the meditation began. I was filled with so much love as we meditated.

Some months later, she landed in the hospital again. When I went to see her this time, she was unconscious, on a ventilator. She looked swollen and purple, and it hurt just to see her that way. I sat beside her, talked to her, and prayed with my hand on hers.

The next day, I went back to visit her again, but she had died. The celebration of her life was held in her beautiful, big backyard. The gathering was a great send-off, with friends and family sharing all kinds of remarkable stories about her. Then we partied, as she would have wanted.

Not long after Nancy died, Steven came over and we went out to lunch. He broke the news that Lou and he were now lovers. Apparently, before either Max or Nancy had died, they had each given their blessing to Steven and Lou to be together. I was surprised and greatly disappointed, but I was touched that he took me to lunch to tell me. I told him that I had wondered if he and I might have a relationship one day, and he said, with that shy smile of his, that he had wondered the same thing. Afterward, I grieved the death of the dream I'd had of the two of us as lovers.

Lou sold that beautiful house off Mulholland, and he and Steven moved to Santa Fe, where Lou opened a restaurant, and Steven took care of their little girl as well as the beautiful home they bought there.

I wasn't sure yet that I could trust how well I was feeling. AIDS was like a roller coaster. First, we plunged into illness, and then we crawled back up to "heights" of wellness, only to plunge farther down each time until we died. I saw this repeatedly in other people with AIDS, so it was natural to wonder how many hills on the roller coaster I had left. There had been the plunge into illness in 1982 and 1983, with hepatitis, pneumonia, herpes, shingles, and that fungal infection on my foot. Then I felt well for a few months before being diagnosed with stage 4 lymphoma and KS. I worked at staying well and at creating the conditions for healing until suramin took me down again. Now I'd fought my way back. How long would I stay well?

About this time, the denomination's Northwest District coordinator, David, offered me the opportunity to be the pastor of the Metropolitan Community Church of Maui. The district sent me there for three weeks, to lead worship and preach, to see if it would be a good "fit" and to see what it would feel like to live on a rock in the middle of the Pacific Ocean.

I had not spent time on any Hawaiian island since I was twelve. I loved Maui right away, its tropical beauty, the great beaches, the lovely people who hosted me, the gorgeous road to Hana, and of course, the "Maui Wowie" marijuana. I preached each Sunday for the small parish.

They met for worship in the small Episcopal church in Lahaina. The back wall, behind the altar, completely opened onto the beach. It could not have been more beautiful, and I could not have been better treated.

On Thanksgiving, my hosts took me to a potluck at a large home on the slopes of Haleakala, the volcano. This was where many in the LGBT community of Maui came together every Thanksgiving. The house was packed, and my hosts told me that while the LGBT community was largely closeted on Maui, they considered the Metropolitan Community Church's pastor to be the community's pastor, even though only a handful of people were regulars at church.

I was offered the position, but I realized that I could not accept it, as much as I'd enjoyed my time there. I had already begun to get "rock fever," the antsy feeling that I had to get off the island, after only three weeks. More importantly, I would have to fly to Honolulu for any medical care, and I didn't want to be on an island where medical care for a person with AIDS was then unavailable. Finally, the church could not afford to pay me any salary. I would have to earn my living in some other way while being their full-time pastor. I just didn't know whether I had the energy to do both. So I reluctantly turned down their offer.

As 1987 began, I wasn't sure what my future held. How long would my cancers stay in remission or my good health last? For now, I was glad to be back on the mainland with my two cats and near my gym and, of course, my dear Dr. Levine. I started to look and feel healthy, even after all I'd been through since the spring of 1982.

Years later, I learned I was one of only two survivors of the now noto-rious suramin trial. The other man, a patient in San Francisco, only took it for four weeks. He told me he quit after suramin killed his life partner. He saw what it was doing to the patients who had been taking it longer than he had. Dr. Levine told me I'd taken the drug for thirty-six weeks, longer than anyone else. My cancers had gone into remission while I was on the drug. I was the "one complete clinical response," as Dr. Levine reported in the peer-reviewed article on the suramin trial.

I heard there had been ninety of us in the suramin trial. Aside from the one other survivor I knew of, everyone else died from AIDS.

CHAPTER SIX

Building an International AIDS Ministry

THE 1987 UFMCC GENERAL CONFERENCE WAS HELD IN MIAMI Beach in July. Troy Perry always liked to open the conference with a video of something that had happened since the last General Conference. He then gave his opening address, using that video as a jumping-off point. At this conference, he opened the week-long conference with the video of my interview with Tammy Faye Bakker.

When it started, people laughed at Tammy Faye's opening credits, but as the interview got going, people began paying close attention. They reacted with loud, appreciative "Amens" and "All rights!" to a lot of what I said to her. They laughed a lot when Tammy said I did not look gay. The audience soon became completely spellbound by the twenty-four-minute interview. At the end, everyone jumped to their feet and applauded and cheered. People were all turning to look at me. Ken Martin, seated next to me, gave me a big kiss on the cheek. Troy had me come down to the podium as the standing ovation continued. He whispered to me, "You can wave, but you're not going to speak." That was fine with me. I was so surprised by the audience's reaction I wouldn't have known quite what to say.

As the week went on, people stopped me everywhere I went and complimented me on the video and on my articles in *Journey*. Many pastors invited me to preach at their churches. My calendar started filling up with engagements.

I was due to be ordained at this conference, and my parents came down for the ceremony. In the Metropolitan Community Churches at that time, a person was first licensed as clergy and after a few years that person could be ordained. A lot of clergy were forgoing ordination because it was quite a process and you could still do almost everything with a license that being ordained allowed. But the powers that be in MCC decided all of us licensed clergy needed to get ordained. As a result, that summer there were close to twenty clergy to be ordained in the one worship service.

The day of the ordinations, Ken Martin, on behalf of MCC in the Valley, gave me a beautifully embroidered red stole, which I wore for the service. My friends from MCC Maui gave me a fragrant, full, fresh lei, which I also wore. Troy Perry posed with me in the robing room.

We were ordained in alphabetical order. When it was my turn, my parents came up with me as my witnesses. Mom was holding my pink fairy wand. After I took my ordination vows, I knelt amid the elders while they all laid hands on me, and Troy prayed. When he said an enthusiastic, "Amen," I turned my head toward Mom. In a stage whisper, I said, "Now, Mother!" and she tapped me on the head with my fairy wand. The crowd let out a roar of approval and gave my parents and me a loud, cheering, standing ovation as Mom, Dad, and I left the stage.

I felt like quite a celebrity at that General Conference. Everyone was talking about the miracle of my complete recovery from five years of illness, as well as the triumph of my Tammy Faye interview and that special ordination moment with the fairy wand. After so many years of illness and dark nights of the soul, it felt amazing to me that things were going so very well.

That Saturday night, there was a dance for the conference attendees. Rev. Delores Berry, a beloved singing evangelist, asked me to dance. It was one of the most joyous moments of that whole joyful week, just locking eyes with her as we danced in total sync with each other. We were both on top of the world.

That fall, I started traveling almost every weekend, which I would do through the end of 1997. The board of elders appointed me to be the field director of our newly created denominational AIDS Ministry.

In the first years of my time as AIDS Ministry Field Director, I worked from home, which I had mixed feelings about. I had been so isolated at home throughout the years of my illness that I would have loved having the company of coworkers in an office. Plus, I felt on some level that they did not value my work much if they couldn't find money for a salary or room for an office space. On the other hand, it was nice to be at home and to be able to take a break, eat, or take a nap, which I found I needed just about every day.

Don Eastman and I soon became founding board members of the AIDS National Interfaith Network (ANIN), on whose board I sat for most of the next twelve years. In the first full meeting of that board, we went over a proposed mission statement. Despite the many line items in the mission statement, there was no mention of ministry to people living with AIDS. Barely controlling my anger, I pointed this out to the gathered board. Silence. Finally, one of the other board members quoted the cartoon character Pogo saying, "We have met the enemy, and he is us."

The chair of the board asked me to write a new section dealing with our mission to people with AIDS and present it at the next day's meeting. That night, I wrote and polished and rewrote and repolished that section. It was quickly accepted by the board the next day. That gave me a great sense of accomplishment, but I also felt annoyed that the mission for ANIN's ministry to people with AIDS had to be written by a person with AIDS. On the other hand, who better to do it? It did get in the way of my kicking back that evening. I often felt addicted to time off. I was always looking for the next time when I would get to relax and be irresponsible. And smoke dope.

Despite the lack of salary and office space, I continued to create and do AIDS ministry for the denomination. My typical week began on Friday when I would fly to one city or another in the United States or Canada. Usually, there was a press conference to introduce me to the region and create publicity for my appearances at the church. Sometimes I was also interviewed on local radio or TV news shows.

Saturdays, I would do workshops and visit people with AIDS. Sometimes I preached at a special service on Saturday evenings. Sundays, I preached at each service. At some point during these weekends, I would show my Tammy Faye Bakker interview, much to everyone's delight.

In sermons or lectures, I always carried my fairy wand as a prop. I talked about how I'd been called a "fairy" ever since I was seven, but when

I came out, I learned to be proud of being a fairy. I told my audiences the profound effect it had on me as a little boy to learn from *Peter Pan* that a fairy is born when a baby laughs for the first time. When that baby gets older and says they no longer believe in fairies, a fairy dies.

I reminded my audiences of that famous scene in the play *Peter Pan* when Peter turns to the audience and says, "Tinker Bell is dying because people don't believe in fairies. If you believe in fairies, clap your hands, and bring Tink back to life!" Of course, for over a century now, audiences everywhere have applauded like crazy, and Tink comes back to life.

I preached, "Now, a lot of good fairies are dying. So, we need to believe in fairies more than ever. We need to believe in ourselves enough to do the work of healing, whether that be healing into life or healing into death."

I tried always to preach about the love of God for each one of us and usually ended my sermons with a paraphrase of a Pauline scripture, "There is nothing in this life, not AIDS, nor cancer, nor diabetes, nor heart disease, nor anything else that can separate us from the love of God in Christ Jesus."

Since I received no salary from the MCC denomination in the first years of my time as field director, my parents sent me a small check each week to help me with rent and groceries. Every weekend when I traveled to different churches, they would take a love offering after I preached. Some, of course, were larger than others, but I was grateful for every one of those offerings. I certainly needed them.

I would fly home to Los Angeles on Sunday evening or more often on Monday morning. I stayed stoned and rested on Monday and Tuesday, and then Wednesday and Thursday I caught up on correspondence and phone calls. I would attend board meetings of APLA and the AIDS Interfaith Council of Southern California, and of course, I had at least one or two doctors' appointments each month, even though I was, according to Dr. Levine, "Clinically well in all respects." Rev. Elder Jeri Ann Harvey began to lovingly call me "NED," because of another phrase Dr. Levine used about me: "No Evidence of Disease."

Sometime over these years when I was so well, I once asked Dr. Levine if I really needed to see her every month. She said, "You may not need to see me, but I need to see you." Being a hematologist, with a specialization in HIV/AIDS, it was apparently quite special to her to see her longtime patients doing well, while also learning about the new illness of AIDS by listening carefully to our experiences. I loved my hour-long visits with Dr. Levine every month, so I was more than willing to honor her wishes to see me.

One of the highlights of 1988 was a dinner in Chicago honoring Christie Hefner for her work with the City of Hope in the creation of a fellowship in AIDS research. Many of Chicago's wealthiest citizens got on board to honor Christie with the first Spirit of Life Award and to raise money for the Christie Hefner Fellowship in AIDS Research. Christie invited me to come and speak at the dinner, and I gladly accepted.

The banquet was held at one of Chicago's fanciest hotels, and it was packed. I was honored to be seated at Christie's table. There were introductory remarks and toasts, followed by dinner, which I could hardly touch because of my nervousness. My speech came right after dinner.

I told the assembled dignitaries how appropriate it was for the City of Hope to present her with the Spirit of Life Award, for she certainly brought me hope when all seemed hopeless. She saw life in me when so many others saw only death. I told them how she had been one of the only friends to insist that I could live through this, and when I went into complete remission, she had the good grace not to act surprised, but simply celebrated with me and sent me balloons. I told them the story of when I visited Chicago last and had been so very sick and close to death, how she had cared for me so lovingly all the way onto the plane to make sure I was comfortably seated. Bottom line, she was the best friend a person with AIDS could possibly hope for. For me, she WAS the Spirit of Life.

There was silence as I began to make my way back to Christie's table. Then she got up and walked toward me and gave me a long, tight hug, as the room stood and applauded for what seemed like an eternity.

After the program was over, many people thanked me and complimented me on what I had said about Christie. Film critic Gene Siskel, who was married to one of Christie's best friends, spoke to me very tenderly and gave me his famous "thumbs up." Irving Kupcinet, whose "Kup's Column" was a mainstay of Chicago journalism, asked us to pose for a photo. The next day, Christie and I headlined his column.

The author meets with his good friend Christie Hefner after his speech at the Spirit of Life banquet, honoring Christie and raising money for City of Hope's Christie Hefner Fellowship in AIDS Research. COURTESY OF REVEREND PIETERS'S PERSONAL COLLECTION.

Christie's fundraiser for City of Hope was repeated at the Playboy Mansion West the next year. This time, Morgan Fairchild was the emcee. I had suggested her to Christie, and Morgan made a point of thanking me for this opportunity. I did my tribute to Christie's abiding friendship again. Dr. Levine and her husband, Dr. Victor Levine, attended the event, and I was excited that I was able to introduce them to Christie, who graciously expressed her gratitude to Dr. Alexandra for all she'd done for me.

As I got ready to leave the event, Beatrice Arthur, whom I had noticed in the front row of tables, came up to me, and said, "Let's walk out together, shall we?" She took my hand in hers as we walked, patting it with her other hand while she raved about my speech and my attitude. That was one of my favorite celebrity encounters, since I love *The Golden Girls* so much.

That year, I visited Tripp, who had moved to Portland, Oregon. On a drive to the Oregon coast, he said he liked to buy a pack of cigarettes now and then, smoke one, and then throw the rest of the pack out. So he bought a pack, and I joined him in smoking just one cigarette each. It tasted and felt great. When I flew home, I bought a pack in the Portland airport. I smoked one, and again, I loved it. I didn't throw the pack out. When I got back home, I smoked another, and then I threw out the rest of the pack.

A few hours later, the cravings got so strong, I dug the cigarette pack out of the trash and had another cigarette. I decided to smoke the whole pack, but then stop. Of course, I bought another pack, then a carton, and soon I was smoking a pack a day again.

When I was on the road, I would present my holistic plan for healing. Then I would sneak off to the back door of the church to have a cigarette. The delight of the people with AIDS who smoked was obvious. To the nonsmokers, I paraphrased Paul and said, "God's grace is made perfect in my weakness" (2 Corinthians 12:9). The smokers crowed in delight. I felt guilty for giving smokers with AIDS a scriptural excuse to smoke, but I was hooked.

During these years of AIDS ministry, I also did several longer tours than my usual weekend visits to cities in the United States and Canada. I did two-week preaching and teaching tours of the mid-Atlantic and the deep South, as well as several tours of Europe and Australia.

These trips certainly appealed to the love of traveling that I'd inherited from my father. I enjoyed seeing the different cultures and learning about the people. At the same time, it was tragic to see how AIDS was impacting the cities and countries I toured.

Most often, both on overseas tours and in cities and towns in the United States and Canada, I stayed in people's homes, which had its ups and downs. Sometimes I liked my accommodations and, more importantly, my hosts. But there were times when I slept on the floor of tiny apartments and had little to no privacy. Sometimes I had to deal with hosts who didn't keep very clean homes, or whose homes were so cluttered that I felt like I couldn't move or even breathe, or hosts who were simply not very friendly or hospitable.

All this was a small price to pay for meeting all the great characters I met, for seeing all the sites I saw, and for the opportunity to touch many lives, particularly the lives of people with AIDS, their pastors, and caregivers.

In the summer of 1989, our General Conference was held in St. Paul, Minnesota. We knew that AIDS numbers had increased so much that there would be many people with HIV/AIDS in attendance. We designed a full program, with daily support groups and a variety of workshops. In one I taught the ten principles of long-term survival. I had written them up in a pamphlet for churches, called "Spiritual Strength for Survival: Finding Hope to Be Fully Alive with HIV/AIDS." It was based on a study of long-term survivors of HIV/AIDS, which in those days was defined as those who had survived twice the average life expectancy of eighteen months. So, a long-term survivor was a person who had survived three years past diagnosis. Even in 1989 I was considered a long-term survivor.

The biggest moment for all of us concerned with AIDS was the AIDS Forum. This year it was held in a plenary session during a business meeting instead of on the delegates' day off in the middle of the week.

I invited six speakers, each of whom represented a different perspective on the issue of AIDS in our churches and our denomination. Each speaker was more powerful than the previous one. The one thousand or so people present were in the palm of our hands.

Finally I got up to speak. After summarizing the issues before us, including the lack of funding for a denominational response, I asked everyone present to participate in an exercise to highlight the prevalence of HIV/AIDS among us. I said, "Would each of you who has lost someone to AIDS, please say their name. Then get up and leave your seat empty in memory of that person and go to the back of the ballroom." It seemed like a big gamble, but I felt a clarity about calling for it, a rather transcendent feeling that this is what it would take for us to respond as a denomination.

At first a few people said names and got up and walked to the back. Soon more and more people said names and left their seats empty. After about five minutes, most of the seats in the ballroom were empty, and everyone crowded into the back of the large ballroom. Many were crying, but there was an eerie silence behind the tears.

As I stood in the back with everyone, something possessed me to say, "Now look at all those empty seats. This is what AIDS is doing to our denomination. In the name of God, respond!"

I didn't know what would happen or how people would react, but Rev. Larry Uhrig, the Senior Pastor of MCC Washington, D.C., said, "I had put aside money to take my lover and me out to a nice restaurant while we're here. But I cannot in good conscience do that anymore. I'm going to give that money to fund our AIDS Ministry." He walked down the aisle and placed his money on the stage beside the lectern. Then another delegate did the same thing, then one more, then almost everyone poured back down the aisles and piled money, and even jewelry, at the center of the stage beside the lectern from which we had spoken. After everyone went silently but tearfully back to their seats, Troy Perry prayed over the money. Then Don Eastman and several ushers began putting all the money and jewelry in big buckets and took it all to the side to count. We had enough money to begin to fund our AIDS Ministry.

Afterward, Rev. Nancy Radclyffe said, "You just conducted your first altar call!" The whole forum became the talk of the conference.

The next day was the business meeting to discuss and pass the budget for the next two years. Rev. Elder Freda Smith, the vice-moderator of the board of elders and one of the most powerful preachers I've heard, was to be given a new salary to become the third full-time elder, alongside Troy Perry, the moderator, and Don Eastman, the treasurer. However, Freda announced she was going to forgo that salary so the field director of AIDS Ministry could have a salary. I was stunned. The budget passed overwhelmingly.

And so I began to be paid a salary, and the denomination's AIDS Ministry was finally funded as a program of the denomination. It was an overwhelming victory for people living with and affected by HIV/AIDS, which essentially was everyone in the denomination. I shall always be grateful to Rev. Elder Freda Smith for giving me a salary as AIDS Ministry Field Director.

They still didn't have office space for me at our headquarters, but I had a new energy for the job, now that I was being paid. Sometime in 1990, they finally were able to expand the headquarters at 5300 Santa Monica Boulevard. So, I got an office. I brought my laptop in to have a computer. The move into the office made all the difference and once again reinvigorated me.

By this time, there were increasing numbers of churches dealing with leadership who were living with HIV/AIDS. My job became more intensive, as I was spending a lot of my time on the phone with clergy and lay leaders all over who were in various stages of living with AIDS. I also began providing pastoral care by phone for clergy and lay leaders living with cancer. My monthly reports to the board of elders became longer and longer. I began reporting so many deaths to Troy and Don and the elders that Troy started calling me his "angel of death." He said, "I dread the times when you come into my office, because you always seem to have news of another leader diagnosed with AIDS, or worse, one who has died."

On December 4, 1989, the AIDS National Interfaith Network organized a special, interfaith conference to be held at the Carter Presidential Center in Atlanta. The purpose of the conference was to pass an Interfaith AIDS Declaration, signed by leaders of many different faith communities. Rev. Ken South, now the executive director of the AIDS National Interfaith Network, organized the whole event, and he was able to book us into the Carter Center, next to the Carter Presidential Library and Museum. That gave the event a certain gravitas. President and Mrs. Carter sent a supportive, congratulatory message to us.

There were over one hundred thirty delegates from many faith communities. Ten leaders from the Universal Fellowship of Metropolitan Community Churches participated, including Rev. Troy Perry and me. The declaration was the first time a positive, affirming statement about people living with AIDS and those affected by AIDS was made by diverse communities of faith. We declared ourselves to be opposed to the religious right's attitude and, indeed, any theology that spoke of AIDS as God's punishment.

The MCC denomination's delegation to the Atlanta Declaration: Rev. Steve Fund, Rev. Reid Christensen, Rev. Elder Jeri Ann Harvey, the author, Rev. Karen Ziegler, Rev. Emmett Watkins, Rev. Elder Troy Perry, Rev. Elder Freda Smith, Rev. Ed Helms. December 4, 1989. COURTESY OF REVEREND PIETERS'S PERSONAL COLLECTION.

My weekly travels to preach in different churches around the United States and Canada continued, as did my pastoral calls on clergy and lay leaders with life-threatening illnesses. As more and more faith leaders were diagnosed, those calls took up even more time. The near-constant drumbeat of death after death was felt all over the denomination. Rev. Jim Mitulski, the pastor of MCC San Francisco, reported that he and his staff were doing multiple funerals a week. MCC San Francisco, and indeed the entire MCC denomination, was starting to be known as "The Church with AIDS."

Sometimes I met people who were skeptical about my "miracle" and others who were angry at me for getting well. These people sought to confront me with my own bravado and my cockiness and certainly fed my own doubts about what had happened to me.

One time, a man called me on my home phone and threatened to kill me. He was angry that I had gotten well when his partner had died, and he was angry that I had never visited his partner in the hospital. How could I when I didn't even know them? Even though I knew his anger came from his grief, I had my phone number changed to an unlisted number.

Another time, I was speaking at Marble Collegiate Church in Manhattan. I was honored to be invited to speak at Norman Vincent Peale's church. They treated me very well, paying for a limo to bring me in from the airport and giving me a beautiful suite in a fancy hotel.

After my talk, a beautiful, well-dressed woman approached me. She was shaking with anger and told me she did not understand why I survived when her beloved son did not. In this case, and whenever I was confronted like this, I tried to listen carefully and assure her I did not understand it either. I tried to honor her feelings and didn't try to argue her out of them.

Once, I went to an event for APLA's major donors in a beautiful home in the Hollywood Hills. My dear friend Randy was with me and he was ecstatic when Dionne Warwick came up to us and introduced herself. After she moved on, Randy and I turned to each other and squealed with delight.

At that same reception, we met Estelle Getty, "Sophia" on *The Golden Girls.* She asked me why I was on the APLA board, and I told her I was the client representative. She asked me when I was diagnosed, and when I gave her a brief version of how I got well, she said, "I don't believe you." Randy told her it was all true, but she would have none of it. "People with AIDS do not get better," she said.

Years later, at my niece's wedding reception, my brother, a physician, said to me, "You know you never really had AIDS. You were misdiagnosed. Everyone knows that anyone who had AIDS in the eighties died." I smiled at him in disbelief. I was so stunned that I didn't know quite what to say, but I somehow found the words, "I'm sure my doctor will have something to say about that."

Sure enough, when I told Dr. Levine, she was insulted and angry. "I'll send him the slides of your tumors and your lab work that proves your diagnosis, with your written approval, of course." I told her not to bother. As it turned out, my brother never said another word about it anyway.

The truth is, I did not truly understand it myself. I've asked myself many times, "Why did I survive what hardly anyone else did?" Despite all my efforts at creating conditions for healing, with everything from good nutrition and exercise to laughter therapy and prayer and meditation, I certainly knew many people who worked harder at getting well than I did. They took better care of themselves, had greater faith than I did that they could get well and survive, and I felt had more to offer the world. For some reason, they did not make it. It was a mystery why I was the one to get well and survive.

Despite the people who were angry that I survived, or the ones who simply didn't believe my story, most people I met all over the world were thrilled by the story of my miraculous recovery. I know my testimony gave a lot of people hope at a time when there was so much hopelessness. I often thought of Scott, the ex-marine who was my nurse before and during the suramin trials, who, when my cancers went into remission, told me, "It's no mistake that this has happened to a highly visible clergyman. God needs a vehicle of hope, and you're it."

My dear friend Randy who attended that APLA reception with me was the love of my life. We had a tempestuous, long-distance relationship when we first knew each other in 1979 and 1980. He lived in Los Angeles when I lived in Hartford. For years, I harbored hope that we would yet become partners. I loved his beach boy sexiness, his intellect, and his great sense of humor.

When I finally moved to Los Angeles in 1982, I was disappointed that Randy moved to San Francisco and then Cincinnati for his executive position with AT&T. In early 1988 Randy moved back to Los Angeles, and I was excited that we were finally living in the same city. He found a beautiful, big apartment in Silverlake, my neighborhood, and we began visiting back and forth almost every day. We smoked a lot of marijuana together, which I usually provided. He cooked for me and fed me all kinds of wonderful meals, so it seemed like a fair exchange. I loved his cooking, and he loved trying out different recipes on me.

Randy liked to drink. A lot. It bothered me that I couldn't join him, but I would smoke a joint, which he shared, or smoke a cigarette. Sometimes I would root for him to get drunk enough to want to have sex with me. That happened a few times. Each time, it reinforced my desire to see him drink a lot. Talk about codependence.

I was thrilled to have Randy close by. I found myself stimulated by his intellect, and he seemed to enjoy my presence as much as I enjoyed his. I had come to accept that we would not be partners, but I thoroughly enjoyed having him as my best friend.

My favorite fundraiser each year was the annual S.T.A.G.E. event, with musical theater performers presenting a concert of a particular Broadway composer's works. At the 1989 event I had been asked to introduce the cochairs, one of whom was Betty Garrett, costar of the movie *On the Town* and other great musicals. After the brief soundcheck, I went out to the lobby where I met Randy, and we began to mingle with other friends.

Suddenly a blaze of video lights and flashbulbs went off in another part of the lobby. I saw an unmistakable head of red hair moving through the crowd. Lucie Arnaz was singing this year, and so, of course, I knew that had to be Lucille Ball. I said a silent prayer that I would have the opportunity to at least see more than her hair.

After my short speech to introduce the show, I went to my seat next to Randy. I was on the aisle, in the fourth row. As soon as I sat down, I saw that Lucille Ball was seated in the third row, directly in front of Randy. I must admit I couldn't think of anything else. All I could do was watch her watch the show. With as many movie and TV stars as I'd met, seeing Lucy two feet in front of me totally blew me away.

At the intermission, I asked Randy if he wanted to go out to the lobby. He said, "If you don't introduce yourself to Lucy right now, you will regret it for the rest of your life." I knew Randy was right, but I was terrified. I was sure I would nervously mumble at her, without making any sense, just the way Lucy Ricardo did when she met William Holden in the Brown Derby episode.

Nevertheless, I got up and moved a foot or two down the aisle and said, "Lucy, I just want to thank you for helping me laugh my way through AIDS."

She said, "Oh, you got that idea from Norman Cousins."

"Yes, but you're the one who made me laugh." She offered her hand, which of course, I shook. Oh my God, I was shaking hands with Lucy!

"This fellow over here said the same thing. Do you know him?" I didn't, so she introduced us.

Others were waiting to meet her, so my moment with Lucy ended. Randy joined me as we quickly moved up the aisle to greet other donors, my job as a board member. But I couldn't wait to get back to my seat to watch Lucy watch the show. When her daughter sang in the second act, Lucy daubed her eyes with a handkerchief. She was so proud of her daughter.

I had a hard time sleeping that night. I couldn't stop thinking about my encounter with Lucy. There was no other celebrity (except maybe Julie Andrews) who could have thrilled me more in meeting them. Not only was she the first actor I fell in love with, but she had indeed helped me laugh my way through AIDS. It was watching her "Vitameatavegamin" episode that got me through that first evening with what I thought was a terminal prognosis. As I thought about our encounter, her current resemblance to my mother made me realize I had always thought of Lucy's characters as a funny version of my mom.

The next morning, I flew to the East Coast for a board meeting of the AIDS National Interfaith Network. When we landed, all I could think of doing was finding a phone booth to call Mom to tell her all about meeting Lucy the night before. Mom and I had shared so many episodes of *I Love Lucy* and *The Lucy Show* throughout my childhood that I just had to share with her this miraculous moment in my life.

Lucy died two months later. When the news broke, I sat in front of my TV all day long, crying as I watched the wall-to-wall coverage the local channels gave to her. So many of her friends shared wonderful stories about her. I was grateful that Randy made me introduce myself to her.

∼✥∽

Gradually, I felt that I needed to be more on the frontlines of AIDS ministry. It wasn't enough for me to fly to a different city every week, where I would teach, show the Tammy Faye interview, preach, visit people with AIDS, and then fly home. I knew what it was like to be on your deathbed with AIDS, so I felt I was suited to be a chaplain for the people who were dying from the complications of AIDS.

I had been present for the deaths of several friends before volunteering anywhere as a chaplain. I had learned that I had a gift for helping people make their transitions. I found that simply paying attention to my friends was enough. It was that "ministry of presence" that I remembered learning about in seminary. "God with us" became my model for ministry. I couldn't rescue or save my patients or my pastoral care parishioners from AIDS, but I could certainly be *with* them. I could accompany them for the ride as they faced the roller coaster of AIDS that usually ended in death.

I had already volunteered for a year as a chaplain at the AIDS ward of the Hollywood Community Hospital, where I first attended someone's death. He was a young gay man named Tony. I had visited with him any number of times during his stays in the hospital. As he became more comfortable with the idea that he was dying, he told me, "Remember *It's a Wonderful Life*, and how the little girl says, 'Whenever a bell rings, an angel gets his wings'? When I pass, listen for the first bell to ring, and you'll know I got my wings."

The hospital called me one morning to come in because Tony did not have much time left. When I got there, his brother was pacing up and down in Tony's room and was obviously having a hard time watching what was happening with his brother. I could see it was bothering Tony, who was awake but too weak to talk. I suggested his brother take a walk around the block. He looked relieved and left, so it was just Tony's sister-in-law, his nurse, and me standing around his bed. With his brother out of the room, Tony calmed down and closed his eyes. His breathing became more and more shallow, until it stopped altogether. Tony was gone.

The bell on the phone by his bed rang. I looked at the others and said, "Tony got his wings!"

I picked up the phone, and said, "Hello." It was his mother. "I'm terribly sorry, but he died a few minutes ago." I tried to bring that ministry of presence to his mother, by simply saying yes to her weeping.

When a hospice for people with AIDS was opened, I decided to volunteer as a chaplain. The Chris Brownlie AIDS Hospice was near my home in Los Angeles. An AIDS hospice was controversial before it even opened. Some people believed that we create our own reality through our thoughts, beliefs, and actions. So they argued that opening an AIDS hospice would create the reality of more death and dying. In the end, though, that resistance did not stand in the way of opening the facility.

My work at hospice reminded me of Mark Larner, a friend in prep school, with whom I had had an ongoing discussion about theology. He was Jewish and told me one day, "You Christians are a death-centered religion. You center your faith on a man who was executed by the Romans. You believe that there's life after death. We Jews believe when a person dies, that's it. It's over." That made me stop and think.

A week or two later, Mark died during a mountain-climbing expedition to Mt. Washington, led by one of the faculty. It's not clear whether he slipped and died from the fall or if he had a heart attack and died before he fell off the trail. The family would not allow an autopsy since they followed the Jewish custom of burying him within twenty-four hours of his death.

I felt haunted by our conversation for a long time after that. I thought long and hard about Mark's comments about Christianity being a death-centered religion, and how he, as a Jew, believed that death was the absolute end.

Remembering that conversation with Mark, I made a point of finding out what my hospice patients personally believed about death and dying, to give them hope in the face of death. For those who thought death was a passageway to heaven, I encouraged their hope for eternal life. For those who thought death was the end, with no afterlife, I encouraged their hope that their pain and suffering would soon be over.

Sometimes, there was no calming their fears. Many patients asked me, "Pastor, am I going to hell?" I would assure them that they were not, and try to help them see that AIDS, their illness, their suffering, and their impending death were not a punishment from God, but simply an eviction notice. God would welcome them home, no matter what their "sins" may have been, and certainly being gay was not a sin.

I worked hard at reassuring people who were dying that God loved them unconditionally. I would tell them, "My favorite name for Jesus is Immanuel, which means 'God with us.' It doesn't mean God over us, or God under us, or God punishing us, or God rescuing us. It means God is with us, suffering right along with us, grieving with us, loving us, and going for the whole journey with us, even into death and beyond."

I took guidance from Stephen Levine, whose work I had studied since my bodyworker, Linda, handed me his book *Who Dies?* I would talk about "healing into life or healing into death," a concept I learned from his book *Healing into Life and Death*. We do the work of healing, whatever that might mean, wherever we are in the process. There's no guarantee of the outcome, but our lives and our deaths will be easier because of the work we've done on healing ourselves, physically and/or emotionally.

Sometimes, people dying from AIDS at the hospice told me they felt as if they'd failed somehow. They should have been able to heal themselves. They just didn't work hard enough or believe fully enough, and so they had brought on their own death. Of course, I told them that it wasn't their fault, that sometimes the work of healing can end in the healing of death.

As the years went on in the AIDS hospice, I saw that patients who did the work of healing as they faced the end of their lives often died in peace. I always found it moving.

Four of the many patients I followed at the Chris Brownlie Hospice stuck with me to the end. First was Johnny, the young man I tried to comfort in Jane Pauley's 1991 profile of me. When he died, which happened not long after her crew recorded that scene, I was invited to his memorial service, held in the garden of the Brownlie Hospice. All his family was there as well as many of the hospice staff and several of his friends. However, the family's pastor, who was to conduct the service, didn't show up. Unfortunately, this was not the first time I'd seen this happen. So, I was prepared for it when the director of the hospice asked me to step in and lead the service. I was honored to do it, although I was sad for Johnny's family.

Another patient I will never forget was a middle-aged man who had Kaposi's sarcoma and AIDS. The flesh on his feet and legs was rotting, and we could smell it from far down the hall. I called on him often and was moved by the level of suffering this man was enduring. He was understandably in a bad mood most of the time, and I know he looked forward to the day when he would be released from this body that had betrayed him so badly and caused him so much agony. I remember telling him that he was getting "a hell of an eviction notice" and assured him that he would soon be released from his suffering and pain. That always seemed to calm him. I was relieved for him, and for the staff, when I arrived one morning and learned he had died.

Another patient was a young Filipino American woman whose husband had left her at the hospice to die, away from his or their children's eyes. She said she understood why he had done that, but she was also grieving. Before she arrived at the hospice, she had had to say goodbye to her three young children. She was abandoned and alone. My job was to be there with her in her grief, and to try to offer some level of comfort. It was not long before she died, but I always felt she died of a broken heart as much as the complications of HIV/AIDS. We never discussed this, but I wondered if she had been infected with HIV by her husband. Unfortunately, that was not uncommon.

Perhaps the most memorable character I attended at the AIDS Hospice was Connie Norman, a well-known trans woman about my age, who had written a regular column for the *San Diego Update*, an LGBT newspaper. She had had her own talk show on the radio, and was a highly visible, powerful activist.

She had stopped writing her column when she became a patient at the hospice. After a period of calling on her to get to know her better, I suggested she could dictate new columns to me as I typed them into my laptop, and I would then send them into her editor at the paper. She was skeptical but decided to give it a try. So, I started bringing my laptop in on my hospice visits, and she started dictating. Being a fast typist, I was able to capture her dictation accurately. We would always go back over it, so she could correct or edit what I had typed. Then I went home and emailed the new column to her editor. This was a great solution for all involved, especially her audience of devoted fans. Best of all was how much pleasure it gave Connie. It gave me a lot of joy, too, to be of service to this amazing activist.

Connie was still a patient at the AIDS Hospice when it came time for me to leave for the 1996 International AIDS Conference in Vancouver, British Columbia. I told her I'd be flying up there the next day. She angrily told me, "While you're circling Vancouver, do me a favor and open the door of the plane and piss all over the conference." I laughed, but I knew she was deadly serious. She was angry that she was dying, and she was angry at all those scientists who could not do anything to help her at this late stage.

At the conference, I was in the plenary session when researchers announced that a combination of protease inhibitors and antiviral drugs, commonly called "the cocktail treatment" was successful in managing HIV disease. I started to cry when it dawned on me what the reporting researchers were telling us. This would change everything. People would start getting better, and the galloping rate of death would slow way down. I wept for all my friends who had not lived to see this day. I cried in relief that so many others, including me, had lived to see this day. I remembered how Dr. Levine had told me when I was first diagnosed, "Your job is to stay alive long enough for us to find a way to manage this disease." I did it. What a bittersweet triumph.

When I got back to Los Angeles, I went to the hospice to tell Connie about the conference. She was in bad shape. She was still conscious, but she knew it was indeed too late for her, and she bitterly told me to stuff the good news. She died not long after the conference ended.

I realized that I was burning out. To protect my health and my sanity, I ended my chaplaincy at the Chris Brownlie Hospice. It had been one of the most rewarding things I'd done as a minister, but after six years of it, I was tired of witnessing the deaths of so many young women and men with AIDS.

CHAPTER SEVEN

Into the Spotlight

BACK IN THE SPRING OF 1990, I WAS EXCITED TO BE INVITED TO PLAY myself in a new play, *AIDS US II*. It gave me a creative outlet that I didn't even realize I'd needed, and it was thrilling to be a part of a stage production once again, which I hadn't done since around 1978 in Chicago when I'd been in our church productions of *Norman, Is That You?* and *The Mousetrap*.

When the opportunity to appear in *AIDS US II* arose, I grabbed it. I had seen the first *AIDS US*, produced in 1986. It featured twelve people, most of whom were living with AIDS, telling their stories. One of these people with AIDS was the actor Steve Tracy, who had portrayed Nellie Oleson's husband, Percival Dalton, on *Little House on the Prairie*. He died a few months before the first *AIDS US* closed, and an understudy assumed his role in the AIDS play.

In *AIDS US II*, I was one of eleven people affected by AIDS, telling a variety of stories. The great ensemble cast included Alison Arngrim, who played Nellie Oleson in *Little House on the Prairie*. Alison would be telling her story about becoming an AIDS activist because of Steve Tracy.

Michael Kearns, the director, and James Carroll Pickett, the writer, interviewed each of us, with a series of common questions, ranging from things like, "How did you first hear about AIDS?" to "What's the best sex you ever had?" Pickett then wove together our stories in his script, using our actual words, from our recorded answers.

We rehearsed the play for a couple of months. We performed it all over the Los Angeles area, but only did one performance a week. We were a big hit right from the start, garnering critical raves and prolonged standing ovations. We were the *LA Weekly*'s "Pick of the Week" for many weeks that summer.

We felt like family. It was that old familiar feeling I'd had when I was playing in one show after another in my teens. Working on this project, being creative, and engaging in something both joyful and tragic was such a bonding process for all of us in the cast. Of course, in *AIDS US II*, we had the added level of sharing the AIDS experience.

Two of the people in the show, Shevawn and Aidan, were an unmarried straight couple whose son contracted AIDS as an infant through a blood transfusion. In the play, the two of them told of their little boy's decline and death. As the emotional climax of the show, it always had the audience, and some of the cast, in tears.

The cast of *AIDS US II*, summer 1990, includes Alison Arngrim, "nasty Nellie Oleson" from the long-running TV series *Little House on the Prairie*. All the other men in this photo have died. COURTESY OF MICHAEL KEARNS.

Shevawn and Aidan decided to get married that summer, and they asked me to perform the ceremony after a performance. The audience was invited to stay for the wedding. This time, we were all awash in tears of happiness.

One of the great joys of being in *AIDS US II* was making friends with Alison Arngrim. We hit it off right away and began hanging out with each other all the time, if not in person, then on the phone.

One time, I was driving her home from a rehearsal, when she said, "You know, I first remember you from when you taught 'Homosexuality and the Bible' to my hotline training class at AIDS Project Los Angeles in 1986. I had stood up and asked, 'Why do we have to learn this? I thought we just politely excuse ourselves if someone calls in saying AIDS was God's punishment against homosexuals.'"

I said, "YOU!!!" I almost stopped the car and threw her out in the middle of La Brea Avenue. Her question had made sense to the hotline director, Bob Schoonover, and it was the last time I was invited to teach homosexuality and the Bible to the hotline training class. To be fair, when we got back to her home, she showed me her notebooks with my entire lecture taken down in outline form.

After the show closed, the other men living with AIDS in the cast died over the next year or so. Shevawn, Aidan, and I stayed in touch for a long while. When their first baby was born, they asked Alison and me to be godparents. Alison and I are great friends to this day.

I was incredibly excited when the following spring, one of Jane Pauley's segment producers Susan Farkas called to ask if I'd be willing to be profiled for a piece marking the tenth anniversary of the first published report on AIDS. I readily agreed.

Susan came out to Los Angeles in April 1991 and spent ten days following me around with a camera crew, including going with me to Pueblo, Colorado, where I did one of my weekend gigs, this time with the camera crew and Susan recording my workshops, as well as the sermon I preached on Sunday. Back home, they also followed me speaking at a prison, dancing at an AIDS Dance-a-thon, and attending patients, including Johnny, at the AIDS hospice. They filmed me visiting Tony Gramaglia, a friend from the cast of *AIDS US II*, and they filmed me watching *I Love Lucy* at home. All but my presentation in prison ended up in the finished piece. They recorded over forty hours of footage for the eleven-minute segment.

The high point of that time with Susan and the camera crew was the day Jane Pauley flew out to Los Angeles to interview me. She met us at MCC Los Angeles. Rev. Elder Nancy Wilson let us do the interview in the sanctuary. My friend Randy came with me, and before Jane arrived, he served as her stand-in while they set the lighting and cameras.

I was extraordinarily nervous. It's not as if I'd never met a celebrity before. It's not as if I'd never been interviewed on camera before. But Jane Pauley was someone special to me. When I was housebound with multiple illnesses in 1983, watching her on *The Today Show* every morning made me feel as if she were family. When she first sat down with me at MCC Los Angeles, I said, "When you went out on maternity leave with your twins, I missed you terribly."

She said, "That's what I usually hear from elderly people in nursing homes."

When we were done, it felt like one of the best interviews I'd ever had, and I'd done plenty by that point. There's a reason why Jane Pauley was at the top of her field. She was the best.

After we finished the interview, Susan asked us to shoot some B-roll footage for possible use in transitions. We all went out to the front of the building to shoot some footage of Jane and me walking into the front door of the church. We were told to wait down the street a bit, while they set up the shot of us walking down the street before entering the building. While Jane and I waited, she asked me to show her a tap step. "I took tap as a little girl, but I don't remember much." So I taught her a tap step. We tried it slowly, then a little faster, and then she broke into a fast and furious, out-of-control tap dance, and I joined right in.

Later Susan took me aside, and said, "You better believe I captured the two of you doing your tap routine!" They didn't use the footage in the final piece, but when I asked for it, Susan got Jane's permission and sent me the footage.

When the piece aired in June 1991, I had Randy and Alison over to watch it with me. We were all delighted with how it turned out. I wrote thank-you notes to Susan and Jane and was so pleased to hear back from them both. I was so impressed with the whole team, and everything I'd assumed about Jane from watching her on *The Today Show* during the time I was a shut-in turned out to be true. She was as sweet, fun, and smart as she seemed on TV.

Mom and Dad were thrilled with the broadcast. I was so happy that I made them proud. Just as Mom and Dad had carried around their audiocassette recordings of my high school performances in musicals, they carried around the Jane Pauley videocassette for all their friends and our family to see.

Knowing how much my parents and friends loved it, I began showing the Jane Pauley profile instead of the Tammy Faye interview when I traveled to churches. It didn't take long for me to learn that people were far more interested in seeing my appearance on *Tammy's House Party* than they were in my profile on *Real Life with Jane Pauley*. I often showed both, but everyone's questions were always about Tammy Faye.

In 1991 a collection of my articles, a sermon, and my pamphlets about living with AIDS was published by Chi Rho Press as a book, *I'm Still Dancing: A Gay Man's Health Experience*. It never sold very well, but Chi Rho Press was a small publisher, primarily putting out books by people from the Metropolitan Community Churches.

In the summer of 1991, the Metropolitan Community Church's General Conference was held at a resort in Phoenix, Arizona. I invited Alison to do a presentation on "AIDS and Safe Sex." People came out to see Nellie Oleson, but they came away knowing a lot more about AIDS and safe sex.

Dr. Levine flew out one day to do the Medical Update on AIDS. It was well attended, with AIDS on everyone's mind in those days. The numbers of cases and deaths were mushrooming all over the country and in almost every MCC all over the world. My parents drove over from Sun City, and it was wonderful to bring them together with Dr. Levine. Of course, she charmed them as no one else could, and they were so grateful to meet the physician who'd saved my life.

There was plenty of programming specifically for people living with AIDS, including daily support groups that were well attended. At the end of the week, the people living with AIDS gave me a stuffed coyote, lifting its head in a howl. It still holds a position of honor on my plush toy animal shelf.

After the 1991 General Conference, Alison started booking weekends at different MCCs around the United States. We went together some weekends, and we took great delight in doing dialogue sermons, as well as various workshops, including one on laughter as therapy. Alison was, and is, an accomplished stand-up comedian, and I knew enough about the importance of laughter in living with AIDS, that between the two of us, we were able to get everyone to see how important laughter was in facing AIDS or any other life-threatening condition. In these workshops, we had people literally laughing on the floor. We would have the audience members lie down on the floor in a long line, with each one laying their head on the belly of the person before them. Then, the first one would start laughing a big belly laugh, and that would get the next person laughing, and on, and on, until we literally had people rolling on the floor in laughter. Not exactly what they were expecting from a workshop on an AIDS awareness weekend.

Indeed, a response I frequently got, with or without Alison, was people's surprise that workshops or sermons on AIDS could be so upbeat and positive. I always stressed hope and joy.

Alison came back to the General Conference in 1993 and was again greeted with great love and admiration for her AIDS activism, not just because of having played Nellie Oleson. Her bookings in MCC churches continued, and I joined her on many of those. We had great fun together out on the road and hardly ever stopped laughing.

She taught me a lot about women's health during those tours. Having never had a sister or a wife, I knew next to nothing about the female anatomy. Even my mother had not taught me much about the female body. So, on one flight to some MCC, Alison proceeded to educate me, and I learned a lot. The woman in the row in front of us started squirming with discomfort when Alison told me about the dilation and curettage procedure. That just egged Alison on.

On November 6, 1993, I officiated at Alison's marriage to Bob Schoonover. It was a wedding full of magic. They had a friend who was a magician at the Magic Castle, David Taylor, professionally known as Damien. He made their rings appear in a ball of fire in mid-air, and I grabbed the rings (after the fire went out) out of the air and continued with the ring portion of the wedding service.

At the end of the ceremony, I touched each of them with my fairy wand as I pronounced them husband and wife. Then I said, "Poof! You're married!" as I threw a handful of glitter over their heads. The large gathering of their families and friends laughed and cheered. A big glob of glitter stuck to the front of Bob's sweaty scalp (it was a warm day), and he sported that through the entire reception.

The wedding was covered in the *National Enquirer*, *Hello Magazine*, *Ola*, and as one of the "Best Weddings of 1993" in *People Magazine*. I believe that was the only time I was in the *National Enquirer*!

Back in 1987, Dr. Levine had started asking me to join her in a lecture for the first-year medical students at the University of Southern California's Keck School of Medicine. As a Distinguished Professor of Medicine at USC, she was responsible for a two-hour lecture given to first-year medical students. The first hour was a formal lecture on the scientific aspects of HIV/AIDS. In the second hour, she "interviewed" me in front of the class about my experiences as an AIDS patient. She asked me to give my patient's perspective about being a good physician. I would talk about physicians who had tried to take away my hope. She loved to have me tell the story of the neurologist who told me I could never again work out with weights. I also told stories about Dr. Levine and the doctors on her staff, who always gave me hope and who didn't hide behind their white coats but made a point of being human and accessible.

These presentations have continued for over thirty-five years, though the topic has been modified a bit. The first hour is now spent with Dr. Levine discussing the scientific data proving a relationship between mind and body, and in the second hour, I'm interviewed about my experiences as a patient. The lecture is called "Medicine: The Power of the Art." She always ended our interviews by having me sing a song I'd written to the tune of the Gilbert and Sullivan song "I am the Very Model of the Modern Major General" from *The Pirates of Penzance*. Before I wrote it, I'd been thinking about how church people considered my story of recovery from AIDS a "miracle." However, in medical circles, they referred to my story as an "anomaly." One day, as I thought about this conundrum, I had the inspiration to write these new lyrics to the Major General's song. The words came pouring out of me in less than an hour.

> I am the very model of a medical anomaly.
> I've had KS, lymphoma, hepatitis, thrush, and CMV,
> Bacterial pneumonia and adrenal insufficiency,
> All this and more because I caught a virus that's called HIV.

> And then I took an antiviral, just like chemotherapy.
> It made me sick, my hair fell out, I suffered neurologically.
> But, hey! It worked! It stopped all of the HIV activity:
> My lymphoma's in remission, and there is no more KS to see.

> Lymphoma's in remission, and there is no more KS to see!
> Lymphoma's in remission, and there is no more KS to see!
> Lymphoma's in remission, and there is no more KS, KS to see!

> Now many years have passed, and I'm as healthy as a horse can be.
> It's certainly a miracle for anyone with faith to see.
> But still in journals medical, in science and oncology,
> I am the very model of a medical anomaly!

The medical students always roared their approval and delight.

I've sung this song throughout the English-speaking world. Inevitably, someone comes up to me afterward and says, "I never thought anyone could put AIDS and Gilbert and Sullivan together, but you did it!"

Dr. Levine loved my ditty so much, she pulled out her cell phone one day and recorded me performing it. She's played it many times for her colleagues at the National Institutes for Health and the Centers for Disease Control and Prevention, including for Dr. Anthony Fauci. She has reported that those colleagues often ask after "that survivor of the suramin trials," and they're always "surprised and delighted" to know I'm doing fine.

At Christmas 1991, Dad was getting very thin, and we weren't sure he would live much longer. He'd had open-heart surgery after a heart attack in the late 1980s, but it was chronic lymphocytic leukemia (CLL) that was bringing him down now.

Dr. Levine told me that his CLL was directly related to my type of lymphoma, proving we were indeed related. When I told Dad that, I immediately regretted it, because I could see the pain in his face. He apologized for passing on the genes that would cause me to suffer. I assured him that I felt no apology was needed since it wasn't anything that he could control.

On Christmas Day, Dad asked me to drive him out into the desert so we could have a good, private talk. When we got out there and parked with a close-up view of the mountains west of Sun City, he started the conversation by saying, "I'm afraid of death."

"You mean you're afraid of dying?"

"No, I'm dying now, and I'm not afraid of this. What I am afraid of is being dead."

I responded with words I'd used with many others who were dying, but it took on whole new depths of feeling when I addressed them to my father: "Dad, I know you to be a man of great faith. You believe in Jesus Christ, and Jesus says, in John 11, 'I am the Resurrection and the Life. Those who believe in me, even though they die, they shall live.' Dad, there is nothing to fear in death. I have died, and I've lived close to death, my own and others', for years, and I know that what awaits us on the other side is perfect peace and perfect love. It's literally 'the peace that passes all understanding.' And all the folks who have loved you and gone before you will be there, surrounding you with love. Your mother, your father, your brother, and all the rest... They will be there to guide you to that great Light, which is the perfect love of God."

"I wish I had your faith."

"Do you believe that I believe?"

"Yes."

"Well, then, here—just borrow my faith."

As much experience as I had at helping people face death, I felt I was now teetering on the edge of feeling helpless. I was so scared that I wasn't getting through to him, that I wasn't really helping him face his fears about being dead.

As we drove home, he said, "Please try to get along with your brother. It's one of the great disappointments of my life that you two aren't close. I hope you will work on your relationship."

Finally, he asked me not to abandon my mother after he was gone. He told me he knew she and I had a difficult relationship, but he hoped I would visit her regularly and write or phone her as often as I could. I reassured him that I would, as much as I knew it would be challenging. Mom had, in recent years, become angry and bitter, and often it was directed right at me. Mom resented the way I had become closer to Dad than to her. She had been my best friend when I was a child. Now it was very different, and I know she felt rejected.

My cousin David pointed out that Mom had always had at least one person in her life at whom she focused her anger, beginning with her abusive father. Now, she focused her anger on me. I know she was disappointed that I would never present her with a daughter-in-law who could take care of her in her old age, the way Mom had taken care of her mother-in-law. Worse, I would never present her with any grandchildren. I believe that deep down, she was furious with me simply for being gay.

When Christmas was over, I was careful to say goodbye to Dad before I drove home to Los Angeles because I wasn't sure I would see him again. We both got choked up when I told him how much I loved him and what a good father he was before saying goodbye. Dad went into a nursing home not long after that Christmas Day and was put into hospice care.

On January 24, 1992, my cousin David called from the hospice in Sun City and said I should get there as soon as possible, as Dad was close to death. David and Nancy had arrived the day before to visit Mom and Dad since they feared the end was coming soon for Dad.

I packed up as quickly as possible, called Don Eastman to tell him I had to leave for Sun City immediately, and I called my pastor, Nancy Wilson, to ask for her prayers. She asked me to call her right after Dad died, no matter what time it was.

I tried not to smoke a lot of grass as I drove across the desert, but I did get stoned as I set out from Los Angeles. I stopped smoking joints halfway across the Mojave Desert, so I was no longer stoned when I arrived in Sun City. I went directly to the nursing home to see Dad. Mom, David, and Nancy were there by his bedside. Dad was awake but didn't have the strength to talk. I kissed him on his forehead, and then I held my forehead next to his.

A couple of hours later, Rick arrived from Boston, and being a doctor as well as the first-born son, he immediately took charge. Not long after he got there, a nurse came into Dad's room and asked us if we were expecting any other family. Rick told her no. She suggested that it would be a good time for her and another nurse to make Dad more comfortable, and she asked us to wait in the corridor right outside his room.

When we were invited to come back in, Dad looked clean and comfortable. He was still awake and looked at each of us in turn. I could see in his eyes he was afraid, and I tried to reassure him, as I reminded him of our talk in the desert. I was scared, too, afraid of the grief to come, the feeling of not having a father anymore.

Mom told him, "You'll see your beloved mother soon." This surprised me since I'd never heard Dad talk much about his mother, who died long before I was born. It seemed he had told Mom how much he had loved her. I was touched by this sign of their emotional intimacy.

We each told him it was okay to go, encouraging him as we could and reassuring him of our love. Everything we said was highly charged with emotion, since Dad kept looking at each of us with such fear in his eyes. Very soon, his breathing became shallow, and he finally took his last breath with his eyes wide open, as if looking at someone in front of him. He was gone.

Rick closed Dad's eyes. I was grateful David and Nancy were there with us. Of course, they were grieving as much as any of us, since they had been so close to Dad, but they had an inner strength and peace I could lean on, and I knew Mom and Rick felt much the same.

Dad died around 1 a.m. on January 25, exactly one month after our talk in the desert and exactly one month before he would have turned eighty-two. We each said goodbye to Dad and then went back to Mom

and Dad's house. Despite it being around 2 a.m., I called Rev. Elder
Nancy Wilson, but reached her answering machine. When she called me
back the next day, she apologized profusely for not answering the phone,
but I assured her I completely understood.

Even though it was the middle of the night, Mom immediately put
us all to work. She threw things at us from his closet and his dresser. We
took what we wanted and put the rest in piles to donate. I took some
of his shoes. We wore the same size, and I wanted to walk in his shoes.
David, Rick, and I went through his jewelry box, splitting his cufflinks
and tie clips among us.

It was all so strange to be sorting through his clothes, jewelry, and
other possessions so immediately after his death, but it was Mom's way
of dealing with Dad's death, and we all just followed her direction. The
house was finally all hers, and she wanted to claim it all. Her incredible
energy in the middle of the night, as she threw everything out of his
closet and his dresser, was her way of expressing her anger at Dad. She
had told us that she was angry that she'd had to spend her whole life taking care of people. In these last years, it was particularly difficult to care
for an increasingly frail husband. Now she just wanted to be done with it
all, hence her frenzy to get rid of Dad's things in the hours immediately
following his death.

There were two services for Dad; one in Sun City and one back in
Andover at the Phillips Academy Chapel, followed by burying his ashes
in the garth at the Phillips Academy cemetery.

I don't remember much about the memorial service in Sun City. Dad
had asked me to officiate at his memorial services, but I declined, saying
I expected I would be too emotional to do the whole service. I did, however, tell him that I would be willing to speak at the services. That pleased
him, although I know it disappointed him that I wouldn't officiate.

When we gathered at the Chapel in Andover later in the spring, I
was glad to see many of the men Dad had hired to teach math at Phillips Academy. I hadn't seen most of them since I graduated in 1970. I
was surprised when several of them commented on how I'd grown to
look so much like Dad. That pleased me, remembering how, when I
was growing up, I was always told Rick looked like Dad and I looked

like Mom. As a child, I had taken those comments as judgments on my fragile masculinity.

I was pleased to see the Schneiders there. Mr. Schneider had played a major role in my early life. He conducted the choir and the school musicals. He also recommended I go to Northwestern, his alma mater, and he got me into summer stock at the College Light Opera Company on Cape Cod.

I was so glad to see my "substitute mother," my mother's best friend, Diz Barker, and her daughter Bobbi Winter there, as well as my beloved cousins Lucia and Lawrie, and of course, Rick, his wife Edie, and my niece Jen. Once again, Rick and I both spoke at the service, as did one of Dad's former students, whom I didn't know. Dad's student told the gathering what a great teacher Dad was and what a huge impact he had on his life as well as the lives of so many others. Dad would have been surprised and pleased to hear that.

When I spoke, I talked about how Dad had changed after I'd come out. He became more comfortable with his feelings. He even wrote a whole new, long addition to his autobiography about his emotional reactions to the facts of his life. That had touched me deeply. I also talked about Dad's final month, focusing on the talk we had out in the desert, and how Dad was surrounded by his family when he passed away.

Many of us walked down Chapel Avenue to the cemetery. I carried the urn with Dad's ashes, while Mr. Penner, one of the teachers Dad had hired, talked to me about playing the baker in Andover's production of *Into the Woods*. It seemed so weird to have that conversation as I was carrying my father's ashes to the cemetery.

After the burial ceremony, Mom grabbed Rick's and my arms and the three of us led the way out of the cemetery back to the reception. As we walked away, out of the corner of my eye I saw Jen, who was fifteen, sobbing in Lucia's arms while they stood on the garth where we had just buried Dad's ashes. I felt pulled toward Jen and wanted to go back to help comfort her, but Mom, sensing my feelings, tightened her grip on my arm. Realizing my place at this moment was at Mom's side, I was grateful that Lucia was there for Jen, who had been so close to her grandfather.

The reception was a blur of faces and words of comfort from many of the Phillips Academy community. It was great to see so many of them paying their respects. Everyone seemed so practiced at saying the right words for a reception after the burial of a faculty member. Even though Dad retired and left Andover in 1975, he had taught there for thirty-eight years, and he certainly made his mark on the school. I was deeply touched that so many of his colleagues came to pay their final respects.

My grief unfolded over the next year. I had taught about grief in workshops and sermons, but it still surprised me how it washed over me now. Just as I thought I was done with it, it would break over me again, like waves of the ocean. Dad taught me to body surf when I was nine or ten, and he told me then not to fight the wave, but to give myself over to it and let it carry me into shore. If I fought the wave of grief over Dad's passing, I knew it would pull me under. If I rode the wave, I knew it would carry me through all the feelings and into a place of healing. I reminded myself of all the times in teaching about grief I'd quoted Robert Frost, "The best way out is always through."

A little over a month later, I was scheduled to take a cruise to the Mexican Riviera. The company that ran the cruise specialized in catering to the LGBTQ community. I had been paying for the cruise for over a year, and so I felt I had to go, even though I didn't feel up for it.

My cabinmate was my friend Ralph, also a patient of Dr. Levine's, as well as an influential member of Christ Chapel MCC in Santa Ana. As many people with AIDS were doing at the time, Ralph had sold his life insurance policy in a viatical settlement, a way for people with AIDS or other life-threatening illnesses to get a lot of quick cash. Ralph's settlement gave him the cash to buy the Jaguar he'd always wanted and a ticket for this cruise, among other things. He was a real self-starter and a good friend. He was my unofficial assistant with the denomination's AIDS Ministry. I became depressed when he moved to Dallas the next year. He died soon after that and I grieved his passing.

Despite Ralph's friendship, I was miserable through much of the cruise. There were some stunning men on board, showing off their chiseled bodies as they sunned in their Speedos, but they all felt unavailable and unreachable. There was a lot of sex going on all over the ship, which some were referring to as a "floating bathhouse," but none of it involved me. This made me even more bitter and resentful.

During the cruise, Ralph became perturbed and frustrated with me and my foul mood. I couldn't blame him, and I tried to perk up. But I was still grieving Dad, and I knew that I shouldn't have come on the cruise. I was so relieved when we disembarked for the final time. This was one time when I did not ride the wave of my grief, but fought it and got pulled under as a result. I was miserable throughout, and I made Ralph miserable, too.

I got back to work and traveled to different churches, conferences, and board meetings of the AIDS National Interfaith Network through the summer, but my heart wasn't in it. I got lazy about putting the *ALERT* newsletter together and started copying articles and other resources instead of writing my own. I dragged my feet about calling the clergy and lay leaders with AIDS and cancer so that sometimes my reports to the board of elders were late. I was spending a lot of time just sitting at my home where I stayed stoned and watched endless hours of TV. Most days, I did get to the gym, where I worked my feelings out with furious weight training.

From my studies of grief, I knew that grief was cumulative. All the grief I never allowed myself to feel as more and more friends died from AIDS compounded the grief I felt for Dad.

In the fall, I went on my second tour of the European District of Metropolitan Community Churches. I was excited about that. I started in the United Kingdom, before heading to the European MCC District Conference in Hamburg, Germany.

I preached there with an interpreter. I did my usual routine about believing in fairies, complete with my fairy wand, but while the folks from the United Kingdom got it, most of the people from the continent stared at me blankly. Afterward, the District Coordinator, Rev. Hong Tan, told me that people outside the English-speaking world weren't familiar with Peter Pan and didn't understand the English language connection between fairies and gay men. Live and learn.

At the worship service the next night, Rev. Delores Berry preached and sang. After our dance at the Miami General Conference in 1987,

I felt a special connection with her. This evening, something she sang triggered an enormous wave of grief over Dad. Right there in the front row of the congregation, I doubled over and sobbed. I had a momentary flash of embarrassment and thought I had to pull myself together. But hadn't I been teaching for the last five years that you've got to go through the grief, to feel it deeply, to get through it and move on? So, I continued to weep. I know someone comforted me with a hand on my back, and people expressed their concern and comfort afterward. I had never cried so hard in public in my life. It was the same depth of despair and grief that I felt the night I was given my "terminal" prognosis in 1984, but it was different. Then I was grieving my own life. Now I was grieving all my friends with AIDS and most acutely, my dad.

After the conference was over, my next stop was Copenhagen. I stayed with the pastor of MCC Copenhagen, Rev. Mia, and her life partner, Laurenz, during my time there. It was not a large church, but the members were close to each other and seemed like a tight-knit family.

One night, I had a vivid dream. My father came to me, and I felt his presence as strongly as I did on that drive into the desert. We basked in each other's presence, and then he wordlessly said goodbye, turned away from me, and disappeared into the light. I awoke crying. The dream somehow enabled me to say my final goodbyes to Dad. I knew that he had been set free of his earthly connections and was now living his eternal life with God. I suddenly felt my grief healing, and I felt ready to move on.

I flew back to London, where I had one more weekend of teaching and preaching, this time at the Metropolitan Community Church in Brixton. Feeling newly released from my intense grief over Dad, I preached up a storm.

The next day, I flew back to Los Angeles.

The year ended with a difficult Christmas with my mother in Sun City. I did not want to be there but felt obligated because of Dad's final wishes. It was not the first time I'd visited her after Dad's death. I went out there for her eightieth birthday in May and was grateful that Rick, David, and Nancy were there, too. Their presence helped shield me from her anger. Now, I felt the full brunt of it during my solo Christmas visit.

To be fair, I'm sure I wasn't easy to love, as I took every opportunity to get out of the house and drive nowhere in particular to smoke a joint and a few cigarettes in peace.

The drive back to Los Angeles was a marijuana-fueled relief. I must have smoked three or four joints and half a pack of cigarettes before getting home. It's amazing I survived all those stoned car trips. Talk about miracles.

On the Monday before Thanksgiving 1993, I was working in my office at headquarters when our receptionist came in to tell me that the White House was on the line for me. I said, "Yeah, right." But in case it was real, I took the call, and I'm glad I did. It was, indeed, a White House aide. She invited me to the White House for a prayer breakfast on AIDS on November 30, 1993, with President Bill Clinton and the AIDS Policy Coordinator, or "AIDS Czar," Kristine Gebbie.

I said, "Yes."

I raced down the hall to the office of my supervisor, Don Eastman, to tell him. He stood up and said we had to go right into Troy Perry's office to tell him. Troy was almost as excited as I was. He had been at a White House meeting in 1977 with President Jimmy Carter to discuss LGBT rights, so knowing what it would mean for me and the denomination, he was thrilled.

The White House aide had said they had no budget to help anyone get there. Troy and Don agreed to pay my round-trip airfare and hotel.

The White House faxed all the paperwork required to clear me for a visit with the president. I filled it in as carefully as I could. I worried about getting every answer perfect, lest they catch me in some detail and deny me the opportunity to go to the White House.

I called Mom and Dr. Levine. They shared my excitement, and I could feel their pride at this incredible honor. I was most excited about calling Randy, knowing how much he loved Bill Clinton. His reaction was underwhelming, but he was getting ready to move to New Jersey for his job, so he had other things on his mind. Nevertheless, he had me over for dinner the evening before I left for Washington. He was scheduled to leave Los Angeles while I was in Washington, and so we had to say goodbye that evening at dinner. It was an emotional farewell for me. I knew there would be a big hole in my life now, but Randy was excited about moving so close to New York City. I tried to share his excitement, but it was difficult because I was just so sad about it all.

On Sunday, November 28, I flew to Washington, D.C., and checked into my hotel. The next morning, my friend Jim, the life partner of Rev. Larry Uhrig, the MCC pastor in Washington, D.C., picked me up for a tour of their church and to see Larry. Larry was seriously ill with AIDS but had conducted the service the day before.

Larry had been an important figure in my life since I first met him in the spring of 1979, my last year of being student clergy. He was then the chair of the denomination's clergy credentialing committee. His first words to me were an imperious, "What makes you think you can be the pastor of a Metropolitan Community Church?" I took an instant dislike to him.

Despite that rough start, we became good friends. After I had recovered from lymphoma, Kaposi's sarcoma, and the suramin trial, he invited me to preach several times. He had also been the first to give a significant financial offering to fund our AIDS Ministry at the General Conference in St. Paul, the summer of 1989.

When he himself was diagnosed with AIDS, I called him every month, as I did with all the clergy and lay leaders with AIDS, and he called me many times. He had always been an emotional man. As a pastor living with AIDS in a church filled with people living and dying with AIDS, his feelings became even more acute.

Larry had overseen a huge project: building a gorgeous new church building for his congregation. He was determined to make this happen, and he did it. It was, and is, a stunning tribute to his faithfulness and his determination. After we visited other staff there and toured the church, Jim drove me to the home he shared with Larry.

When I saw Larry lying in his big bed, he looked so wasted and frail. As I did with other people who were close to death, I crawled into bed with him, and we had a good visit. At one point he said, "I want a Steve Pieters-type miracle."

I nodded and said, "I hope you get it."

"If I have to die from this, I want to die in the pulpit." He did not want to resign as pastor, and he was determined to preach and lead worship as long as possible.

"I hope you get your wish."

We talked about my trip to the White House. He said, "I'm so proud of you, this kid I met long ago, who wanted to be a pastor."

When it was time to leave, I said goodbye, trying not to show I suspected this would be our final goodbye.

Then Jim took me for a drive around Washington before we stopped for dinner. As evening fell, he drove me past the White House. I became emotional suddenly, just so sad that Dad didn't live to see his son go to the White House. When I shared that with Jim, he simply said, "He knows." I wanted to believe he was right.

I did not bring any marijuana with me on this trip. That was unusual for me when traveling in the United States. I was always paranoid that I would get caught, and sometimes my anxiety about that was huge, but I usually traveled with it anyway. This time, however, I certainly did not want to risk being arrested for possession on my way to the White House. Also, I wanted my brain to be as clear as possible for my encounter with the president. I worried that I would not be able to sleep the night before the prayer breakfast without marijuana, but I did manage to get to sleep.

I awoke early the next morning and was ready to leave long before I needed to. I did not want to be late! I took a cab to the east entrance gate of the White House. I was the first of the attendees to show up. I knew the other guests were leaders of their denominations' AIDS ministries. Rev. Ken South, executive director of the AIDS National Interfaith Network, had been instrumental in putting the guest list together, so I knew most of the twelve guests from my work on their board of directors.

When a few more of us arrived, we went through security at the gate, and they ushered us through the East Wing to the hallway beneath the main building. As we waited, we were invited to inspect some of the downstairs rooms.

One of our number said, "Look, there he is!" In sauntered our president in his sweats, just in from his morning run. He waved at us and said, "I'll be right down after I change." I was so surprised to see the president dressed like that, but it made him more human, somehow. My heart was in my throat as I thought about talking with him.

We were taken upstairs to the first floor. It was quiet in that big entrance hall. I peeked into the Blue Room, the Green Room, and the Red Room. The East Room was closed off while they prepared for some event.

The only other time I had been there, I was nine and a tourist. I had glowing memories of seeing this part of the White House back then, filled with other tourists. It all seemed so beautiful and historic. After that visit, I studied all I could about the White House, and even built little replicas of it out of cardboard. Now, here I was, about to meet the president.

An usher told us Vice President Al Gore would be joining us, too. I had developed a crush on him during the campaign, so I was delighted. Then we were ushered into the State Dining Room, where butlers served us orange juice and coffee as we mingled. There was no furniture in the room, which made that great portrait of Abraham Lincoln over the mantel even more powerful. A harpist played Broadway show tunes. Kristine Gebbie, our AIDS Czar, arrived and greeted us.

There was a little table with a place-setting diagram, and we all looked for our names. I was stunned to see they put me between President Clinton and Ms. Gebbie and directly across from Al Gore. One of my colleagues speculated that I was seated there because I was the only person with AIDS among the twelve guests.

We were told we would be eating breakfast with the president and vice president in the Family Dining Room, adjacent to the State Dining Room. I hadn't realized there was a Family Dining Room on the first floor. Soon, Clinton and Gore appeared, and we were each introduced to them, while the White House photographers took photos of every encounter with the president and vice president. They both knew something about each of us. Now I realized the paperwork I had filled out was not only to clear us with the Secret Service but to brief Clinton and Gore before we met.

Finally we were ushered into the Family Dining Room, and I took my place next to the president at the table. The room was magnificent. There were handsome portraits on the yellow walls and a gorgeous chandelier over an elegant, long table set beautifully with White House china and arrangements of yellow flowers in the center. Someone told me that seated on the other side of the president was Rev. Ed Dobson, an architect of the Moral Majority and Jerry Falwell's right-hand man for many years. He was currently working on a "compassionate" AIDS ministry, although he disapproved of homosexuality.

As the White House ushers put fruit cups in front of us, Clinton turned to talk to Dobson, seated on his left. So, I turned to Kristine Gebbie and talked with her. I thanked her for including a representative from

The first AIDS Prayer Breakfast at the White House, in the old Family Dining Room. The author is third from the left (with a White House butler standing between him and President Bill Clinton) and across from Vice President Al Gore, with AIDS "Czar" Kristine Gebbie on the far right. November 30, 1993. OFFICIAL WHITE HOUSE PHOTOGRAPH BY WHITE HOUSE PHOTOGRAPHER SHARON FARMER.

the Metropolitan Community Churches, and she said, "Are you kidding? I insisted!" She told me how much she had learned about AIDS from Rev. Gary Wilson, our pastor in Portland, Oregon, when she lived there. After a few minutes of conversation, she said, "You should make yourself available to talk with the president. He'll really listen." She turned to talk to the person on her right.

I picked at my fruit cup while I waited for the president to turn toward me. I was as full of self-doubts as I'd been in years. I was about to have a conversation with the president of the United States. Here was my opportunity "to speak truth to power," literally, and suddenly, I could not think of anything to say. I felt as if I were an awkward adolescent at the table with my father's math colleagues, with no idea how to join the conversation. Now, here I was in the White House, next to the president of the United States. As I looked around, I was the only one at the table not engaged in some discussion or other. I felt totally out of place, worried that I was a fraud, and it seemed like this moment would never end.

I didn't think Clinton was ever going to stop talking to Dobson, so I started to listen in on them. Dobson was saying how sexuality is not a concern to him in doing AIDS ministry. He believed in ignoring a person's homosexuality while ministering to people with AIDS. Trying to be agreeable, I said, "Sexuality doesn't matter too much when you're dying, except in terms of who you want to have with you at your deathbed." Dobson froze, but Clinton smiled at me.

Finally turning his full attention on me as the ushers served scrambled eggs, bacon, sausage, potatoes, and toast, the president said, "Reverend Pieters, I hear you're quite a miracle." He was charming and warm, if a little reserved. We talked one-on-one for about fifteen minutes while we ate breakfast. I briefly told my story. He asked, "How do you explain your miracle?"

"Well, first I give the glory to God. My doctor says it was the suramin, but suramin didn't work for anyone else." I explained to him about the toxic side effects and the casualties it caused. He asked if I'd experienced any side effects myself, and I told him all about the adrenal insufficiency, the wasting, the nerve damage, and the inflammation in my eyes that compromised my sight. When I told him how meaningful "Amazing

Grace" was to me, quoting "I was blind, but now I see," he gave me one of those glowing smiles.

I told him I was treated at the University of Southern California by Dr. Alexandra Levine, and he made a note of that. I offered Dr. Levine's observation that the only effective vaccine on the horizon was education. He really liked that line. He later invited her to be on his AIDS Advisory Board.

I went on to report how heavily my denomination had been hit by AIDS and told him all the things we were doing in AIDS Ministry. I thanked him for including us, and he smiled and nodded. Then I mentioned Rev. Larry Uhrig, and how he was still working as the pastor of our D.C. church despite how sick he was with AIDS.

He then asked me about the latest on safe sex and, specifically, about how to keep oral sex safe. I started talking about what that meant for gay men. He interrupted me and said, "No, I mean between a man and a woman." I proceeded to teach him about how to have fun with condoms and dental dams and keep oral sex safe. This was several years before the Monica Lewinsky scandal led to his impeachment.

After the meal, he addressed the group and said, "I want to bring AIDS off the back burner on World AIDS Day." He asked us what our denominations were each doing and how worshiping communities can help the government. He reminded us that unfortunately, there were limits to his powers as president, but that he could certainly use the "bully pulpit" of the White House.

He gave everyone a chance to speak, as we went around the table. When I spoke, he was very attentive, as he had been in our one-on-one, fixing those serious blue eyes on me with full interest. He took notes on things that each of us said, underlining key words. People spoke about the need for education, for consensus, and for action. I talked about hope, and how helplessness breeds hopelessness, and action creates hope. I told him, "We're tired, we're burning out, and we need hope. Please give us reason to have hope."

I said he could give us hope by reaching out and touching us, embracing not just babies with AIDS, but adults with AIDS. I urged him "to lift the immigration ban against people with HIV, which is inconsistent with the principles on which this country was founded." I could see a wall go up when I mentioned that. I moved on to education and being an advocate for hope in the face of all the hopelessness.

After we each shared our comments, the meeting ended. It was supposed to end at nine thirty, but it was already about ten o'clock. One of the guests remarked how odd it was to have the conservative Rev. Ed Dobson on the President's left and the representative of the liberal, largely LGBT Metropolitan Community Churches on his right. Clinton said, "This would be a great photo op. We should send a copy to Rush Limbaugh." As we all laughed, he reached back and put his hands on Dobson's and my backs, but I've never seen a photo of that moment.

When the president rose to leave, Dobson suggested we pray. We all stood and joined hands. As Dobson prayed, Clinton held my hand with great intensity. I could not believe it. I was holding the hand of the president of the United States, the most powerful person in the world.

I presented Clinton with my book and pamphlet, and he said he'd be "very interested to read them." He pocketed them, which pleased me, since he'd given my colleagues' documents to an usher.

Knowing that it would be important to the others to see the president embracing a person with AIDS, I asked him for a hug. He rolled his eyes and said, "Oh, all right," and gave me a hug. He was so tall that my head was on his chest. He held me tight. The others did, indeed, notice, and one of the Episcopal priests at the breakfast told me, "That was arguably the most important moment of the whole prayer breakfast." The moment was not photographed, although moments before, the White House photographer was busily shooting photos of the whole group. He resumed shooting after the hug.

As we stopped hugging, I said, "Thanks. I need all the strength I can get!"

And he said, "You've given me strength. Thank you for bringing hope to the table."

We moved out of the Family Dining Room back into the State Dining Room. As people gathered around Clinton and Gebbie, I noticed Gore standing by himself. I went over and thanked him for being there. He said he was very moved by the meeting. We talked about how AIDS was connected to the environment. "The earth has AIDS," he said. We ended up talking for about five minutes. Then he said Clinton and he had to get out of there because they had Helmut Kohl on hold down in the Oval Office. Finally, Clinton came over and put his hand on Gore's shoulder, and the two of them went to the elevator next to the State Dining Room, and the doors closed on them.

Our delegation was shown to the front door. When we got outside, I asked everyone if I could get a photo of us all. One of the security guards who'd come outside to show us the way out, volunteered to take the photo. I was so glad I brought my camera with me! No one else had, apparently, and everyone, even Ed Dobson, asked for a copy, which I gladly sent them.

We went to the nearby building where Kristine Gebbie had her office, and we were debriefed on the whole prayer breakfast. She told us she thought the breakfast went "wonderfully well." Aides to Clinton had told her it was the best prayer breakfast yet: "good communication, substantive, honest, no games, and no pretense." One aide asked us how he should brief Dee Dee Myers, who would be giving her daily press briefing at one o'clock. I suggested she talk about the diversity of religious support for the president to bring AIDS "off the back burner."

I was itching to get out of there so I could call Troy, Don, and Randy to tell them each about it all. Soon enough, we dispersed. I called Troy and Don from my hotel room. They were almost as excited as I was. Then I called Randy. He was now in New Jersey, and he was thrilled to hear all the details.

I was so excited about the whole experience that I hardly needed an airplane to fly back to Los Angeles. It was good to get back to my home and my cats, who were always lovingly cared for by friends during my many absences, and it was a great relief to light up a joint and get stoned again. As often happened with the first joint after some days off, I got very stoned very quickly and suddenly had all the energy in the world. I called my pal, Lucia Chappelle, and chattered away endlessly, telling her the story of my time with the president. Soon, more marijuana began to bring me down. I crashed hard and slept long.

The next day, World AIDS Day, President Clinton gave his first speech on AIDS. He talked about the prayer breakfast and specifically mentioned me. "Rev. Steve Pieters, who's been living with AIDS for over a decade, is one of America's longest survivors. He credits his survival to his faith and hope." C-SPAN carried it, as we had been told they would, and Mom, certain that he would mention me, videotaped it live, and every time it was rerun over the next twenty-four hours so that she would have multiple videotapes to distribute to her friends and relatives, as well as to have one for herself. Our relationship was complicated, but it felt great to make Mom so proud.

At the Los Angeles World AIDS Day interfaith service that evening, a pastor of one of the Los Angeles area Metropolitan Community Churches, Joseph Gilbert, dragged me into the robing room when I arrived and announced to the fifty or so clergy there, "Here he is, direct from the White House!" Rev. Elder Nancy Wilson, my longtime friend, pastor, and vice moderator of our denomination, knelt and kissed my hand.

In my journal, I wrote, "I get the feeling this will change things in my professional life." Kristine Gebbie had told us in the debriefing, "This event will give you each more credibility in your work." It gave me more self-confidence, more joy, more hope, and, feeling everyone's respect and affection, I felt more connected. I told Lindsay, my bodyworker, "Even if I die young, I've led an amazing life, full of blessings. I've really lived!"

Rev. Larry Uhrig died on Tuesday, December 28, 1993, exactly one month after I visited with him. He preached his last service two days before, the day after Christmas. His ashes were interred in the columbarium he'd designed on the second floor of the church building he built. I was sad that this great friend had passed away. I was grateful I'd had a good, in-person visit with him before he died.

One of the biggest events of 1994 happened the same month I joined the Gay Men's Chorus of Los Angeles. On January 17, the Northridge earthquake destroyed the Metropolitan Community Church of Los Angeles's building we had so lovingly renovated over seven years. Thankfully, there was no loss of life since it happened in the early morning hours. But our building was gone.

There were some members who said they thought this was God's punishment against our church for LGBT people, and they dropped their membership. Our beloved pastor, Rev. Nancy Wilson, pointed out, "If losing our church building was God's way of condemning our church, then God was also delivering judgment against all the other denominations' churches that were destroyed in this earthquake."

Most of us believed that our church was not the building, but the people. Rev. Ken Martin, my first mentor in ministry, always said in his benediction: "Remember, you have not been to church. You are the church. And when the church is the church, it is nothing more, nor less, nor other than Christ's presence through people. So, go into the world and be the church."

And so, the earthquake forced us out into the world to be the church. The first challenge was finding a place where we would gather to worship together. Fortunately, a prominent member of the church was a Hollywood executive, and he arranged for us to gather every Sunday on the church set from the popular situation comedy *Home Improvement*.

We continued to be a church "on the move," worshiping in different locations from 1994 through 1996. Meanwhile, I continued to travel all over the world for my preaching and teaching engagements.

In 1996 the Metropolitan Community Church of Los Angeles and the denomination's headquarters together bought a property on Santa Monica Boulevard in the heart of West Hollywood. My commute became much longer, but the facilities were beautiful. Headquarters was in a multistoried office building, and our local church was in a former furniture store next door.

I joined the West Hollywood Athletic Club, a popular gym right up the street, so that I could work out during my lunch hours. Being in the heart of Boys Town, it had a largely gay clientele, making for a steamy locker room.

In the fall of 1994, the AIDS National Interfaith Network announced that the Centers for Disease Control would be offering grants to denominational AIDS ministry programs, so Don Eastman and I set about to get one of those grants. We got it, and I went to work on the project we'd proposed, a Peer Education Program on HIV prevention and awareness, to be called PEP-MCC.

This was based on the Peer Education Program created by Wendy Arnold, a friend from when she was the director of the Speakers Bureau at APLA. The program taught young people how to educate each other about HIV awareness and prevention. She not only established this program in Los Angeles, but in other places around the world.

With the grant, we created a training video and manual for use in our churches. In the spring of 1995, we mailed them to every Metropolitan Community Church around the world. We came in under budget, and I was proud of this whole accomplishment.

Our General Conference in the summer of 1995 was in Atlanta. When the AIDS Ministry report came up in a business meeting of the whole conference, only one delegate rose to make a comment. Barely controlling her anger, she asked, "Why did you send out these unsolicited peer education program packages, and where did you get the money to do this, without it being authorized in the previous General Conference's budget?"

She was hoping for a big fight. I remained calm and said, "It is the job of our denomination's AIDS Ministry to develop resources for the local church. A grant from the US Centers for Disease Control paid for the peer education program materials and all associated costs." The conference delegates applauded. The delegate who'd challenged us said, "Oh," and sat back down.

Rev. Jim Mitulski, the Chair of the denomination's AIDS Ministry Advisory Committee, suggested that I be given a sabbatical: a fully paid three months off to do as I pleased. I knew exactly what I wanted to do. In mid-August, I put my cat Preshy in her carrier and drove to New Hampshire, where Mom let me stay at the farm for three whole months. It was the best three months I had had since before AIDS. I spent countless hours in my rocking chair on the front porch, as I watched the lush green of summer change into the riotous colors of fall. I even enjoyed seeing the skeletal trees after they dropped their leaves, as the weather got cold. I read many books I'd been wanting to read, mostly fiction and memoirs.

'Ihe day I arrived at the farm, I opened my laptop, plugged the modem into the phone line, and dialed into AOL. I had an email waiting for me from a man named Daniel who wrote that he liked my profile and wondered if I would be interested in corresponding with him. I read his profile, which I found hard to believe. He claimed to be an accomplished Broadway performer, having sung and danced in many Broadway shows since he first landed in New York in the early 1970s. It turned out to be true. He worked with Michael Bennett in *A Chorus Line* on Broadway. He went on to work with Bob Fosse in *Dancin'*. He was now living in Los Angeles. He wrote of his loneliness. I explained I was in New Hampshire for a few months but would enjoy corresponding with him.

We started writing every day, sometimes two or three times a day. I loved reading all his stories of being on Broadway. He loved hearing about my life in the church. He came from a religious family, and he yearned to meet gay men who were people of faith.

I found myself falling in love for the first time in years, and I hadn't even met the man in person. Online relationships were new to everyone, and we both succumbed in no time to the other's online persona.

During those three months, I enjoyed my local friends and got a kick out of welcoming friends and family to stay with me at the farm. I discovered I loved to entertain, something I couldn't do in my tiny home in Los Angeles. My guests all loved the farm, and we had some amazing conversations on the porch and over lobster dinners. I found it healing not to think about AIDS for three months.

When my sabbatical ended in November, it was starting to snow at the farm. I drove back to Los Angeles with Preshy in only four days. I could not wait to meet Daniel in person. I knew we were going to fall into each other's arms and live happily ever after. When I got back to Los Angeles, he was singing in the ensemble of the musical *Candide*, at the newly refurbished Ahmanson Theater at the Music Center.

The day after I got home, he came to my house on his way to the theater. He had a big, bright smile and was just as handsome as the eight-by-ten glossy he'd sent me. We fell into each other's arms. We made mad, passionate love, and I could not have been happier. He was everything I'd dreamed he would be, and more. My love for him was sealed.

The next afternoon, he came back to my place, on his way to the theater again. He sat down and said, "I can't do this. It just scares me too much to be with someone who has AIDS."

My heart plunged. I knew there was no fighting this. He was already scared to death that he had caught HIV from me the day before. We had played safe, but fear is not always rational.

I sank into a depression that lasted for months. Watching him in *Candide,* I deeply regretted leaving the theater and wondered if I could have had a career like his. I suddenly missed everything about the theater and decided to attend every play and musical I could afford. Each show I saw deepened my despair that I'd stopped pursuing a theater career.

I felt that I would never have another chance at a relationship. I fell into the bitter trap of feeling I was damaged goods, not just in terms of having AIDS, but as someone who was not psychologically capable of forming a lasting relationship. I started joking in sermons and lectures that I was "romantically disabled." That always got a big laugh, but deep in my heart, it wasn't funny, because it was painfully true.

Despite my depression, or maybe because of it, I worked very hard at staying in touch with this now ex-boyfriend. I tried to be such a good friend that he would change his mind and decide we should be life partners after all. It didn't work, of course, but I kept trying. At the same time, I was grieving the loss of what I had foolishly thought was a sure thing. And this grief was cumulative: I was grieving not only all my failed efforts at relationships but all the wonderful friends I'd known over the past fifteen or so years who had died from complications of HIV/AIDS. I just could not shake the sadness, the grief, and the despair.

I was still traveling to churches and conferences all over, and with my theater training, I was somehow able to share my story of surviving AIDS and to inspire others to live with AIDS as fully as they could. Yet, when I got home, I would fall into such despair that all I could do was smoke endless amounts of marijuana and zone out in front of the TV, although nothing much made me laugh or cry.

One good thing did come out of this. Daniel referred a friend who was also in the ensemble of *Candide*. This man's name was Timothy Smith, and he, too, had had an extensive career in Broadway musicals, but recently had become HIV positive. Daniel told me Timothy was having a hard time with his diagnosis. He thought talking to me could help. To please Daniel, I met Timothy for dinner in West Hollywood. He, too, was a handsome man with a bright smile. I don't remember much about the dinner, except that he was very kind and grateful.

In the spring of 1996, Timothy and Daniel were cast in the national tour of the Andrew Lloyd Webber musical *Sunset Boulevard*. I helped Daniel pack up his belongings to be stored at his parents' home in northern California. We said goodbye, which broke my heart all over again, because I knew my efforts at being his best friend were not going to work long distance as he toured the nation.

After months of my depression, someone on the board of the Gay Men's Chorus of Los Angeles kindly suggested that I call his therapist. I saw this psychologist on a weekly basis for quite a few years. He had his office in the beautiful home he shared with his husband, also a psychologist, high in the hills above West Hollywood. I loved driving up the mountain to see my therapist, who spoke to me of "accepting life on life's terms." I argued with him that acceptance felt too much like resignation, but my depression began to lift.

Several times during the late eighties and early nineties, Louise Hay had me come speak to her weekly Hayride at West Hollywood Park Auditorium. I had accomplished what so many of her devotees wanted: to recover from full-blown AIDS. I was happy to speak, I was flattered, and as I told my story, I outlined all the things I had done to "create the conditions for healing." I always emphasized that I'd known others who had worked harder than I did and who had greater faith they could survive, but they did not. So, I grappled in front of the Hayride audience, not knowing why I survived when so many others did not.

One time, I brought my fairy wand and shared with the Hayride my *Peter Pan* story about the importance of believing in fairies. This got the usual roar of approval, complete with applause to bring dying fairies back to life. When I finished, Louise Hay came back to the mike and told how she had played Peter Pan when she was younger. Somehow that seemed right, for now she was leading a huge group of lost boys and good fairies.

Rev. Ken South, who had referred Tammy Faye Bakker's producer to me in 1985 and then helped secure my invitation to the Clinton White House, now invited me to introduce Coretta Scott King when she addressed the Minority AIDS Project's Skills Building Conference in Atlanta.

The night before she spoke, I sat in my room and wrote out my speech. It had been steeping in my brain ever since Ken asked me to do it, and now the words just poured out onto the page. I had to do a little editing to get it just right and to ensure it didn't take more than a couple of minutes to deliver.

In her introduction, I read some of her recent accomplishments. Then I said, "Here is a person who can well understand what we go through in living with AIDS or caring for people living with AIDS. She knows what it's like to live with the near-constant possibility of dying, and she knows what it's like to experience the premature, tragic death of a loved one. It is my extraordinary honor to introduce Coretta Scott King,"

She came from behind the ballroom door, up the stairs to the stage, and gave me a prolonged hug while the audience cheered. As she took the podium, I stood back and joined the applause. When the ovation ended, I sat down in the chair beside the podium and watched her speak from three or four feet away. It was another surreal moment, being so close to this historic person. After she was done, she gave me another hug and then left the stage.

In one of the press reports on the speech, a journalist quoted one of the conference organizers, "When King embraced Pieters, it was the moment when the African American community finally embraced the lesbian and gay community over AIDS."

CHAPTER EIGHT

A Cocktail Changes Everything

WHEN THE "COCKTAIL TREATMENT" OF PROTEASE INHIBITORS AND antiretroviral therapies became available in the fall of 1996, people with AIDS began to get healthy. One of my friends in the chorus, who was thin from wasting syndrome and who had large KS lesions on his face, suddenly started looking better. It was truly remarkable to see how the new cocktail treatment was visibly making him well. His lesions disappeared, and he soon was back to his normal weight. He's still alive and going strong.

This story was repeated, not just throughout the chorus, but all over the developed world. It was a time of great celebration for many people. I felt jubilant to see so many people suddenly getting well. IV poles disappeared from chorus rehearsals and grocery stores. Funerals and memorial services gradually became few and far between. We no longer saw people with KS lesions around the LGBT neighborhoods. Activists began to shift their focus to marriage equality and issues other than HIV/AIDS.

Sadly, to this day, HIV/AIDS continues to ravage places in the world where it's almost impossible to get aspirin, let alone highly active anti-retroviral treatments. But wherever these treatments could be accessed, the rapid pace of death from HIV/AIDS slowed so much that by the late nineties people began to question the need for AIDS social service agencies and AIDS ministries. By 1997 I could see the handwriting on the wall, but I stayed in denial about the inevitable closing of our AIDS Ministry and the end of my job.

When I realized I could very well live for a good, long time, suddenly, I had to figure out what to do with my life. How would I support myself? Would I want to go back to being a pastor? I had to worry about retirement, about growing old, and about who would be there to care for me when I did.

I wrote a new pamphlet for churches to hand out. "So, You're Going to Live" had advice and scriptural support for the dramatic shift from living with the prospect of an early death to living with a manageable disease. As I was experiencing in my own life, it wasn't at all unusual for many people with AIDS to experience this seemingly happy news as depressing. When you expect to die in the short term and then discover you're going to live, it's a huge psychic adjustment. Many people had maxed out their credit cards and spent all they had. Now they were going to live and had vast amounts of debt. Career-wise, people newly recovering from AIDS worried about what they would do now.

During this upheaval, I accepted my niece Jen's invitation to join her for her spring break in Paris. She was taking her junior year at Vassar at the Sorbonne. April in Paris—who could resist? I asked Caroline, the pastor of the Metropolitan Community Church of Paris, and her partner Cathérine if I could stay with them. Caroline said I could, but only if I preached for her church. Of course, I was more than happy to do that.

The first Sunday I preached in Paris, I met a nursing student named Ludovic. He was charming and good-looking, and we hit it off immediately. I was shy about staying over with him, worrying that I might offend Caroline and Cathérine if I did. After a few evenings of dropping him off, Caroline turned to me in the backseat and said, "Why aren't you staying over?" I gave some fumbling excuse about not having my medications on me, and she replied, "So, tomorrow you will."

Ludovic and I strolled through the parks, with flowers blooming everywhere and new, young leaves on the trees. We walked along the Seine, holding hands and occasionally stopping to kiss. We climbed Montmartre where he took me to his favorite restaurant, tucked away in an alley I never would have known was there.

With Jen joining us, we explored Notre Dame and Île de la Cité. We gazed at the amazing stained-glass windows of Sainte-Chapelle.

We went to see the new Baz Luhrmann *Romeo and Juliet*. The ending wrecked the two of them. They leaned on each other, and I tried to comfort them, unable to cry myself.

Then, on a day that Ludovic couldn't join us, Jen and I took the train to Versailles. It was even more magnificent than I remembered from seeing it in December 1966, when my parents and I toured France. Now the gardens were alive with beautiful flowers in full bloom. Jen and I bought a picnic lunch and dined on the lawn of the Petit Trianon.

Jen had a dinner party for me one evening, with four or five of her friends, as well as Caroline and Cathérine. Jen cooked up a marvelous dinner, impressing everyone with her culinary skills. Her girlfriends loved hearing my stories of kissing Ludovic on the banks of the Seine. One said, "Gee, we've lived here for almost a year, and we've never kissed anyone on the banks of the Seine!"

When it was time to leave, Cathérine took me to the airport. She cried when we said goodbye, and I gave her a big hug. She said, "Your French has improved tremendously." There's nothing like total immersion to refresh one's foreign language abilities. I gave her another big hug, then boarded my plane.

Back in Los Angeles, I was not enthusiastic about returning to my job. In May I flew to Washington, D.C., for another meeting of the board of directors for the AIDS National Interfaith Network. Several of my friends on the board tried to persuade me it was time to resign from my job. They could see I was burned out, but I also had a suspicion that someone had asked them to do that. Their arguments just seemed so canned and rehearsed. But I had to agree. It was time to announce my resignation.

When I returned to Los Angeles, I dragged my feet for a few days, but I finally went in to see Ravi Verma, the administrative director, who had recently been made my supervisor. I told him I would resign my job, but not until the end of 1997. That would give me time to find another job as well as finish my AIDS ministry.

He rushed me down to the conference room where the board of elders was having a meeting, as if he wanted me to tell them before I had a chance to change my mind. When I told them, Troy Perry cried.

I was touched. I felt appreciated and loved. Everyone seemed fine with my staying on to the end of the year. General Conference was coming up soon, and then it would be fall, with time to finish up whatever business I had to do, get some closure with the clergy and lay leaders I had been calling every month, and spend some time finding a new job.

The General Conference in July 1997 was held in Sydney, Australia. I had designed a full program for people infected and affected by HIV/AIDS. The HIV support groups were well attended, although there was less interest in HIV/AIDS programming in general. In the support groups, people with HIV/AIDS mostly talked about the challenges of getting well.

The AIDS Forum in Sydney was not well attended. Troy Perry presented me with a beautiful plaque, "In Special Recognition of Rev. A. Stephen Pieters . . . whose remarkable journey of faith has provided heroic and prophetic leadership to the UFMCC and other communities in the global battle against HIV/AIDS . . . Thank God for his witness and gifts, which have been a source of healing and hope to the many thousands of lives he has touched since the beginning of this pandemic." It ends with, "You Are the Light of the World," from Matthew 5:14. I was touched and honored, but my ego was bruised by the fact that while others who were leaving their ministries were celebrated in the big worship services that one thousand people attended, I was recognized in front of maybe one hundred people at the AIDS forum. It felt as if they were trying to hide the fact that when I left, they would end the AIDS Ministry program altogether.

There was a small party for me later that afternoon, held in Ravi's suite at one of the conference hotels. Don Eastman and Nancy Wilson were there, but not many others. Once again, my nose was out of joint. I plunged into the pool of bitterness and resentment that had long been a part of my psychological makeup. I was working on it in therapy, but my experiences at this General Conference exacerbated my negativity.

One thing that got me through that week was meeting the men from the Metropolitan Community Church of Melbourne, where I was scheduled to preach a week after the conference ended. We hit it off as soon as we met, and they took great pleasure in getting me stoned almost every evening. Of course, I was relieved and happy because I knew better than to bring any marijuana with me to Australia.

For the time between the conference and my preaching gig in Melbourne, I had scheduled a short vacation in Fiji. A dozen of us from the conference stayed at a beautiful resort on the shore of one of the islands. I had a great time lolling about, drinking kava, posing for pictures with my sculpted torso on full display, and touring the main island. For a long time, I had been getting snow globes everywhere I went to give to Alison for her collection. We were both surprised and tickled that I found one in Fiji.

On my last day there, I began to feel very sick. A particularly nasty flu had gone around the General Conference. I had managed to avoid it, but now, on Fiji, I came down with it, and I was as sick as some of the scrawny dogs we saw around the islands. I had to get on a plane that evening to fly back to Australia.

The plane ride to Brisbane, where I would change planes for Melbourne, seemed endless. I had a window seat, but I could not get comfortable. As tired as I was, I couldn't sleep. I couldn't read and I couldn't eat, although I did try to stay hydrated. I felt for the poor Australian couple seated next to me. I'm sure they were unhappy to be seated beside someone as sick as I was.

When we got to Brisbane, I could barely stand in line for customs inspections. I got through it, but then I had to carry my big suitcase to a waiting area. It would be hours before the morning flight to Melbourne. I tried to sleep on a row of chairs, while keeping an eye on my bags. Fortunately, nothing happened to my bags. As sick as I was, I couldn't get much sleep anyway.

When I arrived in Melbourne, I still felt sick, but I was met at the airport by one of the men I'd enjoyed so much at the Sydney conference. When we got in his car, he handed me a big baggie of marijuana. He said it was mine to enjoy while I was in Melbourne! He even gave me rolling papers. He had already rolled a couple of joints, and we lit one as we drove into Melbourne. It was such a relief to my aching body to get stoned.

I stayed with the pastor of the Melbourne church and his partner. The first thing I did was lie down and take a long nap. When I got up, I went out on the little balcony off my bedroom and smoked another joint. I still felt sick with that awful flu, but the joint brought me some relief.

The pastor and his partner didn't smoke marijuana, but they didn't object to my habit. They fed me that evening, but even with the pot I'd smoked, I didn't have much of an appetite.

The next day, I taught a workshop at the Melbourne AIDS social service agency and another at a special meeting of the Melbourne Interfaith group. Somehow, with the way I was feeling, it didn't feel right teaching a class on getting healthy, but that's what they were paying me for. So, I resisted the temptation to just lie down and moan, and I delivered my "Spiritual Strength for Survival" lecture.

The next few evenings, the men I'd enjoyed so much in Sydney took me out to get stoned and play. I probably should have stayed at the pastor's and rested, but I really enjoyed my time with these men, and after a couple of days there, I was beginning to feel a bit better.

After I preached at the Sunday service, the guys took me to a dance bar to celebrate my forty-fifth birthday. We got thoroughly stoned and danced the night away. The leader of the crowd, Tex, was the DJ, and he played an excellent mix of dance music, culminating with "Oh Happy Day!" Perfect.

After being gone for almost three weeks, it was wonderful to get home to my cat Preshy. I rested a couple of days. Then, I was back in my office at headquarters.

One day, I met a friend for lunch at a restaurant up the street from my office. As we were eating, who should walk in but Timothy, the friend of my ex-boyfriend, the Broadway performer. I stopped him, and we chatted for a few minutes. He told me the national tour of *Sunset Boulevard* had ended prematurely in Chicago. He was glad to be back home where he could see his young son more regularly than when he was on tour. I asked him if I could call him later to talk longer, and he said, "Of course." We began talking almost every evening, much to my delight. I enjoyed learning all about his life's journey, and I think he enjoyed hearing about mine.

I quickly discovered his gift for compassion, born of surviving the trauma of his years in a conservative Christian ex-gay program. I found him attractive, and after a while, I told him I wanted to date him, but Timothy said, "No, I'd rather be friends, because that will last. Being lovers won't." Once again, I accepted that, but fell back into my pattern of trying to be such a good friend that he would realize we should be lovers after all. That never happened, and later I came to realize that he was right all along. We never could have made it as a romantic couple.

In December 1997 I invited him to attend our Gay Men's Chorus holiday concert, and I was thrilled to have him in the audience. Afterward, he told me, "When the curtain went up, and I first saw and heard all of you sing, I finally knew what 'gay pride' meant." That was the nicest compliment I'd ever heard about the Gay Men's Chorus of Los Angeles.

The chorus board had elected me chair in the summer of 1997, a position I held for two years. The stress of my duties as well as dealing with two board members who tried to stop my agenda at every turn challenged my recent return from depression. It became so bad that I almost left the chorus, but I realized that would be letting them win, and leaving the chorus would take away the joy I felt about singing with my brothers. So, I kept struggling with my nemeses on the board.

Meanwhile, the end of my employment as field director of AIDS Ministry was getting closer and closer. I looked for a job, first as a pastor, but also in the AIDS world. Unfortunately, I couldn't find work anywhere. From churches, I kept hearing that I was so associated with AIDS, that they were worried I wouldn't be able to be "just a pastor" nor to preach about issues beyond AIDS. I couldn't find a job in the AIDS world, because with the new cocktail treatments, every agency was downsizing and laying off staff.

One evening, I had dinner with Christie, who was in town on business. I told her about my employment dilemma, and she said, "Why don't you come to work for me at Playboy?" I thought about it overnight and then said, "Yes."

And so, my time in AIDS ministry ended, and my employment with MCC ended. I decided to take time off from going to church. That time off turned into five or six years. After being so devoted to MCC and ministry, I realized I was burned out on it all. I walked away. I missed some of the people, but I did not miss church or the ministry for a long time.

On January 5, 1998, I reported for work at Playboy's offices in Beverly Hills. I worked in the public relations department where I answered phones and copied and filed all the international press clippings about Playboy or Mr. Hefner. When someone called the Beverly Hills offices of Playboy and asked for Mr. Hefner, they were sent through to me. One of my jobs was to interview the centerfold each month and then write a press release about her. I always enjoyed that. Working the press desk at the Playboy Mansion parties, Playmate reunions, and Playmate of the Year events was a trip. I had a great vantage point to see the guests arrive, including the celebrities.

When I'd been at Playboy for six months, Dr. Levine hired me to be her "recorder" at the International AIDS Conference, in Geneva, Switzerland. So I took a week's vacation from Playboy and flew to Geneva. Dr. Levine wrote her daily summaries for an online reporting service, and I was her copy editor. I enjoyed the work. After six months at Playboy, it was refreshing to do some intellectually challenging work alongside my beloved doctor.

I didn't bring any marijuana with me. I knew the risks were too great to carry it when I flew internationally. But I missed getting stoned in the evenings when my work was done.

After the conference, I went to Zermatt to see the Matterhorn. I'd been there before, in 1972, and I'd always wanted to return. I'd had romanticized notions about Zermatt since Tripp and I were seven and saw Disney's *Third Man on the Mountain*, a feature film fictionalizing the first ascent of the Matterhorn.

This weekend in Zermatt, I had a room with a view of the Matterhorn. Dinner was included. So the first night I was there, I sat down for dinner at my table for one, and there was a glass of white wine at my place.

Dr. Levine and the author at the International AIDS Conference in Geneva, Switzerland, June 1998, in front of the AIDS National Interfaith Network (ANIN) booth.
COURTESY OF REVEREND PIETERS'S PERSONAL COLLECTION.

I thought, "I'm way up in the Alps. No one will know. Certainly, I can have one little glass of wine. I won't have any more after tonight."

I tried to reason with myself. "You know your alcoholism is off doing pushups in the next room while you're sober."

I continued to rationalize it. "It's been twenty-three years since I've had a drink, and I'm much healthier psychologically than I was in those days. Then I was so filled with shame about being gay. Now I'm out and proud. What harm could one glass of wine do?"

So I took a sip, and oh my God, it tasted good. Something clicked in my brain, and I relaxed and enjoyed the buzz.

After dinner, I had a great time walking around Zermatt, and I slept well that night. I had a delicious glass of wine, and nothing bad happened. That was bad.

I had a glass of wine with dinner again the next night, but there was no click. So I had a second glass, and then that release happened again. I had such a great sense of well-being. That near-constant hole in my soul, that deep grief over all my friends who'd died of AIDS, and the anxiety I often felt in the pit of my stomach all magically disappeared.

After a massage, I wasn't as buzzed as before. I went to my room and thought, "One of those little bottles of wine in the minibar would get that buzz back, and I'll be so much better able to sleep." So I drank that little bottle of wine in the minibar. I went to bed and slept soundly.

The next day I took the train back to Geneva. I stayed in the airport hotel Sunday night, as I had an early-morning flight home.

In my room, I could not stop thinking about the minibar. "Oh, hell, I've already started drinking again. I might as well get drunk the way I want. I'll stop when I get home." So, I drank all the wine in the mini-bar and then asked for a bottle of wine with the dinner I ordered from room service. I got drunk and passed out.

The next morning, I was hung over, but it seemed a small price to pay for getting so delightfully drunk in my hotel room the night before. Besides, I knew that once I got on the plane, I would have more wine, and that would make me feel better.

I had glass after glass of wine as we flew back to Los Angeles. I decided that if I only drank wine I would be fine. I had bought a big bottle of wine in the duty-free shop in Geneva. Back home, I drank my first glass while I rolled a joint. I lay back on my couch with my second glass of wine, turned the TV on, and lit up the joint., I was wide awake with jet lag for a few hours, until I drank enough wine and smoked enough marijuana to pass out.

Soon, I drank to get drunk every day. When I was drunk, all I wanted to do was lie on my couch with my cat Preshy curled up on my chest while I watched TV.

I was usually hung over the next morning, if not still drunk. To go to work, I had to steady my nerves by smoking a joint, or part of one, before driving to the Playboy offices in Beverly Hills. Being a little stoned became the norm for me. I was pretty good at covering it up, but I couldn't help being paranoid that people could tell.

By quitting time, I was antsy to get back home and start drinking again. I craved that first glass of wine, which I knew would lead to more.

On weekends, I could start drinking wine first thing in the morning, along with that first joint and first cigarette. I loved getting drunk and stoned first thing in the morning. It just felt so wickedly wonderful. I hadn't realized quite how much I'd felt constrained by not being able to drink. Now I was free to drink all I wanted almost every day. It felt great.

My drinking escalated when I switched to vodka on the Gay Men's Chorus of Los Angeles's concert tour of Russia and the Baltics. When the tour was over, Timothy picked me up at the airport. During my absence, he had had to put my beloved 19-year-old cat Preshy to sleep. He had called me in Estonia to ask my permission, and I reluctantly gave it when he told me she wouldn't survive long enough for me to get home and take her to the vet myself.

When we got to my apartment with no cat to greet me, Timothy sat with me for a while. He gave me a framed tribute to Preshy. I'd left my unwashed hoody for her to sleep on, and the photo showed Timothy wearing it as he held her for the vet to put her down.

As soon as I could, I opened my carry-on, pulled out a bottle of vodka, and poured myself a glass. I hesitated, but I was in so much pain over Preshy's death that I couldn't help myself. If ever I had a good excuse to drink, this was it.

The next morning, I was hung over. I wasn't going to work for a couple more days, so I drank more vodka to cure the hangover. I stayed drunk the rest of that day and the next. It felt so good to be free to drink all day the way I really wanted to.

Finally, I did have to go to work, but I was hung over, so I smoked some grass and drank a little vodka to get me going. When I got to Playboy, I explained to people about Preshy, and mostly just hid at my desk. My coworkers were understanding and left me alone.

I had stopped going to church when I started working at Playboy. After I started drinking, I felt spiritually bereft, unable to make any contact with God, and I stopped praying altogether. I rationalized it as a vacation from church and all things spiritual, but I was angry at God over all the suffering and death I'd witnessed. Also, I wasn't sure God wanted to hear from me drunk and stoned.

I was miserable. I knew I was in trouble with my drinking and that I should stop, but the disease of alcoholism won. I was depressed and hopeless, but I could not stop. I was seeing my therapist, but I hid my drinking. I didn't want him trying to stop me. So, I lied. Drinking trumped mental health.

Timothy and I were in the habit of talking almost every evening, but I was often drunk now. One Sunday morning, he picked me up for one of our hikes. I'd already been drinking. He said he could smell it on me, and I lied and said it must be from what I'd drunk the night before, but he knew. I knew he knew. And he knew I knew he knew.

Sometimes, I decided to have just one drink after I got home from work, but that never worked. After I'd had that one drink (always a tumbler full), I simply had to have more. I kept drinking until I passed out.

When I visited Mom in Sun City for her birthday in May 2000, I got a motel room so I could drink the way I wanted to after spending the day with her. I know it hurt her, but I just could not face the prospect of spending time with her without drinking. I don't remember how I rationalized the motel room, but somehow I manipulated her into paying for it.

Back home, I was having a lot of anonymous sex. I would spend hours in AOL chat rooms that catered to gay men in Los Angeles. Sometimes, I walked to a gay bar down the hill from me. I would invite a guy to my apartment, but usually I was too drunk to perform. So, I had more vodka.

I kept getting sicker from all the alcohol, and my monthly appointments to see Dr. Levine became increasingly difficult. I lied to her, too, about how much I was drinking. I had never told her about drinking my way into a recovery program when I was twenty-three. And I didn't tell her how much I was drinking now, just that I had an occasional drink.

By the late summer of 2000, I had lost a lot of weight, and Dr. Levine could see from my lab tests that I was developing liver problems. She certified that I was disabled and now that I didn't have to go to work anymore, I was free to drink and smoke marijuana the way I really wanted to: all day, every day. One morning a week, I stayed sober long enough to go stock up on gallon jugs of scotch, vodka, and, oh yeah, food.

Dr. Levine saw me just before I left for a two-week vacation at the farm in New Hampshire to see the fall foliage. She asked me not to have anything to drink while I was there, to see if that would improve my liver tests. Despite having lied to her about the history and extent of my drinking, I knew she knew I was in trouble, so I agreed. While I was at the farm, I smoked a lot of marijuana, but I didn't drink. I also smoked a lot of cigarettes until a friend read me the riot act. I used the patch to quit, and it worked. I hoped quitting cigarettes would solve my problems. It didn't.

When I got home, my lab work showed my vacation from alcohol had helped. So of course I started drinking again. I stumbled around my apartment, sometimes falling on the floor, my couch, or bed. From there, I watched the room spin, a feeling I loved.

I continued to be desperately lonely. I couldn't call anyone because I was too drunk. Even Timothy was tired of talking to me when I was drunk, and I was drunk all the time. But my drinking was more important than my loneliness.

Once, when I'd miscalculated and run out of vodka, I knew I was too drunk to drive. I stumbled down the hill to the nearest liquor store. There, I stood at the checkout stand and pointed to a bottle behind the cashier. I was too drunk to say more than "vodka." The cashier looked at me with contempt and sold me the bottle. I felt subhuman.

At Thanksgiving, Timothy had me over for brunch, but he told me he wouldn't be available the rest of the weekend. After the brunch was over, I stocked up on liquor and stayed drunk for the next nine days. Friends called and left messages, but I was too drunk to talk. I ached with loneliness, but I didn't dare talk to anyone lest they try to stop me from drinking.

Eight days after Thanksgiving, I was drunk early in the morning, as usual. I knew this would be another day of feeling demoralized. That feeling of freedom to drink all I'd wanted had turned into a feeling of enslavement. As I staggered around my little apartment, I howled in despair. I couldn't ask anyone for help because I didn't want anyone to know how much I was drinking. So I drank some more. I finally closed my eyes and prayed, "Help."

My prayer was answered the next morning. I was sitting at my desk, with an open half-gallon of vodka by my side. It was ten o'clock, and I had already drunk half the bottle. Suddenly, Mitch appeared at my side. She grabbed the jug and said, "This has got to stop."

"I know!" I started to cry. I felt such remorse and shame. Mitch poured the bottle down the kitchen sink. I knew it was over. Someone had answered my prayer for help, and I was demoralized enough to know it was time to accept it. I later heard people call this the Gift of Desperation aka G.O.D.

After Mitch emptied my vodka bottle, she asked me if I'd taken my medications recently, and I could not remember. She didn't think I had. That would certainly have contributed to my physical deterioration.

She brought me slices of orange and some milk, and I took my medications. She insisted I take a bath, since she was sure I would fall if I tried to take a shower. It felt good to bathe, but I was so weak, Mitch had to help me get out of the tub.

Mitch called Barbara Bailey, the woman who had been my psychotherapist in the first years after my AIDS diagnosis. She came right over, and I wept as my pent-up feelings of shame and remorse came pouring out. She listened patiently. I called Dr. Levine to let her know what was going on. I confessed that I had been drinking alcoholically for a couple of years. Mitch got on the phone with her, and they discussed getting me into rehab, but nothing was decided.

When Barbara and Mitch left, I was on my own. Mitch was right upstairs, but I wanted to be alone so I could smoke marijuana. I smoked part of a joint but didn't really get stoned. There was no alcohol in my apartment, so I couldn't drink.

I lay down in the afternoon for a nap but could not sleep. I hoped I would sleep through the worst of the hangover I was starting to feel. I silenced my phone but left my answering machine on at my desk, with the volume turned up in case I got an important call.

As I lay in bed, I heard someone leave a message saying that was a friend with whom I'd smoked a lot of pot and occasionally dropped acid. Her message said, "You really don't have to go to rehab. You're not an alcoholic."

After a bit, I heard Dr. Levine leave a message saying I was doing the right thing by stopping my drinking and all my drug use. "I'm thinking of you and doing some research on the right rehab."

Variations of these dueling messages repeated a few times as I tried to sleep. I finally got up and went out to my desk to listen to the messages more carefully.

There were no messages on my answering machine. I'd had an auditory hallucination, or I'd just dreamed it all.

Later, Mitch, Dr. Levine, and I discussed where I should go into rehab. I decided I wanted to go to an LGBT rehab, Alternatives Inc. It was a program for dually diagnosed LGBT people. You had to have both a major mental health disorder as well as alcohol or drug addictions. I didn't want to admit to any mental health disorder, but the executive director, Jann, said I could easily be diagnosed with major depression disorder as well as alcoholism, so I would qualify. It would mean being in a locked ward for a couple of weeks, or longer, and then in their Intensive Outpatient Program for three months. I said, "I have to think about it."

As the afternoon and evening went on, I felt worse and worse. I tried smoking another joint, but I couldn't get stoned enough to feel better physically. I had the shakes, and I ached all over.

I had a bad night. By the next morning, I was vomiting in my bed. I didn't change the sheets because I didn't have the strength to do it. I was weak, I couldn't eat, and I could barely walk to the bathroom. I was still shaking badly. I felt sick, and I was terrified. I knew I had to be hospitalized, but I still didn't want to go.

I called Tripp to tell him what was going on. I wanted to feel his calm, steady presence, the way I'd felt it so often when I was sick in the 1980s. I told him, "I've been drinking a quart of vodka a day for over a week, and Mitch stopped me yesterday. Now I'm having a horrible time withdrawing."

"Yeah," he replied. "I was actually kind of alarmed when I was down there visiting you last year, and you were drinking wine."

I suddenly had to excuse myself to go vomit. There was nothing left in my stomach, but I still had horrible dry heaves, which I told him about when I got back to the phone.

"Shit, Pieters. You need medical attention. Please go to the hospital." I assured him I would ask Mitch to take me to the emergency room. "Call me when you're admitted. Please."

I assured him I would. It really meant a lot to me just to hear his voice.

I asked Mitch to take me to the hospital. We got Jann back on the phone, and she told us to go to the emergency room at Glendale Memorial Hospital, and they would evaluate me for the Alternatives locked ward, 4 South. I called Timothy to tell him I was headed to the hospital. Mitch drove me to the emergency room, and they saw me quickly. Soon, Timothy arrived, and Mitch took off.

I was glad to see Timothy. By this time, a cheerful nurse had put in an IV and hung a bag of yellow liquid. She told me, "This is a banana bag, filled with vitamins and minerals that you need, and it will help you feel better. It's a common treatment for alcoholics. The doctor also ordered a good dose of Librium for you, to help prevent any further DTs [delirium tremens]." She administered the Librium, and I suddenly began feeling a whole lot better. I was relieved.

I told Timothy, "Getting sober is going to change everything. I'm done with alcohol and marijuana."

"I know relapses are possible, or even probable. I've been talking with my therapist about your alcoholism. He urged me to drop you as a friend."

"I'm so glad you didn't."

"Everything is changing for me, too. I'm getting serious about Robert." I knew he'd been seeing him for a while. "So, I won't be as available as I've been."

This would have flattened me if I weren't on a good dose of Librium. I felt the fear of abandonment creep up, but I knew I had to focus on getting sober.

I guessed Timothy chose this moment to tell me about his new relationship to get it over with while I was in the hospital, on good drugs, and with psychotherapists to look after me.

The nurse came back in and told me that I had to be medically stabilized before the locked ward would take me. I understood, since I still felt so fragile and weak. I was taken upstairs and put in a hospital room just outside the locked ward. Timothy made sure I was settled and then went to fetch a few things from my apartment that I thought I'd need.

I called Tripp. "I've been admitted to the hospital before I can get into the rehab."

"I'm so relieved," he replied. "I really thought you were going to die right there on the phone with me."

"I'm feeling much better with the drugs and supplements they've given me." With great emotion, he wished me well, and I promised to be in closer touch now that I was getting sober.

Not one to be alone at times like this, I began calling a lot of my friends. Alison and Bob were the first to visit. The former executive director from the AIDS hospice where I'd been a chaplain came by as well, and she brought me two books of fairy tales retold for gay men. Somehow, these fairy tales made sense of things at a time when there wasn't a lot that made any sense.

After a couple of nights in that hospital room, I was admitted to the locked ward. They took everything from me that I could possibly use to harm myself.

I began attending group sessions and was seen by a psychiatrist. He prescribed Ativan for my anxiety and kept me on the Effexor I had been taking for depression. Now that I wasn't drinking or smoking pot, the Effexor began to work better. I still felt weak and was almost as thin as when I was on suramin, back in 1985.

I got a call on the ward's pay phone from Daniel, the Broadway performer I'd fallen in love with online during my 1995 sabbatical. When he'd finished the *Sunset Boulevard* tour in Chicago, I helped him get a job at Playboy, putting in a good word for him with my friend Christie. He worked in Playboy's human resources department.

Daniel assured me that everything, both my inpatient care and outpatient therapy, would be covered by Playboy's insurance. I was deeply grateful for his caring and his kindness as well as for Playboy's excellent benefits. He called me several times at 4 South so he could report to Christie on how I was doing, and it was always a joy to hear from him.

Christie herself called a couple of times and was so warm and supportive, telling me how happy she was that I had reached out for help. She sent a huge bouquet of balloons to cheer me, but I wasn't allowed to keep them in my room or anywhere we patients could harm ourselves with them. So, they were kept in the locked nurses' station with its big windows so we all could see them.

Jerry, a friend from the chorus, called. I knew he had been in recovery for some time. He was both kind and challenging. I told him something about being "in this rehab." He said, "You're not in rehab. You're in a psych ward." That shook me, because I really thought this was a rehab facility, but of course, he was right.

As the days in the locked ward progressed, deep shame grabbed hold of me. For years, I had been in demand internationally as a speaker, preacher, and chaplain. I had been on news and talk shows all over the world. I'd been profiled by Jane Pauley and interviewed by Tammy Faye Bakker. I'd been to the White House for a prayer breakfast with the president and vice president of the United States. Yet here I was in a locked psych ward. How had it come to this?

I don't remember much about the required therapy groups. I found it hard to participate. I felt all these other guys had so many more problems than I had. I had a car, an apartment, and a job to go back to. Most of the others didn't. So, I kept quiet.

Finally, the group psychologist confronted me. I tried to participate more because he made my discharge dependent on my starting to share. I did want to get out of there after the two weeks they had suggested for me.

As I began to talk about my drinking, I realized I had big questions for God. "Why did You let all those people die from AIDS, God? Why did so many friends die who took better care of themselves and had greater faith than me? Why did I survive when there were so many who had far more to offer the world but who didn't?"

I began to understand that I drank to medicate myself against my survivor's guilt and my grief. It felt as if I'd been in a horrible war. I'd seen terrible suffering in so many people with AIDS. There was the steady drumbeat of death of so many friends, not to mention the roller coaster of my own illnesses and near-death experiences. I'd hardly acknowledged all these losses when they happened, and I never cried through most of it. Drugs and drinking helped me ignore all this, at least at first.

I began to read the basic literature about recovery. One of the stories about a recovering alcoholic who had a white light experience moved me, and I felt a flicker of faith deep in my heart. It felt very weak, as if it would go out if I blew on it the wrong way.

I prayed for help in keeping that faith alive, and I suddenly remembered all I'd read in my years as a pastor about doubt being a part of faith. I began to give that flicker of faith air to grow. I still didn't want to go to church, but I began to pray again, usually simple prayers like, "Help" and "Thank You."

More feelings began to surface. I sat on my bed during one break, reading another story from the literature that triggered my remorse and shame about my years of relapsing. I sat there on my bed and wept.

Faith, one of the group therapists, happened by my room. She asked, "Why are you crying?"

"I'm so ashamed I lost my sobriety."

"Have you been drinking or drugging today?"

"No."

"Then you're sober today, and today is all that counts."

I felt relieved and stopped crying.

I was fed a steady diet of Ativan while I was on the ward. I thought it a bit odd, since I was in there for my addiction issues. But who was I to argue with the medical authorities? I'd needed the Librium to get me through the DTs, and so, maybe I needed the Ativan to get me through inpatient treatment. Besides, I enjoyed the buzz.

After two weeks, I met with the psychiatrist, who approved my discharge. Concerned that I lived alone, one of the therapists told me I should move out of my apartment, put everything in storage, and live in Alternatives' residential treatment facility. "Then you should live in a halfway house for six months to a year."

I rejected the idea. The notion of moving out of the apartment I'd lived in for almost sixteen years, not to mention getting rid of my new cats, Lucy and Viv, was unacceptable. I would live alone in my apartment and commute to the Intensive Outpatient Program (IOP) daily. It wasn't far from my home in Silverlake.

I was discharged on a Saturday morning, and I went right home. I called a couple friends who were kind enough to come right over. They changed my bed, then vacuumed and cleaned while I tried to rest. Although I had felt fine when I woke up in the locked ward that morning, I was feeling physically weak and emotional when I got home. So after they left, I napped.

When I woke up, I started to cry. I was relieved to be home in my own bed, but I felt overwhelmed with all that had transpired over the last few weeks, and I felt so ashamed. I went up to Mitch's apartment, and I couldn't stop weeping. I told her, "I'm so embarrassed about what I've put you and all my friends and family through."

Back in my own apartment, I called Jerry, that sober friend from the chorus. He had already arranged for a friend to pick me up and take me to a large gathering for recovering alcoholics that evening. I resisted, because I was still crying, but he was quite firm with me and told me I had to go. Finally, I agreed.

I managed to stop crying for a bit while I ate some soup and watched the news. As soon as my ride arrived, I started crying again. I cried all the way to the gathering, and my new friend kindly held my hand. At the gathering, he introduced me to many of his friends, including the main speaker that evening, a sweet, soft-spoken, older man named Paul. He was wearing a hat with an abundance of chiffon draped all over it. Paul invited me to come to the recovery group at the AT Center, every morning at seven-thirty. That quickly became my "home group," and I attended it every single morning. Much to my delight, Paul wore different flowers, chiffon, and ribbons on his hats every morning.

But that first evening, I couldn't stop crying. This was so unlike me. I'd been crying for hours. I hadn't cried at all the funerals and memorial services I attended or led. And now I couldn't stop crying.

I still could not stop crying at my first morning groups. At the first one I attended, a man my age introduced himself and said he couldn't stop crying either when he was newly sober. He said it happens for a lot of people. It really helped to know that my crying was not unusual for a newcomer.

I was told by one of my therapists at 4 South to find someone to guide me through recovery as soon as I could. At the next evening group, the speaker was a fellow named Jeff K. I liked how he talked about God. He said someone had told him to make his God so big that He could handle anything Jeff couldn't and to make his God as loving and caring as God was big.

Jeff was a tall, handsome man, about ten years younger than me. He had such a vivacious, joyful manner about him that I was sure he probably had lots of guys asking for his help. I asked if he would take me on. To my surprise, he said yes.

Jeff went with me to most of the groups I attended and held my hand or rubbed my back through them all, since I was still so shaky and insecure. He was patient and gentle with me, although sometimes he reminded me, with a teasing laugh, "You're a mess."

I did manage to stop crying after a couple of days. I wondered then why I had cried so much. Maybe it was about how ashamed I felt about my relapse. Maybe it was the huge accumulation of grief that had finally come to the surface. Or maybe it was both.

I had been so wrapped up in my own drama in recent weeks, that I neglected to call Mom. When she couldn't reach me, she began to worry that I was lying in some hospital somewhere, dying from AIDS. She called my cousins David and Nancy. David told her I was in the hospital, but not why. When David told me about this after my discharge, I called her and told her that I had relapsed on alcohol. She was angry that I had cut her out of the loop, but she was glad that I finally got help. She was supportive of my sobriety throughout her remaining years, despite the anger she felt toward me about being gay.

I went to see my therapist of the past four years and told him why I had disappeared. I told him all about my drinking and my history with alcoholism. He told me later, "I kicked myself all over the room for not realizing you were drinking."

"I worked very hard at making sure you didn't put it together, because then you might have tried to stop me."

My time in Alternatives' Intensive Outpatient Program (IOP) began the Monday after I got out of the hospital. I attended every weekday for the next three months. I once again found it difficult to share more than the brief check-in required. The others in my small group seemed to have it so much worse than I did. Finally, my therapist confronted me about it; he got me to see that my issues, and there were plenty, were as important to discuss as any of the others'. So I began sharing more, and I found it was indeed helpful.

One day, a couple of months into my outpatient program, the therapists announced they were going to show us the movie *Hook*, starring Robin Williams as a grown-up Peter Pan, with Dustin Hoffman as Hook. Of course, I was delighted. After the film, one therapist asked us all to think about which character we most related to. I said, "I've always related to the Darling children, wanting to follow Peter and fly off to Neverland."

In a firm voice, he said, "No, you're Peter Pan." I was surprised, but when I admitted I'd always wanted to play Peter Pan, I knew he was right. All my life, I wanted to go live among the fairies and the lost boys, lead them in adventures, and never grow up. Ironically, admitting I was a Peter Pan helped me grow up.

After almost three months, I knew my time in the outpatient program was coming to an end, but I was terrified of being discharged. I didn't think I was ready. The therapist tried to get me to realize how much stronger I was than three months before. After a lot of resistance on my part, he finally got me to say, "I'm enough."

"That's right. You're enough." I felt something in me shift for the better.

Next thing I knew, the team of therapists was preparing me for discharge, and I knew I was ready.

My first day back at Playboy, Christie was in Los Angeles. She called and said she wanted to take me out to lunch to celebrate my graduation from rehab. We walked down to a fancy Beverly Hills restaurant nearby.

The head of the public relations department was already there in a booth with someone else. Christie and I said hi and then the two of us were shown to our own booth. Before we had a chance to order anything, our waiter appeared with a bottle of champagne chilling in a bucket full of ice. He said, "This is with the compliments of the lady over there," and pointed to the PR director.

Christie firmly said, "Take it away. We'll both have sparkling water." She gave a withering look to the PR director. Christie had always been fiercely protective of me, ever since I first got sick with AIDS, and she was now fiercely protective of my sobriety. She knew that graduating from rehab did not mean I would now know how to drink like a gentleman, as apparently my boss thought. I felt deeply loved and cared for.

I continued to attend two or three recovery groups a day. The morning meetings were always packed with forty or fifty gay men, lesbians, and transgender persons. And every morning, at the head of the table, there was Paul with his fabulous hats.

As 2001 began, Jeff joined the chorus, much to my delight. It made me feel secure to have him there. At our annual retreat, which had been a drunken, stoned weekend for me in the last few years, Jeff and I asked the retreat organizer if we could start a sober support group. There were only three of us at that first group, but it helped get me through that retreat without getting drunk or stoned. That sober group grew with each subsequent retreat.

Jeff continued to be a strong and caring friend. I told him I wanted to go back to school to get my master's degree in clinical psychology and become a therapist. One of my strengths as a minister had been in pastoral care and counseling. I thought getting an advanced degree in psychology would be a logical next step. Jeff told me I shouldn't do it in my first year of sobriety. The general rule was not to make any major changes for at least a year. I knew he was right, and so I bided my time, focusing on doing what I needed to do to stay sober.

CHAPTER NINE

Return to the Land of the Sick

LIKE MANY PEOPLE, I AWOKE THE MORNING OF SEPTEMBER 11, 2001, and watched a plane fly into one of the towers of the World Trade Center. By the time I had to leave for my morning recovery group, a plane had crashed into the Pentagon, and one of the twin towers had fallen. We had our group anyway because we all needed it.

The events of September 11 snapped me to attention again, just like when I was diagnosed with cancer and AIDS. The shock of all those people dying so suddenly reminded me of the fragility of life, and I felt an urgency to apply to graduate school and start my work toward becoming a psychotherapist.

In March 2002, I enrolled in the master's program in clinical psychology at Antioch University–Los Angeles. If all went according to schedule, I would have my master's degree in September 2003. I loved being a student again.

During my time at Antioch, my dear friend Randy died from the complications of HIV disease. He had refused to believe that HIV caused AIDS, and so he wouldn't take any of the medications that would manage HIV infection. I could not persuade him to take the "cocktail." I knew for years that he had a self-destructive streak. One of his favorite movies was *All That Jazz*, Bob Fosse's semiautobiographical film about his own flirtation with self-destruction and death. The Fosse character was a role model for him in some ways. He flirted with death throughout the time I knew him. So, I was not surprised when his partner, Michael, called to tell me Randy had died.

I still miss Randy. In my heart, he lives on as the love of my life, even if we never ended up together.

Now four of the men I had loved the most had died. My first infatuation, Michael Kenna, and my beloved friend in Hartford, John Andy, died from complications of AIDS in the late 1980s. David Templeton committed suicide in the late 1990s, after a long struggle with addiction issues. And now Randy was gone. I never consciously grieved for any of them, although I'm aware that I continue to carry in my heart the cumulative grief of all their deaths, as well as the deaths of so many other friends in the 1980s and 1990s.

One morning in the fall of 2002, Bill Farley, Hugh Hefner's publicist, called me into his office. I liked working for Bill; he was one of my favorite people at Playboy. A Libertarian with a terrific sense of humor, he was caring and supportive of me, always.

On this day, however, he couldn't quite look me in the eye. After we sat down in his office, he said, "Your friend Christie hired a consultant to assess the company. He decided the staff had to be downsized, and so we have to let you go. You need to pack up your desk with all your personal belongings and leave this morning. Security will escort you out because that's how it's done. I'm so sorry, and I'll miss you."

I returned to my desk in shock. Before long, two security guards showed up, went through the box I'd packed, and walked me out of the offices and down to my car.

I immediately called a sober friend, and we met at a coffee shop near my home. As we were talking, Christie called. "I'm so sorry about this. Are you okay?" I was so touched.

"I've survived much worse. Are you okay? I know you had to let some of your longtime colleagues go today."

"That's very kind of you, but I'm all right. I really wanted to check on you."

"I'm having lunch with a sober friend. I've got good support, and this will let me focus more on my studies." She was so tender and caring. I still get tears in my eyes thinking about that moment in our longtime friendship.

I now focused completely on my schoolwork and was grateful for the opportunity to do so. I applied and was accepted as an intern therapist at the Lesbian and Gay Center in Hollywood. After some introductory training, we were assigned clients and supervisors. I enjoyed meeting with my clients, trying to apply all the lessons I was learning at Antioch and the Center. It was hard work, but it was a great experience and a wonderful supplement to classes.

In the spring of 2003, I had started dating a man who had a small vacation home north of Palm Springs, so after I went to visit Mom on my spring break from Antioch, I stopped in to see him on the drive back to Los Angeles and spent the night. After some half-hearted attempts at sex, we watched a movie and went to sleep. Because of all the medications I was taking, my "equipment" just wasn't working anymore.

After this frustrating encounter, I decided to be celibate, at least for the time being. Over the next months, I realized I was much happier being celibate and I decided to stay that way. Yet if a man were to come along with whom I wanted to get into a relationship, I'd be happy to be sexual again. Meanwhile, life was so much easier after this decision. I was so much more at peace that soon I didn't miss sex or the chase. Especially the chase.

When I graduated from Antioch in the fall of 2003, I was thrilled that I was hired to continue as a therapist at the Gay and Lesbian Center.

During my time at the Center, Timothy took me to the 2004 Academy Awards. He had worked for the Academy for several years, and I was thrilled to accept his invitation. It was so exciting to walk the red carpet and see so many stars. Everywhere I looked there was a famous face. At one point after the awards show, I found myself standing between Clint Eastwood and Pierce Brosnan as we waited for an elevator. They were both so tall they talked over my head. It was the year that *The Lord of the Rings: The Return of the King* won Best Picture. It was also the year that Blake Edwards was awarded an honorary Oscar. I was thrilled to see his wife, Julie Andrews, one of my all-time favorites, in person.

Sharing this experience was a special moment in my friendship with Timothy. He's not star-struck like me, but I appreciated his willingness to indulge me.

My time as a paid intern at the LGBT Center did not last long. Just as I felt a growing self-confidence as a psychotherapist, the Center, facing hard times, had to cut its staff. As the last hired, I was the first to go.

I was unemployed once again. I soon found a job as a group therapist at the Alternatives locked ward, 4 South, the same unit in which I had been a patient. It had been four years since I was treated there, but things hadn't changed much. There were a few of the same staff members, including Jann, the director, and Faith, a group therapist, and the program was much the same.

I quickly got into the swing of things. I enjoyed doing my groups. I got along well with the other staff, and I learned to do notes on patients after each group the way Medicare and MediCal wanted. I enjoyed the nine to five routine. I didn't play the "I was a patient here, too," card too often, but when I did, it seemed to have a positive impact as a sign of hope that the patient could get well and have a job like this, too.

Not long after I started at 4 South, Rick and I visited Mom for her ninety-third birthday. We were both concerned that she could no longer live alone. He wanted to move her to an assisted living facility near him in Massachusetts. Mom agreed to it initially, but the next morning, she changed her mind. We compromised by moving her into an assisted care facility nearby.

Back at 4 South, the days started to blur because of their sameness. I saw many of the same patients repeatedly. They would be discharged after a couple of weeks, but they would start using and drinking again before long. Many of them were homeless, and everything they had went to drugs and alcohol. One of my patients sold the shoes off his feet to get his fix. When they got desperate enough to want "three hots and a cot," they'd check themselves back into 4 South. Although I knew that this was the nature of the disease, it was frustrating that most of our patients kept relapsing.

One Sunday in October 2005, I had a disturbing conversation with Mom. We often talked on Sundays, but this time, she cried through the entire call. She kept repeating that she didn't want to live any longer. She was ninety-three, and her life had become so much smaller, living with a roommate in an assisted care facility. She was plagued with multiple health problems. She cried hysterically, and I was frustrated that I couldn't seem to calm her down. Once again, she told me that she didn't want any heroic measures if something dire should happen. She wanted no nutrition or hydration. She just wanted to be allowed to die. At the end of the call, we each said, "I love you" and "Goodbye."

The next morning, I was not surprised to get a call from one of her friends. She told me that Mom had had a bad stroke the night before and was in intensive care at the Sun City hospital. She needed her sons by her side.

I packed up and drove across the desert to Sun City for what I suspected would be the last time. Once again, I was entering "the valley of the shadow of death."

I found a recovery group that met nearby and made a point of checking in with them every day, as well as staying in touch with sober friends back home.

Mom could no longer speak, and she was paralyzed on one side. I pulled up a chair and sat next to her bed. She reached for my hand with her good hand. I talked to her in pastoral tones, as I'd done with so many hospice patients. Sometimes I would read to her. I would hold her hand and pray for her. I practiced a ministry of presence, being with her in silence, as some people had done with me when I was sick in the hospital, too weak to talk.

Rick arrived a few days later. Being a physician, he didn't understand why nothing was being done to treat her and start her on the road to recovery. I told him about Mom's last call and tried to explain to him that it was Mom's wish to have nutrition and hydration withheld, and eventually, he gave up his quest to get her well.

David and Nancy arrived, and it felt eerily reminiscent of the day thirteen years before when we had all gathered around Dad as he lay dying. My cousin Marianne, David's older sister, also came to be with us. I was so glad to have my three cousins there. I was grateful they all understood and supported Mom's right to die as she wanted.

After a few days, Mom was discharged into hospice care back in her assisted living facility. Her roommate was moved into another room, so that we could have privacy.

We sang to her from time to time, which she seemed to enjoy when she was conscious. We kept singing *Amazing Grace* and *Edelweiss*, since we couldn't think of any other songs we all knew.

Jen arrived from Boston and spent a couple of days with us. She and Mom had been close when she was growing up. She said her private goodbyes to Mom and flew home to get back to her job.

One evening, my three cousins, my brother, and I were all standing around Mom's bed. She had been unconscious for a day or more, and we knew it wouldn't be long now. As we stood there, she suddenly opened her eyes. She looked at each of us and smiled. She closed her eyes, and that was the last time she was awake.

We continued to hold vigil around her bed. I found myself thinking about our complicated relationship through the years. In her later years, her anger and bitterness hurt me on many occasions. However, I also remembered the way she had gone to bat for me as a child and when I was so sick in the 1980s. I remembered the many times she had encouraged Dad to help me out financially when times were hard.

All these memories kept swirling around in my head as we stood around her bed, knowing she would die soon. David and Nancy put her favorite photo in her bed right where she could see it. It was a picture of Rick and me playing in front of my parents' full-length bedroom mirror when Rick was four and I was still crawling.

Later that afternoon, a nurse told us it would not be long now. Soon, Mom's right arm fluttered up as if she were greeting someone. Then she was gone. It was November 3, 2005.

The family asked me to pray, which I was glad to do. We said our goodbyes to her without much emotion since we were all exhausted and relieved. Back at the motel, I called my sober friend, Solomon, and, of course, Timothy. It was late, and I left a brief message for each of them. Solomon called back before too long. He was a great listener as I started to weep, and we talked for a long while. When I talked with Timothy, my tears had stopped, but my voice was still heavy with emotion. He told me he would be unable to attend the memorial service, but that his twin brother, Mike, who lived on the other side of Phoenix, would come to the memorial service to represent him. That made me happy.

I went over to David and Nancy's room. I knew they understood my complex relationship with Mom. They had always shown me such compassion and so much love, and now was no exception.

The next day, David, Nancy, and Marianne decided not to stay for the service, still a couple of days off. They all went home.

Before her memorial service, Rick and I went to Mom's lawyer's office for the reading of the will. She had left almost everything in trust to Rick, including the farm. The only provision for me was a trust fund that could only be used for medical expenses. Mom had said, "We decided to leave most of our estate to Rick, not because you're gay, but because we don't want you leaving our money to some male lover or that church. Besides, when you decided to be a minister, you chose to be poor." And now, everything was said and done. I felt sad and cheated, but there was nothing I could do about it. "God, grant me the serenity to accept the things I cannot change . . ."

In the spring of 2006, the family gathered once again at Phillips Academy in Andover to bury Mom's ashes with Dad's. My friend and Andover classmate, Rev. Mike Ebner, now the school chaplain, officiated. In addition to my family, four of my friends from New Hampshire surprised me by being there. It was so good to see them all and to feel their support and love as we laid Mom to rest with Dad.

Back at 4 South, the daily grind and the seemingly hopeless patients we served were wearing me down. To make matters worse, a whole new administration took over. I did not get along with my new supervisor nor with the new director of the program. I was doing my best in my third year there, but I was totally stressed out by their constant disapproval of almost everything I did.

One stressful day, I was walking down the empty hallway of the ward when I suddenly felt severe chest pains that brought me to my knees. It felt as if someone had tied a metal band around my chest and then kept squeezing it tighter. I weakly called for help, but no one heard me. I finally got to the nurses' station and told them what had happened. The head nurse called the hospital's cardiology tech to do an EKG. I sent the results to Dr. Levine and a cardiologist there at Glendale Memorial who hospitalized me overnight to do an angiogram and possibly put in a stent.

The next day they did an angiogram, which was basically normal. I didn't need a stent after all. Apparently, what I thought was a heart attack was simply an anxiety attack, but while I was in the hospital, I developed septicemia, which delayed my discharge a couple of days.

My supervisor at 4 South allowed me a day or two to rest at home before reporting back to work. I hated going back.

Soon, I got a bad infection in my nose diagnosed as methicillin-resistant staphylococcus aureus (MRSA). It caused painful, crusty sores around my nostrils, and I was hospitalized again. While I was hospitalized for MRSA, I again developed septicemia, this time with explosive diarrhea. They treated me with massive doses of IV antibiotics, but it took several days for me to show any improvement.

When I was released from the hospital, I was exhausted. When I went back to work, I found myself falling asleep in my office chair. Finally, my supervisor and I made a mutual decision that it would be best if I resigned.

I was relieved I didn't have to work at 4 South any longer, but when I started to look for other work as a therapist, I was turned down over and over. There was a lot of competition among intern therapists looking for jobs where they could collect the many hours needed for the Marriage and Family Therapist license.

Finally, I found a position with the Westminster Counseling Center in Pasadena. With this being a nice, suburban clinic, I thought my clients would be much less challenging than those at 4 South, but after looking at my resumé, my new supervisor assigned me homeless drug addicts and alcoholics as my clients.

My health was not great. I was exhausted all the time, and my lower back had become very painful. I kept coming down with bad colds and various infections. I developed type 2 diabetes and painful neuropathy. Dr. Levine finally told me it was time to go out on permanent disability. It was 2008, I was fifty-six years old, and I'd first become sick with HIV infection twenty-six years before.

I announced my departure from the Westminster Counseling Center and began to tell my friends I was going out on disability, although I framed it as an early retirement. I was disenchanted with being a psychotherapist. It wasn't at all what I had imagined it would be. I was greatly relieved to be done with it.

After twenty years of being remarkably healthy, I began to experience even more medical challenges. I asked Dr. Levine, "I'm not as healthy as I once was, am I?" She lovingly said, "No, you're not. You've been through a whole lot of junk between then and now, but here you are and that's what really counts."

After I left my job at Westminster Counseling Center, I applied for Social Security Disability. I diligently answered every question on the thirty-page application, including a list of my twenty-five or so medications, with their reasons and side effects. Dr. Levine filled out the lengthy physician's form, and I was soon approved for SSDI. That was a huge load off my mind.

Even with all my physical challenges, I was still determined to get the most out of life. I continued to sing with the Gay Men's Chorus of Los Angeles. I traveled when I was well enough and, occasionally, still did speaking engagements.

It was, in many ways, a wonderful period. But in 2008 I began experiencing severe pain in my lower spine and my hips. The peripheral neuropathy in my feet and lower legs became progressively worse, and sleep apnea, arthritis, osteoporosis, and type 2 diabetes all became issues, all evidence of the accelerated aging process in long-term HIV infection.

When I traveled, I requested wheelchair assistance at airports because my lower back would become unbearably painful when I stood for any length of time. I also began sitting on a stool for GMCLA concerts. A wheelchair enabled me to enjoy Disneyland. Mark, a friend from church and a Disneyland regular, invited me to join him there one day. I had not been in years. I had so much fun that day with Mark that I decided to get an annual pass.

Alison then introduced me to Richard, a man who took a group, including Alison, to Disneyland every chance he got, and I began joining them. There was always someone who pushed me in my chair. We always had a great time together.

Sometimes, Alison and I would go by ourselves. She kept me laughing all through the park. A couple of times, my cousins Stacy and John and their daughter Payton came down from their home in the Bay area, and we would go to Disneyland together, a great opportunity to see it through a child's eyes.

In early 2011, I visited Mark at his home near Disneyland. As we walked down his front walk, I tripped and fell hard on the pavement. My two hands went out to prevent landing on my face. We heard a huge crack, which I thought was my water bottle hitting the sidewalk when it flew out of my hand. When I got up, my right forearm hurt, and my right hand and fingers didn't work properly.

I had tickets that evening to see Jane Fonda in *33 Variations*, a play she'd done on Broadway, so I refused to go to an emergency room for the inevitably long wait. I drove home from Orange County, and Timothy and I went to the theater. My forearm hurt all the time, but not so badly that it stopped me from enjoying the play.

The next morning, the pain had gotten worse. I went to my usual morning recovery group, where one fellow agreed to go with me to Urgent Care. In case it was broken, he would be able to drive me home. They did an x-ray, and sure enough, I had fractured my right forearm. It didn't warrant surgery or a cast, but they gave me a sling to keep it stabilized. It healed up over the next months, and I felt better with all the rest I got.

In June 2011, Dr. Levine invited me to accompany her to the Los Angeles observance of the thirtieth anniversary of the first published report of AIDS, where she had been invited to speak as one of the pioneers of the early AIDS epidemic. It was quite a gathering, with many noted physicians who had been active in the early years of AIDS. When the program began, Dr. Michael Gottlieb, an author of that first report, spoke. He held up a small, framed picture of a man he told us was his first AIDS patient. He survived only a matter of weeks. Next, Dr. Eugene Rogolsky spoke about his first AIDS patient who didn't survive long either.

Then Dr. Levine got up on the stage and said, "I'm here with my first AIDS patient, Steve Pieters." The crowd roared. At the end of her speech, she asked me to sing my "Medical Anomaly" song, and once again, it was a hit. We were both swamped with attendees afterward.

Once again, I wondered how the hell had I survived. Yes, the feeling of how blessed I'd been was overwhelming, but I couldn't help wondering why I survived when so many others did not. I loved hearing all kinds of people telling me I was special. I wanted to believe them, but on some level, I wondered if it wasn't all a fluke.

Over the next year or so, my various ailments escalated. It seemed that I was always catching a cold. My lower back was hurting so much that I couldn't stand for any length of time and walking any distance was an impossibility. I was in a wheelchair a lot of the time.

Dr. Levine referred me to a spine surgeon at Glendale Adventist Hospital. He diagnosed me with stenosis of the lower spine and suggested surgery. I put it off until after my 2012 vacation at the farm in New Hampshire where I would celebrate my sixtieth birthday.

My friend Barb picked me up at the Manchester airport and drove me up to the home of my good friends Donna and Brad. They had dinner waiting for me. Then they drove me up to the farm and helped me open the place and get the furniture out on the porches. I could see my friends were quite alarmed by my condition. I could barely speak above a whisper.

My time at the farm is always healing. It's my sacred space. Being there always gives me peace, and this time, it was particularly true. My parents bought the place when I was one month old, and I'd been going there all my life. It held so many family memories. This time, all I wanted to do was sit on the porch in my rocking chair while I read novels and memoirs or simply gaze at the trees and the fields, the stone fences, and the little blacksmith shop below the house. I loved hearing the wind in the trees and the brook just inside the woods. I tried to memorize the view and the feelings of peace and joy.

During the day, friends came and spent time with me on the porch. I loved those visits. All that conversation, delicious food, good books, and quiet time strengthened me and gave me peace.

On the downside, my legs had big open sores on them, which often got infected. My skin was so thin, that if I scratched a mosquito bite even lightly, it would open a new sore. My friends in New Hampshire were so caring, and they helped me keep the many wounds clean and properly treated.

One of the best times at the farm that summer was the birthday party my friends threw for my sixtieth birthday. It was a grand celebration, reflecting the triumph I felt at turning sixty. I know many people feel turning sixty is depressing, but considering there was a time when I didn't think I'd see thirty-three, sixty felt like a great achievement. At this pot-luck birthday party, attended by close to twenty people, my friends had me sit in the big easy chair in front of the fireplace, while they brought me a plate with some of every dish on it. Of course, we had birthday cake, although mercifully there weren't sixty candles.

After dinner, my friends helped me out to the front lawn of the farm, where they seated me in a chair and proceeded to light sparklers and dance all around me. The women stood in front of me and sang a special birthday song they had learned with their women's choral group. It was beautiful, and I felt so loved.

When my two weeks at the farm were over, I was surprised by the number of people who came to see me off. Barb put my bags in her car, and I took one last look around. Each of my friends then hugged me tight and long. A couple years later, one of them told me they were all afraid that this was the last time they'd see me.

Back in Los Angeles, I was scheduled to have my spinal surgery at the beginning of October. I arranged for Tripp to fly in to help me out for a few days after the surgery and for Nancy Radclyffe to come out from her home in Canada for the next four or five days.

I had reopened my file at AIDS Project Los Angeles (APLA) a few years before, and my case manager there arranged for me to have a home health-care worker four or five days a week. My health-care worker, Maria, became a trusted aide. Because of all my physical challenges, she came every morning to help me bathe and do my dishes and some light housekeeping. I was glad and grateful to have her help because I was so weak and debilitated.

My back pain had become so bad that the doctor who would do my spinal surgery prescribed morphine capsules. They provided relief, but I kept feeling I needed more, and he gave me more.

One night in late September, a week before my scheduled spine surgery, I awoke in the middle of the night and had to go to the bathroom. On my way out of the bathroom, I tripped over my cat, Lucy, and fell. I couldn't get up because I felt so weak, no doubt from taking too much morphine. I lost consciousness there on the floor. I came to a couple of times, and tried to get up each time, but I couldn't, so I fell back asleep on the floor.

The next thing I knew, Maria awakened me when she arrived at nine-thirty. She was able to get me up off the floor and took me right to my bed. She said she was going to call 911, but I asked her not to, saying I'd get some sleep and then I'd be all right. She knew something was wrong and called 911 anyway.

Within minutes, I could hear sirens approach. The paramedics loaded me onto a portable gurney and started to carry me out of my apartment, but they had to take off the screen door to get me out. They carried me up the stairs and put me in the ambulance. I have only vague memories of the ambulance ride and no memory of being brought into the hospital. The next thing I knew I was in the ICU where everything seemed out of whack, as if I were having a very bad acid trip. Colors on the TV blurred into disturbing distortions, and I had them turn it off.

A neurologist asked me a few questions to test my mental orientation. "Who's the President now?" I tried to figure out the answer, but just couldn't. I guessed Clinton (it was Obama).

"Which hospital are you in?" I could not for the life of me think of it. I kept guessing and getting it wrong. Finally, the neurologist told me I was in Hollywood Presbyterian Hospital, pointing to the sign behind her shoulder, directly in my view, that said so. It felt so weird, knowing that I was giving the wrong answers, but try as I might, I just could not figure out the right ones.

I was unconscious a lot of the time I was in ICU. Many friends came to visit me, including my pastor Rev. Neil Thomas and Rev. Troy Perry.

All they could do was sit there and pray for me. I have no memory of their visits.

Dr. Levine later told me I had been diagnosed with pancreatitis, due to an infected gall bladder. On the rare occasions when I was awake, everything seemed so dark and incomprehensible. I knew I was in trouble physically, and I knew my brain wasn't working right. All I could do was lie there and drift in and out of consciousness. I was depressed, and I felt trapped and hopeless.

Months later, Timothy told me that in my delirium, I somehow got the idea they were putting me in hospice care. When I was alone, I decided to get up and leave the hospital. I pulled out the urinary catheter and ripped off all the different wires attached to me, but before I could get the IV pulled out, the nurses stopped me and put me in restraints. I have no memory of any of it, although I do remember waking up in those restraints. I didn't care. I was giving in and giving up.

A scan of my torso showed my gall bladder had to come out. The neurologist told me that was why I was so out of my mind. But the surgery had to wait until I was stable.

Timothy was there almost every time I woke up. He gently told me what was going on, but I could hardly talk or make sense of it all still. I was so grateful for his continuing presence by my bedside. I felt safe and at peace when he was there.

Solomon came, too, as did Jeff and other friends from the chorus and my recovery groups as well as college friends and friends and staff from AIDS Project Los Angeles.

When the day finally came to remove my gall bladder, Timothy waited with me outside the operating room. Much to my amazement, he prayed for me. I'd never heard Timothy pray before. He prayed beautifully, so meaningfully, and I shall never forget that kindness. As a result, I felt quite confident and hopeful when they finally wheeled me into the operating room. I was hopeful my insane thinking would end once my gall bladder was removed.

When I came to in the recovery room after the surgery, Timothy was there. After I had recovered sufficiently, he accompanied me as they wheeled me out upstairs to my own hospital room, no longer in the ICU.

Not long after getting me settled, he announced he had to leave so that he could get some work done at his job. On one level, I understood, but on a basic emotional level, I felt abandoned, as if I would never see him again. Fortunately, I was thinking clearly enough by this time that I knew he'd be back, and meanwhile, I would be okay. Soon after he left, I fell asleep. He later told me that whenever he said he was leaving for the day he could see my blood pressure and heart rate go up on the monitor next to me.

I totally forgot to have Timothy notify the spine surgeon's office that I was fighting for my life in another hospital. When I finally had the presence of mind to call them, the nurse manager told me they wondered what had happened to me and why I'd disappeared. She said to call them when I was out of the hospital and felt better.

Mitch came to visit me several times. She was a Buddhist nun now and brought me a lovely bracelet of jade-colored beads I wore for a long time. I was particularly touched that my cousin Stacy, in Los Angeles for business, came to visit me several times. It felt so good to have family there with me. Stacy was always a favorite, so positive and upbeat.

Tripp arrived not long after my gall bladder surgery. It was good to see him. He stayed at my apartment and drove my car. When he wasn't at the hospital, he did a lot of work around my apartment. After sleeping in my very old bed, he started raising money among my friends and family to buy a new bed and a used electric recliner and to make other improvements to my apartment. It would all be a glorious surprise when I got home.

Meanwhile, I developed a few hospital-borne infections, including recurrences of MRSA and septicemia. This time, I also got something called Clostridioides difficile infection or C-diff, a bacterial infection that wreaked havoc on my digestive system. I hadn't been out of bed for a couple of weeks at this point, even to get to the bathroom, so I relied on a plastic urinal and a bedpan. The C-diff caused me to have a bowel movement whenever I peed. That soiled my hospital johnny and my sheets. It sometimes took up to two hours of lying in my waste before the nurses' aides had time to clean me.

Once when this happened, Dr. Levine happened to call. I told her I was lying in my own filth as we spoke, and it was often an hour or two before they could help me. She told me to write the nursing director in the hospital. I did, of course, but I never got any response, and it still took time before they changed me. I also had a painful herpes attack on my lips. I tried to keep my spirits up remembering I wasn't out of my mind from toxins since my gall bladder had been removed.

I just lay there, staring at the ceiling, checking emails, or calling friends. I didn't want to watch TV. My friends knew how depressed I had to be not to watch TV.

While Tripp was visiting one day, I stopped breathing. It seemed to happen in slow motion, and I marveled at how my lungs were shutting down, as if I were a fascinated bystander. I didn't have any great fear or anxiety. I simply felt my right lung stop functioning, then the bottom half of my left lung stopped working. As the top half stopped, I managed to say, "I can't breathe."

When I lost consciousness, I was once again in a place of great peace, with love all around me and a great light in front of me. I knew somehow it was not yet my time, but I was so relieved to feel that peace that passes all understanding. Once again, I realized there was absolutely nothing to be afraid of in death. When I came back, orderlies were wheeling me on a gurney back to the ICU.

I lost consciousness again, and I did not regain consciousness for a few days. When I did wake up, Timothy was standing there. He told me I was on a ventilator, and I shouldn't try to talk. I motioned to him as if I were writing on a tablet, and he looked surprised, like "Why didn't I think of that?" He found some paper and a clipboard, and I started "talking" with him.

"Where's Tripp?" I wrote.

"Tripp went home, but Nancy Radclyffe is here." When she leaned over the bed railing, I smiled with my eyes.

It felt so strange to have a machine breathing for me. I had no control over the pace or timing of my breathing, and I couldn't determine the size of breath I took. I began to get a little feisty about being on this machine, since I was beginning to feel better.

Both Nancy and Timothy were there when they took me off the ventilator. The doctor told me to cough while they pulled the tube out. It was painful, but it was good to get it out and breathe on my own.

They took me back upstairs to a private room. I had a sore throat for a few days and a bright red rash on my chin for months afterward from where they had taped the ventilator.

Still in the hospital, I was critically ill, and I had trouble sleeping. All I could do was lie there in the dark and think. I felt so alone during the night. It never occurred to me to invite Jesus into my hospital bed, as I'd done during many lonely nights when I was sick at home. My spiritual resources were not working for me now, during those long nights.

At one point, my liver enzymes skyrocketed to over 8,900; I had bacterial hepatitis due to the infection in my gallbladder. Timothy, who called Dr. Levine in Turkey with all my lab work and numbers, now heard back from her that this was serious. She told me later that she was in a taxi in Istanbul when Timothy called with these numbers on my liver enzymes. She said, "Oh, damn," so loudly that she apparently alarmed both her husband and the driver as well as Timothy.

That night, I dreamed I was facing a big, black wall, but it didn't feel like a dream. I couldn't find my way through this wall. It looked forbidding and awful, and I was trapped. I could not shake this terrible feeling. I was unable to do anything but stare at it. I felt hopeless, defeated, and worst of all, it felt as if the God who had been lovingly present with me through so much was now absent. Or had I completely turned away from God? Despair engulfed me. I was flat up against that dark, impenetrable wall, and there was nothing I could do to escape it. I wrestled with the feeling that God simply was not there.

The next morning, Nancy gave me a bookmark with the famous poem about footprints in the sand. When things were at their worst, and the "I" of the story saw only a single set of footprints, she asked God, "Where were you when things were so difficult?" God said, "That was when I was carrying you."

After my bad night of wondering if God was absent, I wanted to throw the bookmark against the wall, but caring for Nancy the way I did, I didn't. That story just felt wrong, as if it negated my experience of either feeling absent from God or perhaps feeling God's absence. I wanted to believe that God was with me even when I thought I felt God's absence, but I struggled with my faith that day. My attitude about everything was perhaps the worst it had ever been.

Timothy called Dr. Levine almost daily while she was in Turkey, including the last day when she and her husband were in the airport in Istanbul to catch a plane back to New York and Los Angeles. She later wrote me, "When Timothy called this last day of our trip, he said that you were complaining about everything . . . you hated the nurses, hated the food, and no one came when you called them, and on and on. He asked me to call you to set you back on track. By the time we arrived at the airport, and I could get to a pay phone, our flight had already been called. I told you I had very little time to talk, but I was distressed at what Tim was saying about you. I told you to get your head together, that this was not right. . . . I didn't care about the food, I didn't care about the nurses who didn't care about you. This was important, and you had to get ahold of yourself. You'd done it before, and you had to do it again.

"As I heard the attendant announce the last chance to get on our flight to New York, there was a pause, and then you quietly said that you understood and would get your act together."

My attitude improved. I was grateful to have Reverend Nancy there by my side for almost a week. She had always taken such good care of me, and I had always felt so loved in her presence. I was buoyed, too, by the visits of many friends. Somehow, their presence renewed my faith in God's presence.

On the wall beside my bed, Timothy taped a shirtless "beefcake" photo of me from when I was buff, so doctors, nurses, and support staff could see what I once looked like. I was now wasting away since I had no appetite and found it impossible to eat more than a bite or two of any meal. Almost everything tasted terrible. I did enjoy the diet soda that some friends brought me, and I was sometimes able to stomach a spoonful of diabetic ice cream or gelatin or maybe a bite of cling peach.

As sick as I was with C-diff, I kept losing more and more weight. It didn't help matters any that the medication for C-diff was a pill that made me nauseous, as if I wasn't sick enough already.

One of the things that kept me going through all of this was wanting to sing again with my brothers in the Gay Men's Chorus. I wanted to see the curtain go up and hear the tidal wave of applause as we started to perform. I wanted to enjoy the camaraderie of making beautiful music together, to feel the strength of that community of gay men all around me. When I thought of all this, it served as a great motivation for me to try to eat and do the soul work of healing.

After another difficult night when I finally fell asleep about four-thirty in the morning, I awoke at six-thirty or so with Solomon sitting by my bed. I was so pleased to see him and so moved that he had been there since before I woke up. He came to visit many times, and it was always wonderful to feel his caring and support, no matter what time it was.

Timothy kept telling me I didn't need to entertain people, but it seemed to be my instinct to try. The truth is, I was anxious about their leaving, due to my fear of being alone, so I tried to keep them engaged. Dad had told me back when I was homesick in boarding school that I had to learn to be alone. In the hospital now, I still did not want to be alone. Many people want to be left alone when they're sick. I've always been the opposite. I've wanted people there, engaging with me. When I was too sick to engage, I wanted them there just to keep me company.

Finally, I was recovered enough from C-diff, pancreatitis, and all the other medical issues that had cascaded over me that I was deemed ready for physical therapy. I had not walked or stood for over three weeks, and now I could do neither. They wheeled me on a gurney down to the physical therapy ward, and after I'd rested, a physical therapist came in and said she was going to get me out of bed.

With great difficulty and with her strong arms helping me, I managed to stand up with her directly in front of me. Suddenly, I felt a surge in my belly. I projectile vomited dried blood all over her. She put me right back on the bed. I apologized. She disappeared. I've often wondered how she handled having an AIDS patient vomit blood all over her, but I never saw her again. Next thing I knew I was being wheeled back into the ICU.

The doctors diagnosed me with a duodenal ulcer—yet another diagnosis to add to my overly long medical resumé.

Soon, they transferred me back to a hospital ward with no more efforts to get me out of bed for now. I was in a lot of pain throughout my weeks there, and as I was off the morphine, I still felt a good deal of spinal pain, even with the milder opiate they were giving me intravenously.

If the time for my next dose came and went, I got desperate. Once, I sent my college friend Michael out to the nurses' station to pull a Shirley MacLaine in *Terms of Endearment* and demand my next dose. It worked. I got the dose, and I felt a full-body sense of relief.

Unfortunately, Michael couldn't stay with me to demand every dose when it came time. I asked my neighbor Jeff if he would retrieve my opiate pills from my apartment so I could give myself some relief when the nurses were late in getting me what I was prescribed.

Fortunately, Solomon vetoed that, so I did not start taking my own painkillers on top of what was prescribed there in the hospital. I was angry about it at the time, but I soon became grateful that Solomon and Jeff decided not to honor my request. I'm sure that would have meant another trip to the ICU when I overdosed. I would have also had to change my sobriety date.

I recovered enough that they took me back to the physical therapy ward, and this time, a tall, husky woman took charge. The first few days, twice a day, she wrapped a thick strap around me and used it to pull me up until I was standing strapped to her, face to face, body to body. We couldn't have gotten any closer.

Once I got used to standing, she began to make me walk, also on a strap tied to her so if I started to fall, she could pull me up before I hit the floor. That happened a few times, so I was grateful for being on what felt like a leash. Over the next two weeks, I learned to walk on my own, with the physical therapist following me with a wheelchair I could fall back into, which I had to do on occasion. Gradually, she got me to walk down the corridor and back. She had me climb a few stairs with railings on both sides to support me. It was incredibly painful and difficult, but I did it, and it became easier with each effort.

Learning to walk again was some of the hardest work I'd ever done. It was painful and exhausting. Nevertheless, twice a day, almost every day, I did it. I hated how difficult it was, but I kept at it.

Once, I refused my session. I was exhausted, and I needed to rest more than practice walking. The physical therapist on duty that day tried hard to persuade me to do it, but I got my way that once. I knew that my discharge from the hospital depended on being able to walk around the ward and climb those stairs on my own. So I got back to work the next day, as difficult as it was.

All this time, I was getting lung therapy to prevent pneumonia. They had me blow into a plastic "toy" many times a day to make a little red ball float upwards. They also strapped me into a mask to blow an awful mist into my lungs twice a day. I grew impatient with it, but I certainly didn't want to get pneumonia.

On Halloween, Alison and Bob came to visit me, dressed in their costumes: black and white striped shirts and berets. Bob had been to visit me many times and was always great company. It did my heart good to see Alison again.

Finally, the day came in early November when I was discharged from the hospital. A good friend picked me up and drove me home. He helped me down the stairs to my apartment, a bigger challenge than I had anticipated. It felt so good to be home. I hadn't ever been away that long from my cats, Lucy and Viv. When I went to bed, they lay on top of me, as if to say, "You're not going anywhere."

Tripp had raised a lot of money to fix up my place. I now had a brand-new adjustable bed. Another friend, Hollis, had installed safety bars in my bathroom. Friends from church found a used electric recliner.

I soon learned that my friends and family were exchanging a ton of emails about me while I was in the hospital: "Now he's dying."

"Now he's going to live!"

"Now he's dying again."

Alison wrote, "This is the Rev. Steve Pieters. He's not going to die."

The fact is nobody ever told me I was dying. I knew I was seriously ill, but I somehow knew this was not the end. I was aware of crossing over a few times, but in each near-death experience, I knew I had to return to my body. Timothy later told me that watching me through those five weeks "was a study in the will to live."

I was very weak for a long time after my hospital stay. I spent countless hours in front of the TV. I had many visitors who brought me groceries and supplies or just kept me company. I felt loved and cared for.

My first appointment with Dr. Levine at City of Hope after my hospital stay in Hollywood Presbyterian was wonderful. It was so great to see her again, and I basked in her loving presence. We went over my blood work, and she helped me understand what had happened to me over the past months. I was more convinced than ever as we approached the twenty-ninth anniversary of my cancer diagnoses that there could not possibly be any better physician for me.

For my first trip back to Disneyland in late November 2012, Alison pushed my wheelchair all through the park. It was so much fun to be back in the Magic Kingdom and, of course, to share it all with Alison. We had a lot of fun with that wheelchair because of that *Little House on the Prairie* episode where Laura pushes Nellie down a hill in the wheelchair she doesn't need. Alison would pose for pictures in the wheelchair with me behind it as I threatened her, while she did her best terrified Nellie expression.

I was not able to sing in the Gay Men's Chorus holiday concert that year, but I did attend. It was such a joy to hear their beautiful singing and see the delightful production numbers. It made me even more determined to sing in the spring concert.

The holidays at the end of 2012 held extra meaning for me. At Thanksgiving I had for years been invited to the family gathering at Dr. Levine's, and this year, Timothy joined us as well. I was still weak, and I spent most of my time seated on the couch with Dr. Levine's elderly aunts, whom I adored. Everyone in the family was so kind to me, and they pampered me in every way. Not surprisingly, everyone loved Timothy, and that tickled me to no end.

Christmas was very special, too. I spent it at home, where I received calls and cards from many of my friends and family. My niece Jen gave me tickets to see Cathy Rigby in *Peter Pan*. I went to see it several times. I loved it every time. It was a thrill to watch her fly. I'll always have a special spot in my heart for Mary Martin as Peter Pan, but she just didn't fly the way Cathy could.

After one performance, I stood in line to have her autograph the show's poster. There's a photo of the two of us from that encounter. I was shocked when I looked at it later to realize how sickly I still looked a few months after my long hospital stay.

I reminded Cathy how we had met backstage with Timothy after another musical. Timothy had worked with her when she was touring with *The Wizard of Oz*. He had me tell her about my recovery from lymphoma, since her brother had died from it the year before. She was fascinated and gave me a big hug. As Timothy and I walked away, I told him I could die happy now because I'd been hugged by Peter Pan.

I was falling asleep during most of the morning recovery groups I went to. Some people were offended by this, and one or two even made snide comments about it. I was worried about it until Solomon said, "At least you're listening to the music."

Jen and Timothy got me a button to wear around my neck, which I could use to summon the paramedics should I ever fall again or have any kind of medical emergency. It only worked at home, but that was fine since I wouldn't be leaving my home except for chorus rehearsals when I would be surrounded by a couple hundred brothers in song.

Rev. Nancy Wilson, my former pastor and longtime friend, came to visit me when she was back in town. Her very presence was healing. When she had called me in the hospital, it meant so much to me. It was only in retrospect that I knew she had called me to say goodbye to a dying friend. Now, visiting with her in my home, I felt alive with joy. We laughed and had a great time.

Christie Hefner also came to visit when she was in town. I felt a little embarrassed for her to see my tiny apartment filled with Disney figurines and plush toys, but she seemed more amused at that than anything. It was quite a different visit than when she had come to my home back in 1984, right after my AIDS diagnosis and terminal prognosis. This time, there was a lot of joy between us, knowing I'd survived yet another bout with death.

My spine surgery was rescheduled to follow the March Gay Men's Chorus concert, at which I was determined to sing. I felt triumphant singing in that spring concert, held in the First Congregational Church of Los Angeles, with its magnificent stained-glass windows and its glorious pipe organ. A few months before, I prayed that I would somehow, someday, get to sing with them once more. Although I had to sit on my walker for the concert, it felt amazing to sing with them again, and I beamed with joy throughout. Being enveloped in the harmonies of all these powerful men's voices, accompanied by that soul-shaking pipe organ, felt as healing as any medicine.

The week after the concert, I checked into Glendale Adventist Hospital for the laminectomy of my lumbar spine. The surgeon told me I wouldn't be down for long, that I could drive again in two or three weeks and resume all my normal activities shortly after that. After all the time I'd spent in the hospital that fall, I was relieved.

Tripp came down from Oregon again to be with me. That meant the world to me. He was there as they wheeled me into surgery and right after, too. Since the surgeon wanted me walking the same day, a physical therapist came in to get me on my feet. I felt quite fragile taking my first steps, but it was much easier than learning to walk just a few months earlier.

They sent me home a few days after the surgery. I settled into my adjustable bed and enjoyed watching TV. My new physical therapist, Lorraine, gave me exercises to strengthen my legs and my core, and she made sure I knew not to "bend, lift, or twist." I dubbed that the "BLT" orders. She gave me tools to put on my socks and pick things up.

Lorraine had the gift of being a taskmaster with a dry sense of humor. I loved her. She got me up and moving and soon had me taking brief walks, with my walker, just circling the driveway next door or doing tiny laps around the concrete patio out back.

It quickly became apparent that I wasn't going to be driving any time soon and that my recovery was going to take much longer than the surgeon had said it would. When I raised this with him, he simply said, "You're a complicated patient."

I was not supposed to be alone at any time because of the danger of falling and the difficulty of ordinary tasks. I also awoke with night sweats every night, with my nightclothes and sheets soaked. Chorus members spent the night to help me change into dry clothes and change the linens. They also helped me into the bathroom and back. Whatever the task, I was incredibly grateful for these men who took turns doing these all-nighters. During the day, I had home health-care workers assigned by APLA.

I began experiencing horrible headaches almost every day. They would start around three in the afternoon and get worse throughout the evening. It felt like there was a clamp on the right side of my head, extending from my neck, over my scalp, and down into the right temple and eye. The clamp got tighter and more painful as the evening wore on. The doctor at the spine institute was unable to treat it successfully. Finally, a neurologist at City of Hope diagnosed these headaches as migraines and prescribed sumatriptan. If I took this when the headaches were starting, it was remarkable how they would fade away to nothing.

In the fall of 2013, I was still recovering from my spinal surgery, but I finally "graduated" to being able to drive, so I started going to physical therapy up the road from me in Montrose. Lorraine, Kristy, and all the women who worked there treated me like royalty, as befit my queenly self.

My recovery from the back surgery ended up taking six months. I was overjoyed that my lower back no longer hurt. I could stand and walk without pain, although I was unsteady on my feet, primarily due to the neuropathy in my lower legs and feet that had plagued me in recent years.

I did manage some traveling, first to the farm, where I had a rather triumphant return after being so physically vulnerable the summer before. Then in October, I flew to Portland, Oregon, to visit with Tripp and Melinda again. We drove out to Mt. Hood one day alongside the great Columbia River and returned through the countryside. It was always a great blessing to spend time with these two.

I was determined to continue singing with the Gay Men's Chorus of Los Angeles that fall. The chorus had a new artistic director, Dr. Joe Nadeau. He and his husband Eric were so kind, reaching out to me right from the start of their time in Los Angeles. They took me for the walks I needed. With their help, I walked a little farther every week. I loved the sense of progress I was making.

With great joy, I again took to the stage for our holiday concert, Joe's first as artistic director. I was thrilled to be singing with my brothers and bringing joy to our audiences. Just the year before, I had come close to never singing with them again. Being up there on those risers with all those talented men felt like a great gift. I loved singing under Joe's baton, and all felt right with the world once again as 2013 came to an end.

The Gay Men's Chorus of Los Angeles has played an important role in my survival for many years. I first encountered the chorus in the summer of 1984, a few months after being told I would not live to see 1985. I was reeling with grief and anxiety about the diagnosis and prognosis. The concert was held in the Hollywood High School auditorium. I was skeptical about the chorus, wondering if their concert would be campy and silly or just not very good.

When they entered and filled the risers, I was overwhelmed. Here were more than one hundred handsome gay men singing beautifully. I wept. Singing had been an important part of my life since I was a toddler. In recent years the only singing I had done was hymns in church and tunes in my shower or my car. Now, I yearned to be up there singing with these amazing gay men, but I was afraid I would not live to have that chance.

Early in January 1994, I finally auditioned for the Gay Men's Chorus of Los Angeles. I was resistant because of my travels and all my board work. Now Christie urged me to join because she knew I needed something to anchor me in Los Angeles. Remembering how I'd sat in that first concert and wept that I would never get to sing with them, I decided to audition.

I was nervous, but I nailed it. Jon Bailey, then artistic director, invited me to join the chorus. I accepted and quickly became more excited about the prospect of singing with them. It would be wonderful, too, not to be in a leadership role.

At my first rehearsal, I was surprised to see IV poles, but of course, this was a group of one hundred fifty gay men in 1994 when AIDS was ravaging our community. IV poles were common even in grocery stores in those days.

Our weekly rehearsals would often end with a memorial for a member who had died from the complications of AIDS that week. Jon Bailey stopped the rehearsal twenty minutes before the end and gave us all time to share remembrances of that person. At the end, we stood with our arms around each other and sang John Rutter's *Gaelic Blessing*. We hugged and wept for the brother who had just died.

We performed our concerts at the Alex Theater in nearby Glendale. Standing on the risers, watching the curtain go up and hearing the thunderous applause that greeted us even before we sang was a rare joy as I continued my chaplaincy at the hospice and my AIDS ministry throughout the world.

Not long after I had joined the chorus, our board chair, composer Roger Bourland, aware of all the board work I had done for other nonprofits, had me over to dinner one evening to persuade me to come onto the chorus board. I told him I joined the chorus so that there would be one area of my life where I did not have to be a leader, but Roger convinced me, and I began five years on the chorus board of directors.

That June, I traveled with the chorus to New York City to sing at Carnegie Hall for the twenty-fifth anniversary of the Stonewall Riots. We sang Roger Bourland's "Flashpoint: Stonewall!" to a wildly appreciative audience. What a thrill to sing at Carnegie Hall. At our rehearsal there, many of us wandered down to the lip of the stage to pay homage to Judy Garland at the spot where she sat to sing *Over the Rainbow*.

There were so many highlights from my time in the chorus. Singing *Mame* to Angela Lansbury, performing in Tchaikovsky Hall in Moscow with Alla Pugacheva (Russia's biggest singing star), singing at Carnegie Hall for the twenty-fifth and the fiftieth anniversaries of the Stonewall riots, performing in South America, sharing the stage with Lily Tomlin, being coached to perform *Bosom Buddies* by Jerry Herman himself, being supported by other members through my illnesses and my recovery from alcoholism, and simply singing in each concert. We sang at the

Hollywood Bowl for the twenty-fifth anniversary of *The Simpsons* as well as at the memorial service for Debbie Reynolds and Carrie Fisher.

Two days after the massacre at the LGBTQ Pulse nightclub in Orlando when a man shot and killed forty-nine people and wounded fifty-three, we sang on the steps of City Hall at an observance featuring speeches by celebrities and local politicians. Lady Gaga gave a powerful speech and then joined us in singing Holly Near's *Singing for Our Lives*.

I was overwhelmed by the 2016 GALA convention, the Choruses Festival in Denver, where sixty-five hundred LGBTQ singers sang for each other for close to a week. One of our most important programs has been "The Alive Music Project (AMP)" where we sing short concerts and tell our stories in high schools around Los Angeles. If I'd had a gay chorus come sing at Phillips Academy when I was a teenager, it might have saved me from years of depression and shame.

One of the author's favorite moments with the Gay Men's Chorus of Los Angeles occurred when he shared his story at the "I Rise" concert (exploring the intersection of spirituality and sexuality), in front of a sold-out house at the Walt Disney Concert Hall, July 8, 2017. BY GREGORY ZABILSKI.

In the last few years, chorus members have been an enormous help in my ability to stay safe from COVID-19 by doing my shopping, helping with my trash cans, and just keeping me company. I treasure the community we share as gay men who love to sing and dance. The chorus continued to give me hope and joy in equal measure. It's played a big part in my ability to survive and thrive throughout the years.

CHAPTER TEN

Back to Life

THE YEARS FOLLOWING MY SPINE SURGERY WERE A WELCOME RETURN to life. I felt such relief and so much joy about being well again. I was able to fill my life with activities I loved: singing with the Gay Men's Chorus, traveling to visit biological and logical family, and taking great delight in my many local friends. Each new birthday was a triumph, as so many memorable events had taken place. Of course, there were ups and downs in those years.But reading *The Book of Joy: Lasting Happiness in a Changing World*, by Dalai Lama and Desmond Tutu, I learned that joy was not the absence of emotional pain or challenging times, but the presence of faith, hope, and love.

I delighted in each of my many trips to Disneyland with Alison and the gang, evenings at the theater with Timothy and other good friends, and many meals shared with old and new friends at restaurants all over Los Angeles. After food had tasted so awful during my long hospitalization in 2012, I enjoyed eating great food like never before.

My spiritual life, deepened by the physical challenges of previous years, formed the heart of my joy. After the dark night in the hospital in 2012 of questioning God's presence, my faith in God deepened with all I'd survived. I was overjoyed to be back in church after not being able to attend for so long. I was grateful to have my singing voice back. I began belting out hymns as if they were show tunes.

I got on my knees every morning and prayed for help and to know God's will. At night, I gave thanks. I also started meditating twice a day, and that helped me feel a greater peace. All my life, I had "scanned the universe" for something to worry about. I began to lay that burden down by paying mindful attention to my breathing during meditation.

After our pastor Rev. Neil Thomas resigned, Rev. Ken Martin became our interim pastor at Founders MCC. It felt like my life had come full circle. He had been my pastor as I came out, he inspired me to go into the ministry, and he had been my pastor when I was diagnosed with AIDS. He had given me the gift of preaching the Easter sermon right after my diagnosis. Now, here he was, our interim pastor, in my retirement.

About this time, Troy Perry invited me to sit with him at church each Sunday. I was greatly honored. I treasured our quiet conversations as we waited for church services to begin. I know he appreciated not having to explain who the MCC pioneers were.

I nearly died again in May 2015. I accidentally drank contaminated water after a day of sailing on San Francisco Bay. I had dropped my half-full water bottle, cap on, in the murky water where we docked. My host retrieved it, hosed it off, and gave it back to me so I could drink the rest.

Two days later, I awoke unable to hold my head up. I had to crawl to the bathroom. I had little to no control of my muscles. I called Dr. Levine, who told me to come to City of Hope immediately. I knew I couldn't drive myself. I had never felt so out of control of my body. Even with all I'd been through, this was terrifying.

Fortunately, a friend from the chorus was available to drive me out to City of Hope. I was immediately hospitalized. I knew I was in real trouble when I couldn't stand for a chest x-ray. I fell backwards, collapsing into the wheelchair right behind me. Once again, I could feel the life seeping out of me. Timothy came out to the hospital that evening and attended me in his usual caring way.

The doctors diagnosed sepsis, an infection in my bloodstream, and I was started on antibiotics right away. Dr. Levine came and spent time with me, despite her busy schedule as chief medical officer at City of Hope. It meant so much to me that she took the time to sit and talk. Her very presence was healing.

I began to recover within forty-eight hours and was discharged. The next time I had an outpatient visit with Dr. Levine, I was shocked to see how off-the-charts my blood work was from drinking that contaminated water and developing an infection in my bloodstream. I was so grateful to her and to God for my recovery from this quick trip to the brink.

Not long after, a reporter interviewed me for a piece on City of Hope. When I told her about my near-death experiences and how astonishingly peaceful and loving they were, she asked me, "If it's so wonderful, why do you keep coming back?"

"Because I love life! I don't want to miss anything!"

In 2016 I had the unusual experience of seeing an actor play me in a two-person play about Tammy Faye Bakker called *Tammy Faye Tweets.* Charlene Tilton ("Lucy Ewing" on *Dallas*) played Tammy Faye. Sheena Metal, whose drive-time radio show I had been on numerous times, brought Charlene and me together.

The three of us met at a French restaurant and talked about the project. Charlene told me she and Tammy Faye were best friends in the last years of Tammy's life. Tammy told her interviewing me had changed her life. So Charlene and her playwright, Tony Jerris, watched my interview on YouTube many times and it became part of their play, with an actor playing me. Charlene thought it would be great to have me in the audience, so that she could introduce me to the audience after the curtain calls.

It was certainly an other-worldly experience to watch an actor portray me. It had happened once before when actor/playwright Peter Massey wrote a one-man show based on my 1991 book, *I'm Still Dancing!* It was a surreal experience to watch him say my words as he acted the role of Rev. Steve Pieters.

Now I watched another actor, Brian Lamberson, portray me in a play about Tammy Faye. Of course, other audience members assumed that this minister with AIDS in 1985 would have to be dead, so there was genuine surprise when Charlene introduced me at the end of the curtain call. Charlene had me say a few words, and then the audience came up on the stage and mingled with Charlene, Brian, and me.

During the summer of 2017, my sixty-fifth birthday was a bicoastal celebration. I felt so triumphant about reaching this milestone that it became known as "Steve's triumphant birthday." I had multiple parties over ten days in California and New Hampshire. Timothy outdid himself in planning a weekend of celebrations in Los Angeles. Tripp and Melinda flew down from Portland; Alison, Bob, and Michael Vodde joined us to see the Independent Shakespeare Company perform a play in Griffith Park. This has been an annual birthday treat for years. Timothy arranged for reserved seats, and we had a potluck picnic beforehand.

There had been years where my friends had to push me in my wheelchair up the steep hill to the outdoor theater, then get me back down again, but this year, I was healthy and able to make it up that hill under my own steam.

The next morning, Timothy put together a spectacular party for me at The Smokehouse, a historic restaurant near Warner Brothers' Burbank Studios. My cousin Stacy surprised me by flying in for the party. It was a wonderful time, with a spectacular Sunday brunch buffet, a slide show of my life, and a lot of great conversation.

There were tribute speeches by my friends and family, topped by a hysterical, spontaneous routine by two chorus friends Todd and Scott. There were big portraits of famous actresses from the thirties and forties on the walls of our private room at the restaurant. Todd and Scott stood up and gave the backstories for each of these stars, as if they were all my various drag personas. Their delivery was flawless, and we could not stop laughing.

The next morning, I flew out to the farm in New Hampshire. It was such a treat to wake up on my actual birthday in that sunny bedroom, surrounded by the lush beauty of the fields and woods. I meditated in my rocker on the porch and listened to the breeze and the brook just inside the woods. As I gazed out at the sunlit beauty before me, I felt deep peace and great joy.

That evening, five of my local friends took me out for a lobster roll. Then we all went to see *Forty-Second Street* at the New London Barn Playhouse. As an adolescent, I was first exposed to summer stock here, and it was a highlight of every summer visit to the farm.

That Saturday evening, we had yet another party, this time at the farm, and it was thrown by Jen and Stephen. They put on a sit-down, four-course dinner party for eighteen. Jen and Stephen did everything, from organizing, setting the table, cooking, and serving to bringing the wines and cleaning up afterward. They even cooked the entire meal for each of three diets: vegan, vegetarian, and carnivorous. My friends and I loved every bite and every minute of the party.

That fall, my class from Phillips Academy held a joint sixty-fifth birthday party in New York City. I was nervous about my Andover class's birthday dinner. But I was pleased that my senior year roommate, Mel Brown, was there, as I knew I had at least one port in the storm of the reunion. I needn't have worried. I had a great time visiting with any number of classmates I wasn't close to forty-seven years before. One of the jocks from our class approached me and said, "We've been watching you through the years, and we all agree: You are the strongest man in our class." Wow. This guy used to slam me into lockers.

That same year, during our annual lecture to students at the USC Keck School of Medicine, Dr. Levine mentioned that my lymphoma and Kaposi's sarcoma were considered cured. When we were alone, I said, "Cured? I've never heard you say that before!"

She said, "They've been in remission for over thirty years. We consider them cured." I was thrilled.

That fall, when Hugh Hefner died, Christie invited me to her father's memorial service. It was held in the backyard of the Playboy Mansion. It wasn't a large gathering, as Playboy Mansion events went. It was good to see some of the wonderful women I'd worked with at Playboy.

The memorial was a great celebration of Mr. Hefner's life. The most moving speech was Christie's eulogy for her dad. I told her afterward it was the best eulogy I'd ever heard, and it was. I was surprised at how many people knew me. Barbi Benton said, "Hi, Steve," and when I looked quizzical, she said, "You're Christie's friend." I was so pleased to be known as her friend.

As the afternoon closed, I left with Patricia Kelly, Gene Kelly's widow. "How's that memoir coming?" she asked. We talked about it on the van to the UCLA parking garage where we had parked for the memorial. When I went to visit Christie at the mansion in previous years, it was always fun to drive up to the big boulder by the front gate and give my name to security. The gate would swing open, and I'd drive up the steep drive past the sign that said "Slow! Playmates at play!" Now the van drove back down the driveway, and the gate closed behind us for the last time.

⋘∞⋙

On December 30, 2017, I had to put my beloved nineteen-year-old cat Lucy to sleep. Alison drove us to the vet and was right behind me as I sat by the table and patted Lucy while the vet did the deed. I wept. Alison drove me home and stayed while I cried some more.

After the loss of Lucy, Dr. Levine, also a cat lover, urged me to adopt a new cat immediately. Timothy took me to animal shelters. The third day into my search, one of the shelters called and said they thought they had the right cat for me. When Timothy and I arrived, the attendant brought in a carrier with a two-year-old cat named Roosevelt. She opened the carrier, and this handsome, gray and white, tiger-striped cat ventured out. He sniffed the air a bit, then walked over to me and did a face-plant in my hand. I immediately knew this was the cat for me. Timothy and I brought him back to my place, and I renamed him Teddy. He made himself right at home, quickly finding the soft spot in my heart where he belonged.

As 2018 progressed, my life kept expanding. It felt so good to be alive and healthy, and I embraced every moment with joy. I continued to have check-ups with Dr. Levine once a month, and after looking at my labs, she would always say, "Your blood thinks you're healthy." I was always happy to agree with my blood.

I was determined to get back to New York City to see the Broadway revival of *Carousel*, starring Jessie Mueller as Julie Jordan. My friend Beverly kindly agreed to put me up as she'd done before, and I bought orchestra seats for the two of us. *Carousel* had long been my favorite musical, and I had seen the last Broadway revival in 1994, which I loved. Every moment of this 2018 revival was spectacular, and it was special to share it with Beverly, who had played Julie when I was Jigger in the College Light Opera Company production in 1970.

After the show, we visited with Jessie, the daughter of my college friends Jill and Bill Mueller, on the stage of the Imperial Theater, where so many great shows had played. It was thrilling to imagine Ethel Merman, Zero Mostel, and so many other Broadway stars there on the stage where we stood. Jessie was as sweet as ever.

Not long after, I flew to Interlochen, Michigan, to join my National Music Camp friends to celebrate the life and legacy of our beloved operetta director "Dude" Stephenson, who had died a few months before. The memorial service for Dude was as personal, moving, and wonderful as he was. It felt great to share this long weekend with so many of my good friends. What a joy to get all that time with them.

In October 2018, my denomination, Metropolitan Community Churches, celebrated the fiftieth anniversary of its founding by Rev. Troy Perry. The celebration lasted a few days and included a banquet attended by many local officials as well as MCC leaders from around the world. It was great to see so many colleagues in MCC ministry, but they all looked old! How did that happen? It reminded me of a favorite saying, "I thought growing old would take longer."

When I had a moment with Troy, he asked me, "You're going to be at the service tomorrow morning, aren't you? I'm going to talk about you in my sermon."

The next morning, at Founders MCC, Troy preached the fiftieth anniversary sermon. He usually preached through storytelling, and this day was no exception. After many wonderful tales, he finished with my AIDS story and how he planned my funeral with my parents at the beginning of 1985. Now, here I was, miraculously sitting in the congregation, alive and well. I was so honored he ended his fiftieth anniversary sermon with my story. When I thought back to how much he scared me when I heard him preach in my very first MCC service, I got chills; it had come to this.

Later that fall, Dr. Levine invited me to present with her at the first ever Dr. Alexandra M. Levine Endowed Lectureship in Compassionate Care at City of Hope. She titled the lecture "Lessons from Both Sides of the Bed: A Doctor and Her Patient." Between the two of us, we told the history of the AIDS epidemic during the lecture. With specific stories, we presented the lessons we had learned that could be applied by the medical staff who were there. We illustrated the lecture with many photos of ourselves, ACT UP demonstrations, and the last AIDS quilt display on the Washington mall.

A few days after we did this lecture, a very important event happened in the life of my family. Korean Presbyterians honored my grandfather, Rev. Alex Albert Pieters, with a magnificent plaque, unveiled in an all-day ceremony at the mausoleum of the cemetery where my grandparents were buried. They were two of the earliest missionaries to Korea, having arrived there in the last years of the nineteenth century. I was the only grandchild able to make it to the ceremony. Three great-grandchildren and two of their spouses attended, along with a dozen of my friends.

My family and friends were seated in the first couple of rows in the chapel of the mausoleum. The rest of the chapel was filled with hundreds of Koreans. Many had flown in from Korea and others from around the United States. We learned so much that I never knew about my grandfather. A Korean American professor spoke, referring to my grandfather as "the Martin Luther of Korea," since he was the first to translate the Hebrew Scriptures into Korean. He said his translation was still considered the King James Version, not just because it was the first, but because it was the most poetic. It's still used all over South Korea.

It was announced that a Korean hymn for which my grandmother, a concert pianist and surgeon, wrote the music and my grandfather wrote the lyrics, would be sung. I expected a soloist to get up and sing what must be a long-forgotten hymn. However, the entire gathering of Koreans got up and enthusiastically sang the whole hymn from memory.

After that, I spoke on behalf of the Pieters family. I showed the Bible my grandparents gave me on my first birthday. When I held it open to the inscription handwritten by my grandfather, there were gasps of astonishment and then applause. I read the inscription. More gasps. More applause.

After the unveiling of the plaque and a catered luncheon, we gathered at my grandparents' grave. After more speeches and prayers in Korean, we participated in a photo opportunity.

Dr. Park asked me to pose with my Bible, open to my grandfather's inscription. Photographers crowded around me, both amateur and professional. The number of pictures taken over only a few minutes inspired

Alison to quip, "You'd think this was a Star Trek convention, and he's got an original script, autographed by William Shatner." Without missing a beat, my friend Lucia remarked, "That's not Shatner. That's Roddenberry."

⌑

One Sunday during the summer of 2019, Troy Perry told me that a curator at the Smithsonian National Museum of American History had asked him to donate artifacts for what would be the MCC collection at the institution. She also asked him if he knew anyone in AIDS ministry who could donate artifacts and documents from the AIDS epidemic.

Troy asked me to put together a collection of our AIDS ministry artifacts and papers that the Smithsonian could choose from. I went right home and found all kinds of things, including my articles for *Journey Magazine* from 1984 and 1985; a DVD of my Tammy Faye Bakker interview; my 1991 book, *I'm Still Dancing*; the pamphlets I wrote for the denomination's AIDS Ministry; and examples of the *ALERT* newsletter that I had written and edited every month for years.

At the last minute, I decided to throw in the fairy wand that I had carried with me during my years of preaching about AIDS. I had used the wand as a prop to help me talk about believing in fairies at a time when so many fairies were dying. I originally considered not putting my fairy wand in that box. It held so much meaning to me, and I felt deeply attached to it. Then I thought, "Gee, I could leave it on my shelf for me to look at as it gathers dust, or I could give it to the Smithsonian." Into the box it went.

I delivered the box to Troy, and he sent it off to the Smithsonian. I thought they would choose one or two things. Much to my surprise, they wanted all of it, including my fairy wand.

Troy and his husband Phillip would be going to Washington, D.C., the first weekend of October to donate the MCC collection officially at the anniversary service of MCC's founding. I asked him if it would be all right if I went as well, understanding that this was his moment. He was fine with that.

I found a place to stay with my friends Jim and Jeff, in their beautiful house in Georgetown. Then I found an airfare I could afford, and I was all set to go. I called my other friends near Washington, and we made plans to share the weekend's festivities.

Jim and Jeff picked me up at the airport on Friday evening. In the middle of that first night in their home, I woke up drenched in sweat. Jim washed my sheets and clothes the next morning, and the next night, they put a large, absorbent pad underneath my sheets. That was a good thing, because Saturday night, I woke up drenched in sweat again. I couldn't figure out what was going on. I certainly wasn't sick, and it had been six years since I'd last had night sweats. I decided it was stress. I felt grateful my hosts were so gracious. It reminded me of how compassionate many people had been in helping their friends with AIDS.

Sunday morning, Jeff drove us over to the Metropolitan Community Church of Washington, D.C., where Troy would present the MCC collection, including my AIDS ministry collection, to the curator. It was wonderful to be back in the beautiful church that my late friend Rev. Larry Uhrig built with his congregation almost thirty years before. I couldn't help but think how proud he would be of this moment in MCC history.

My entire contingent of local friends took up the second row, right behind Troy's family. Before the service started, many people I had not seen in years stopped to say hello to me. Rev. Ken South was among them, and it was a wonderful surprise to see him. He had come in and out of my life from my difficult years in Hartford, to my time as a board member of the AIDS National Interfaith Network, for which he served as the executive director. Of course, he was the one who got me the Tammy Faye interview, and I was happy to tell him that was going into the Smithsonian, too.

Not long after the service started, the pastor, Rev. Dwayne Johnson, introduced Troy for the presentation to the Smithsonian. Troy gave his usual inspiring talk, focusing on the historic artifacts that he and several of us were donating. He talked about what I was contributing from our denomination's AIDS Ministry, and he highlighted my fairy wand and talked about how I'd taught the Metropolitan Community Churches the importance of believing in fairies. This was met with a roar of approval from the crowd, as Troy invited me to stand and be recognized. My friends got plenty of pictures.

Troy introduced the curator, Dr. Katherine Ott, to whom I took a shine right away. She spoke about the Smithsonian leadership deciding in just the past few years to begin an LGBT collection at the Museum of American History. She went on about what a wonderful thing it was for the Metropolitan Community Churches to be represented in this collection, "particularly that fairy wand."

After the service was over, I approached Dr. Ott to introduce myself. She jumped up to hug me. She said, "I've been looking forward to meeting you! What an important contribution your entire AIDS ministry collection is to the Smithsonian." Of course, there were many others who wanted Katherine's attention, but I felt as if we made a real connection.

The next day, our denomination's delegation met at the south entrance to the Smithsonian Museum of American History for our guided "backstage" tour of the museum. As we all went through security, we saw in

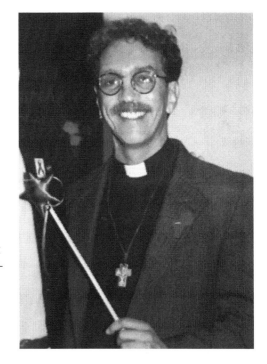

The author poses with his fairy wand in 1997. Used in many sermons and lectures, he says it helped him talk about the importance of believing in fairies: i.e., believing in ourselves and each other enough to do the work of healing. COURTESY OF REVEREND PIETERS'S PERSONAL COLLECTION.

front of us the hall where the flag that inspired "The Star-Spangled Banner" was displayed. Katherine Ott met us there and, to our delight, pointed out the large display of LGBT history immediately to our right. Katherine explained she and other curators had put it there deliberately, "so that all the people in MAGA hats have to go right by it to get to the 'star-spangled banner.'"

Katherine took us upstairs to the floor with all their offices on the perimeter of the building. Storage areas for the artifacts not on display took up the large interior of the floor. We all piled into Katherine's office, where a couple of the other curators were introduced.

A few speeches were made, and then Troy and Phillip signed Deeds of Gift, which legally passed ownership of their treasures to the Smithsonian. Katherine explained that they would mail the rest of us the Deeds of Gift for our artifacts and documents. When mine arrived a couple of weeks later, I signed it in front of the congregation at Founders Metropolitan Community Church. I sent it right back in for the curator's signature. She sent me back my copy, suitable for framing. What a treasure.

Katherine took us into one portion of the interior of that floor where a display of objects had been put out for us to see. These included items of interest to the LGBT population, such as transgender pioneer Dr. Renée Richards' tennis racket, a candle in a Styrofoam cup from an AIDS vigil, and buttons from early LGBT protest marches. Most moving to me were artifacts from Matthew Shepard, whose murder in 1998 galvanized the LGBT community. His tiny sandals took my breath away and brought tears to my eyes. These objects that had belonged to him made his murder even more real.

We all went back to the first floor, where we entered the Archives of the Museum of American History. This is where our documents would be kept, so that researchers and students would have access to them. They had many items they thought would interest us on display here, too, including Matthew Shepard's photo album.

Katherine declared the tour over but invited us to spend as much time there as we wanted. She then approached me and thanked me again for my contributions to the Smithsonian, "particularly that fairy wand. Somehow, that's an artifact that crystalizes the hope and faith that so many people clung to during the worst of the epidemic." I could not have felt prouder.

She asked me if I would be willing to send her my empty medication bottles. She told me they had collections of empty medication bottles from almost every disease except HIV/AIDS. I said, "Of course. I'd be happy to, but there are a lot of them!" I told her I took over twenty medications and seven supplements in different combinations five times a day. She said she wanted them all, and if I'd be willing to write out an annotated list of each one, with the reason I took it, the side effects, the intended purpose, and any interesting stories or notes about them, she would be "extremely grateful."

So I had my assignment, and I was only too happy to work on that over the next month or so. As I emptied each bottle, I put it in the box in which I would send them all to Katherine. I worked hard on the annotated list and sent that in as well. Katherine wrote me, "Christmas came early to the Smithsonian! I just got your box with the medication bottles and that annotated list."

After our backstage tour, we all split up. I ate lunch alone at a deli near Jim and Jeff's house. After the high of the whole Smithsonian experience, it was a letdown to be eating by myself. My loneliness was acute. I yearned to have someone special to share that weekend with.

As I flew home the next day, I was filled with mixed feelings: sadness that the weekend of events was over, anxiety that I would never be able to top this experience, and sheer joy and gratitude that it had happened at all.

I thought about how I'd first been called a fairy in second grade and how that caused me such shame. So much had happened in those sixty years, but perhaps the most amazing thing was the transformation of my shame into something to be proud of. My work as a gay AIDS activist, and my fairy wand, now lay in the Smithsonian National Museum of American History.

You might think that sounds like the end of the story. But happily, it is not. On November 15, 2019, the thirty-fourth anniversary of my Tammy Faye Bakker interview, I posted on social media the link where people could watch it on YouTube. To my great surprise, Jay Bakker, Jim and Tammy Faye's son, saw my post and commented on how that interview had had a huge impact not only on his mother, but on him and his entire family. I responded that it had changed my life as well. He invited me to be on his podcast, "Loosen the Bible Belt."

I accepted and did a forty-five-minute interview with Jay and his co-host, Kristen Becker. It was a full-circle experience that I never expected to have. Of course, we talked about the original interview with Tammy Faye. Jay said that after my 1985 interview, when he was ten, his mother started taking his sister and him around to different MCCs, as well as gay pride parades and other LGBT events. Realizing that she could have a whole new ministry, his mother also started visiting AIDS patients in hospitals and hospices.

I told Jay during the interview how his mother sent me cassette tapes of her albums and how one song cheered me on a few months later when I once again hovered near death. That song was "Don't Give Up on the Brink of a Miracle." I sang it with her over and over to help me get through that period in the first months of 1986 when the toxic side effects of suramin nearly killed me. Jay started crying when I began to sing it, and Kristen had to take over until he recovered.

During the interview, Jay told me that a film was being made about his mother, starring Jessica Chastain as Tammy Faye. The film would feature my interview with Tammy Faye at a pivotal moment. I emailed the movie's production company, writing, "Hey! I'm still alive!" Their publicist emailed me and said they were delighted to hear from me and hoped I would help in the rollout of the film. Since it seemed to be a great cast and creative team, I agreed. Then COVID happened, and everything got put on hold, including the film.

But the Tammy Faye story continued to unfold. A friend alerted me to a podcast interview that a friend of his did with Elton John's husband, David Furnish. In the interview, Furnish talked about how he and Elton were working on a Broadway musical about Tammy Faye and how she had interviewed this gay pastor with AIDS. The friend of the host told him he knew that guy. So he asked me if I'd mind giving my contact info to David Furnish and Elton John. Of course, I said yes.

∽◯∾

On March 3, 2020, not knowing the COVID-19 threat was right around the corner, I had my monthly checkup with Dr. Levine. Once again, she said, "Your blood thinks you're healthy." At the end of our hour, we talked briefly about this new coronavirus that was in the news. No one knew very much about it, including Dr. Levine. However, there was a sense this could affect me with all my underlying issues. I said something philosophical, like, "If it does get me, I've lived a full, wonderful life," and she agreed.

When worries about the novel coronavirus erupted that next weekend, I decided not to go to the Gay Men's Chorus rehearsal on March 9, because people were already concerned about large gatherings, and I didn't want to take any chances. On March 11, Alison and I had lunch together at an outdoor café we liked, but that was the last outing I had. It was fitting somehow that Alison was the last person I hugged for the next fourteen months.

The thought of not going anywhere, just staying home for the next few weeks or months or however long it would take to get the coronavirus under control, was a challenging concept, as it was for just about everybody. I had such an active life that it was difficult to conceive of staying home all the time.

My friends and I began adapting to Zoom meetings and virtual church services. Unfortunately, singing in groups was a high-risk activity, and so, of course, the Gay Men's Chorus stopped rehearsing and performing live.

As the COVID-19 pandemic continued, I found myself doing more interviews than I had done in a long time. Journalists wanted to know what my experiences of the early years of the AIDS epidemic could teach us about what we were facing with COVID-19. I began by quoting my friends Alison and Bob, "This is not my first plague." Then I talked about maintaining hope when it all seemed so hopeless.

Once again, the world and everyone in it was facing the fear of the unknown: fear of how this virus is transmitted, fear of the people who have it already, fear of how this would change all our lives, and fear of the grief when those close to us died from it. This was, however, different in that it was not confined to specific, marginalized groups, as AIDS was first thought to be. This affected everyone because this virus was airborne. I was not the only person who'd lived through the AIDS years to notice how fast research into vaccines and treatments for COVID-19 happened.

There were times in the early months of the lockdown where I went a bit crazy with fear and anxiety. I knew that with all my complicated underlying factors, I was at high risk of dying from COVID-19 if I was infected. Once, when a grocery delivery service sent someone who wasn't wearing a mask, I had an anxiety attack the likes of which I hadn't had in years. I usually turned to friends to talk me off the ledge. When none of them were available, I turned to God through prayer and meditation.

My prayers were simple. I prayed for help to stay safe from COVID-19, frequently adding, "Please don't let me fall into chronic depression and anxiety, dear God." I often prayed a short series of prayers over and over: the Lord's prayer, the serenity prayer, and a prayer to do God's will. When I meditated, I used guided meditations on getting and staying healthy, but I also meditated by paying attention to my breathing, breathing out anxiety and fear, and breathing in peace and joy, breathing out doubts, and breathing in God's love. I often meditated on Isaiah 41:10, "Fear not, for I am with you. Be not dismayed, for I am your God. I will strengthen you. I will help you. I will lift you up with my victorious right hand."

Most days, I was fine emotionally. Alison suggested having a routine, starting with showering and being sure to get dressed. She also urged me to have a project to do. So after I showered and dressed, I sat down at my laptop and set to work on this memoir. I had a job to do, and that routine helped me stay sane amid all the craziness going on in the world.

I did feel a deep sense of loss over not being able to touch or hug anyone. Of course, I had no spouse and no family member in my solitary bubble of safety. Touch starvation became all too real. I learned to cope with it in the routine I set. I reminded myself I had survived without hugs and touch in my early years of living with AIDS. I did not give myself time to dwell on the lack of hugs. As time went on, most days, I felt fine emotionally and physically.

I had several friends who became sick with COVID-19. It seemed to get closer and closer with each new diagnosis. One friend contracted the virus in March and went through ten weeks of severe illness. Although she was never hospitalized, it seemed she would never recover. Finally, she began to get a little bit better, and over the next six months she made incremental improvements. Deep fatigue and the inability to concentrate remained with her for a long time.

One morning in July, right after breakfast, Solomon called. "Jeff died last night. It was COVID-19." I thought he was kidding. I hadn't known Jeff was even sick. He had such a joyful life force that it was hard to believe he was gone. He had been wonderful to me in my first years of sobriety, holding my hand or rubbing my back as I shook with anxiety. He saw me through all that. Now he was dead.

His death sent me into another period of deep anxiety. Jeff had many of the same underlying health issues I did. And he was only in his fifties. If it could happen to him, then it could happen to me. This deepened my resolve to stay in lockdown, minimizing whatever contact I had with other people, making sure I always wore a mask when I encountered anyone. I disinfected every grocery that was delivered to me. I washed my hands for at least twenty seconds whenever I touched anything that came in from outside my home—when I checked my mailbox or held the railings on my outside stairs.

I didn't have a haircut for over a year. I soon had long, curly hair except on the very top, where I'm as bald as the rest of the men in my family. Many people said I looked like a mad scientist. I got tired of that look and finally had it cut much shorter in June 2021.

Chorus and church friends took very good care of me, as did Alison. She came over every Sunday afternoon to get my laundry. She usually brought it back to me the next day, fresh from her dryer. She also brought me all kinds of baked goods and other treats. We always had a chat on the sidewalk, masked and at a safe distance. I felt such gratitude that she took such good care of me and for all my friends who helped me stay safe, sane, and healthy. It took a village to keep this big old fairy safe from COVID-19.

Two weeks after Jeff died, I got word that my mentor and friend, Rev. Jay Deacon, had died suddenly, but not of COVID-19. Once again, I was shocked and deeply saddened. It was only a little over a year ago that

Jay and I had reconnected after almost forty years. He had spent a few nights with me at the farm that last summer before the lockdown. We had talked in recent weeks about his fear of dying: He knew his health and his life were fragile. And now, he was gone.

I helped plan a Zoom memorial service for those of us who worked with him and loved him during his years as MCC clergy. The gathering of his MCC friends ended up being a remarkable time on so many levels. It wasn't just a memorial service for Jay. It also served as a reunion of LGBT religious activists from the seventies, my colleagues, and it was a powerful experience to be together again after all these years, even if it was on Zoom and despite the occasion.

All through this time, I continued to get calls for interviews. Several were not COVID-19–related but were requests for historical information. Historian Lynne Gerber interviewed me for a book about the religious response to AIDS. She also told me about the book *This Is Our Message*, by Emily Suzanne Johnson, a professor of history at Ball State University. It detailed the contributions of women in the evangelical right, and it featured an academic analysis of my interview with Tammy Faye Bakker. Lynne put me in touch with Emily, and she in turn interviewed me for a new article she was writing.

I had seen a couple of documentaries about the response to AIDS in San Francisco and New York and felt disappointed that there wasn't any such documentary about the response to AIDS in Los Angeles. So I was delighted to learn from Alison and Bob that well-respected documentarian Jeffrey Schwarz had set out to do one on Hollywood's response to AIDS. My interview with Jeffrey was one of the best interviews I've had. Even after my two and a half hours on camera, on the way home I kept remembering stories I should have told and things I wish I'd said. I reassured myself that I no doubt told all the right stories and said what was needed for this project.

Alison and I marveled that what we did in the 1980s was now considered history. Even after having my work in the Smithsonian, seeing my Tammy Faye interview analyzed in a history book, and being interviewed for two other history books and a documentary, I still had to pinch myself to realize that what I'd lived through and things I'd done were now considered historic.

My 1985 interview with Tammy Faye Bakker continued to reverberate through the years. Any number of people have told me privately of the positive impact it had on their lives. One man approached me in a restaurant and told me, "My mother always had PTL on her TV when I was growing up. At twelve, I was struggling with my gay identity and was seriously considering suicide, but when I saw your interview with Tammy Faye, I learned I could be gay and Christian. You saved my life."

Jay Bakker told me recently, "I've never stopped thinking about that interview. It had a profound effect on my own ministry, on who I turned out to be."

Jay invited me to speak at the virtual Sunday gathering of his Revolution Church in March 2021. I was honored to share with his viewers' thoughts about my interview with his mother and all its repercussions, also telling the story of my faith journey with AIDS. I called my talk "Jars of Clay" after Paul's words in 2 Corinthians 4:7. It's been viewed thousands of times.

Jay told me more about the feature film *The Eyes of Tammy Faye* starring Jessica Chastain as his mother and Andrew Garfield as his father. Randy Havens, a regular on the Netflix series *Stranger Things*, played me. Jay said my interview was "central to the film," a fact he'd been told by Jessica Chastain herself. Jessica later sent me a private tweet saying my interview was what made her decide to do the film.

After the trailer was released, I heard from all kinds of people, both people I knew and many I didn't. I was delighted to hear from several of Tammy Faye's gay male friends. It was nice to know that she found solace, not to mention good times, with other gay men in the last years of her life.

Various sources told me how the conservative evangelical community came down hard on Tammy Faye for her interview with me. There are those who believe my interview was the "straw that broke the camel's back" for PTL. Apparently, Jerry Falwell saw my interview and was so angry about it that he vowed to finally bring down Jim and Tammy and PTL. A little over a year later, he did exactly that.

After the fall of the Bakkers' PTL empire, Tammy Faye eventually became an icon of the LGBT community, and apparently, that began with my interview. When BBC journalist Jon Ronson interviewed me, he told me my conversation with Tammy was a turning point in the culture wars between the LGBT community and conservative, evangelical Christians. In another interview, a journalist suggested that the way Tammy questioned me about how I was so sure I was gay was her way of dealing with issues in her marriage to Jim Bakker, who was alleged to have had same-sex encounters.

During the summer before *The Eyes of Tammy Faye* was released, I was asked about the interview many times, and interview requests kept coming in after the film's release. These were mostly about my conversation with Tammy Faye, but they also wanted to hear the story of how I survived AIDS in the 1980s.

In September 2021, Searchlight Pictures flew me to New York City to attend the premiere of *The Eyes of Tammy Faye*. I was delighted that my

The author and his beloved niece, Jen Pieters, on the hot pink carpet at the New York premiere of *The Eyes of Tammy Faye*, September 14, 2021.
COURTESY OF REVEREND PIETERS'S PERSONAL COLLECTION.

niece Jen joined me on the red carpet, which was not red but hot pink, Tammy's favorite color. When we stepped out of our limousine, one of the publicists for the film asked me to pose for the bank of photographers lined up on one side of the pink carpet. I worked my way down the line of reporters for outlets like *Access Hollywood, The Hollywood Reporter, The Today Show,* and *Variety.*

Then as Jen and I stood near the theater doors, there was a tap on my shoulder. I turned around, and there was a huge man. "Reverend Pieters, my name is Vincent D'Onofrio. I play Jerry Falwell in this film. What an honor to meet you. I saw your interview with Tammy Faye many years ago, and I have admired your ministry over the years." I was stunned.

A publicist approached me and said, "Jessica would like to meet you now." I could see she was in front of the bank of photographers at the other end of the pink carpet, posing at that moment with a group of drag queens. When the publicist pointed me out to her, she gasped with her hand on her chest and just looked at me with astonishment. Then she ran to me, threw herself into my arms, and hugged me for what seemed like a full minute. She whispered in my ear, "You're extraordinary! You are historic! Do you realize how extraordinary you are?" She turned to the bank of photographers and asked them, "Do you know who this is?!?!" The photographers shouted back, "It's Rev. Steve Pieters!"

When it was time for the screening, Jen and I along with my literary agent, George Greenfield, and Christina Britton Conroy, one of my Interlochen crowd, were shown to our seats, not far from the front and directly behind Jay Bakker. The president of Searchlight Pictures walked up on the stage and introduced "two special guests," Jay and me. The cast, who were all gathered a few rows in front of us, ready to be called up on the stage, applauded us. I will never forget how two-time Tony Award winner Cherry Jones, who plays Tammy's mother in the film, beamed at me as she applauded.

I had seen the film before and enjoyed it but seeing it with Jay right in front of me was a different experience. He understandably found parts of the film quite painful. He twice got up and went out to the lobby during the screening.

At the close of the film, there is a "where are they now" segment. Of course, Tammy, her mother, and Jerry Falwell have all died, and Jim Bakker went to prison. When my photo comes up, the caption read, "Steve Pieters lives in Los Angeles and sings with the Gay Men's Chorus of Los Angeles." The audience whooped and applauded loudly. The gay pastor with AIDS is still alive! Jessica told me later the applause for me has happened at every screening she's attended.

The after-party was a lot of fun, and I danced with the executive producers and a group of the other producers as well as with Jessica. I had a blast.

Jen was a wonderful date, always seeing to my needs. She took my business cards and passed them out to the producers, the screenwriter, the director, and Jessica herself, telling them they should make a movie about my life.

In the days that followed, Jessica did many interviews with all the talk shows, both late-night and daytime. It seemed every time she was interviewed, she talked about me and how she met me for the first time

Stephen Colbert holds a picture of Jessica Chastain and "the real Steve Pieters" as he and Jessica discuss her meeting the author the previous night at the New York premiere of *The Eyes of Tammy Faye*, on The Late Show with Stephen Colbert, September 15, 2021. COURTESY OF REVEREND PIETERS'S PERSONAL COLLECTION.

on the pink carpet. When she appeared with Stephen Colbert on *The Late Show*, they talked about me for a few minutes, with Stephen holding up a picture of Jessica and me on the pink carpet and calling me, "the real Steve Pieters."

Once again, I flew back to Los Angeles wondering how I would ever top this experience. Sharing the New York premiere with Jen amplified my joy. Sharing the Los Angeles premiere with Timothy, during which I sang with other members of the Gay Men's Chorus of Los Angeles, completed my joy.

So many wonderful things happened to me in recent years, and I was the happiest I've ever been in my life. "Rejoice in the Lord always; again, I will say, Rejoice." Philippians 4:4.

EPILOGUE

Bright Lights and a New Challenge

I WAS DELIGHTED WHEN JESSICA CHASTAIN WAS NOMINATED FOR THE Best Actress Academy Award for her performance as Tammy Faye. I was amazed and excited when she invited me to be her "date" for the Oscar Nominees' Luncheon on March 7, 2022. Alison and Jen helped me shop for a new suit for the occasion, and Alison helped me get dressed and ready for the limousine to pick me up. I was as nervous and excited as I've ever been, but somehow managed to keep breathing.

My limo drove me to meet Jessica's limo on a side street of West Hollywood, where I transferred into her limo. There she was, as beautiful as always. She could not have been more loving. I gave her the "God is greater than AIDS" button that I wore during my interview with Tammy Faye. Her eyes welled up, and she couldn't speak for a minute. We talked and talked on the way to the red-carpet event at the Fairmont Century City Hotel. She kept saying how much she loved me and how grateful she was to me for inspiring her to do this film, which had led to this Oscar nomination.

When we got there, we walked together down the red carpet and posed for the photographers. Then we were brought up to a suite where she and I were interviewed and photographed together by Associated Press (AP) reporters. Other interviews and photos followed, and she generously included me in most of them. She kept holding my hand throughout the morning and during the interviews. When she wasn't holding my hand, she had her arm through mine.

She introduced me to her friends, Javier Bardem and Penelope Cruz, and the four of us chatted for a few minutes. Then we went into the luncheon, with photographers flashing their cameras in our faces. It felt surreal.

I was seated between Jessica and Peter Sarsgaard with his wife, Maggie Gyllenhaal, on his other side. Almost every time Jessica would start to introduce me to her friends, they would interrupt and say, "We know who he is." Several of them thanked me for my activism and for my courage in doing the interview during "those times."

There I was in a room full of Oscar-nominated actors, directors, and artists. Everywhere I looked there were familiar faces: Stephen Spielberg, Arianna DeBose, Kenneth Branagh, Penelope Cruz, Benedict Cumberbatch, Will Smith, and Aunjanue Ellis-Taylor. At one point, while Jessica and I sat talking with Peter Sarsgaard, Maggie Gyllenhaal, and others at our table, it dawned on me this was just like hanging out with the theater kids at the Willard Hall dining room at Northwestern. That helped me relax among all these Hollywood heavyweights.

At the end of the luncheon, I asked Jessica if I could meet Andrew Garfield, who played Jim Bakker in *The Eyes of Tammy Faye* but who was unable to attend the New York premiere. Now, he was nominated for a Best Actor Oscar for *Tick, Tick . . . Boom!* Pointing at me, she called him from across the ballroom. He came dashing over, and without a word, he embraced me in a tight, warm hug that felt so good. He told me, "You were so important to this film. You gave the film its heart and soul." Jessica took pictures of us, and then he gave me another warm hug.

I still can't believe how very gracious Jessica was to me throughout the event. As we talked and as we were interviewed, she kept telling me, "You are determined to make me cry and spoil my makeup, aren't you?" We laughed together about that or just held hands tighter. Several times, she told me, "I love you," and I told her, "I love you, too."

The next day, Jessica and I headlined the media coverage. I never had so much press in my life, and it was all due to Jessica's generosity in sharing her spotlight.

Several events over the summer confirmed my awareness of being well-known and loved in Hollywood. On June 9, I did the prayer of invocation and opening remarks at the launch of the Hollywood Museum's LGBTQ Pride exhibit. The event honored my friend Geri Jewell (*Facts of Life; Deadwood*), Fran Drescher (*The Nanny*), and Michael Feinstein, the musical artist and keeper of The Great American Songbook. I met Michael after the program, and we immediately hit it off. I consider myself fortunate that we have become dear friends. He is a strong healing presence in my life.

My seventieth birthday party at the end of July was as wonderful as I possibly could have wanted. Once again, it felt like quite a triumph to reach a milestone birthday when I wasn't supposed to live past thirty-two. Over thirty dear friends gathered at the Smokehouse for dinner. They piled me high with birthday cards and presents, and I treasure the photos I have with each guest at my side.

My beloved Interlochen National Music Camp gang of friends sponsored the party and provided gorgeous floral centerpieces, a rainbow of big balloons, and beautifully enlarged photographs from various eras and/or roles of my seventy years on this earth. They also gave me two gorgeous sets of wind chimes. I hung one on my front porch, and the other outside my bedroom where they help give me deep, peaceful sleep. When I hear the chimes, I feel surrounded by my beloved friends who gave them to me.

A couple of weeks later, I was honored at the Gay Men's Chorus of Los Angeles's summer concert and fundraising gala. They gave me their Humanitarian Voice Award in the second act of the Sondheim concert. I gave a four-minute speech about the impact GMCLA has had on Southern California, the world, and me personally. When I finished by telling them how pleased I was that in the "Where are they now?" segment of *The Eyes of Tammy Faye,* the gay pastor with AIDS' caption said, "Steve Pieters lives in Los Angeles and sings with the Gay Men's Chorus of Los Angeles." The chorus stomped their feet while the audience applauded. I was so happy that I threw my arms around a chorus brother on the front row as I exited the stage.

After the concert, nine of my friends and family were comped for the six-hundred-dollar-a-plate gala dinner under the stars. My out-of-town guests included Jen and her husband Stephen from Boston and Tripp from Portland.

Mine was the last of three awards at the gala. My pal, Alison Arngrim, presented me with the award and gave a funny speech about our long friendship before introducing me. I had a written speech, but quickly realized that the podium lighting was so bad I could not read it. I figured that was God's way of telling me to wing it, so I threw my text in the air. I cracked a few jokes about getting the headlines for Jessica after the Oscar luncheon by virtue of her being the only Oscar nominee to bring an actual character from their movie. I ended my speech by singing my "Medical Anomaly" song. The guests roared their approval and gave me another prolonged standing ovation.

I was swamped with well-wishers throughout the evening, and several times my publicist, Harlan, "rescued" me, telling someone who'd cornered me, "I've been told to fetch Steve." Taking my arm, he walked me back to my table.

The entire evening was a huge success. I had a great time. All my friends and family were thrilled. It's an evening I'll never forget.

I left for New Hampshire a few days later and spent two weeks in my sacred spot at the Pieters's "farm." It was the first time I'd been there in three years because of the pandemic, and returning now comforted something deep in my soul. It was wonderful to see all my local friends there, to meet their grandchildren, and enjoy Jen and Stephen when they visited for our traditional lobster feast. Sitting on the porch while I read, visited with friends, or just gazed at the trees and fields felt so healing. To top it all off, for the first time ever, this 1790 farmhouse had Wi-Fi, and Stephen and I bought a new smart TV to replace the old tube TV.

As the summer went on, I found it increasingly difficult to swallow. Food would get stuck in my esophagus, and it took more and more of an effort to wash it down. Sometimes, I had to force myself to vomit when food didn't go down.

Dr. Levine ordered an endoscopy to discover why. On September 21, 2022, she called to tell me I was diagnosed with stage 4 stomach cancer. The primary tumor extended from my stomach well into my esophagus. The cancer had metastasized to my liver and lymph glands.

I braced myself for yet another fight for my life. This was not my first stage 4 cancer, and it was not the first time I'd faced a potentially terminal illness. I became determined to beat this cancer, too. Dr. Levine told me, "You've done this before, Steve. You can do it again."

Despite all my experience of taking a positive attitude about life-threatening illnesses, I had moments of despair and fear. I wasn't afraid of being dead, but I simply was not ready to give up and die, although I was afraid of the radiation and chemotherapy treatments ahead of me. However, my faith was strong, and I got into my new program of action right away. Once again, I demonstrated to myself that action produces hope.

My radiation oncologist, Dr. Chen, showed Timothy and me the 3-D color graphics from my CT scan that showed in red the extent of my tumors throughout my chest. We could clearly see the long, thick stomach tumor extending into my esophagus where it seemed to get thicker. What shocked us the most was the wall of red in my liver and surrounding lymph glands. My organs were packed with tumors. Timothy told me later, "I went to my car and wept," while I attended to other preparations for radiation.

I learned this cancer often grows and metastasizes without any signs of trouble until it is already advanced. I felt betrayed by my body with this cancer growing unnoticed for months, but I knew my dear Dr. Levine had no way of knowing.

Since this diagnosis, I've undergone two rounds of radiation treatments, two kinds of chemotherapy, and I've been hospitalized twice for a week each time. I've had several severe side effects from the treatments, and I've even had a long bout with COVID-19 and pneumonia. I feel so fortunate to be followed at City of Hope by some of the finest physicians there are, but this has been a challenging fight for my life. Even with all my experience in surviving against the odds, there have been times in the last months when I've thought nothing could possibly be more difficult.

Of course, I have once again been thinking about my mortality. With stage 4 cancer, that becomes a more urgent concern. I am not ready to die. There is still so much I want to do, but should I die from this, I've led an incredible life. So many dreams have come true. My parents gave me a great education, I've traveled the world, and I've been lucky enough to perform on some of the great stages in the world. I've got this amazing village of dearest family and friends, and with them I have loved and been loved. As I have discovered in my near-death experiences, that love is what is eternal.

Shortly before my cancer diagnosis, the BBC radio network asked to interview me again. The other guest was Tony and Olivier Award-winning playwright James Graham. He was writing the book for a new musical about Tammy Faye with lyrics by Jake Shears and music by Elton John. James and I struck up an email correspondence, and he revealed that they were using my interview with Tammy Faye as a crucial turning point in the musical.

I became good friends with the actor who played me, Ashley Campbell. We recorded a thirty-minute dialogue for the theater to use on its website. There was a three-page spread about my interview in the souvenir program. *Tammy Faye* opened to very positive reviews in the *New York Times* and several London papers. James and Ashley both told me how every audience was wildly enthusiastic. In addition to my interview at the beginning of act 2, James told me they brought "Steve Pieters" back at the end of the show, to thank Tammy as she was making her transition to Heaven. The thrill I got from all this helped carry me through my cancer diagnosis.

When I was hospitalized after my first chemo treatment, the entire cast and creative team of *Tammy Faye* recorded a "get well" video. It lifted my spirits when I was particularly depressed about my ill health.

One morning in early December, my phone rang. It was a number from the United Kingdom and thinking it might be one of my two British friends who'd seen the show, I picked it up.

"Hello?"

"Steve?"

"Yes."

"This is Elton."

"Oh, um, hello."

"I want to thank you for your brilliant interview with Tammy Faye. I must have watched it a thousand times during the six years we were writing the show."

He couldn't have been friendlier, and he gave me compliment after compliment. He finished by saying, "I want you to stay healthy and strong so you can come to the opening night when we bring the show to the United States."

"I'll make a point of it!"

As if the feature film and the Elton John musical weren't enough, a documentary about the Los Angeles response to AIDS, *Commitment to Life*, featured me throughout the film. It had its world premiere at the Santa Barbara International Film Festival in February. I was invited to attend the festival to walk the red carpet where I did numerous interviews alongside Jeffrey Schwarz, the director, and my friend Alison Arngrim, who is also featured in the documentary. After the screenings, I did the Q&A panels along with Jeffrey and Alison.

The Los Angeles premiere occurred a couple weeks later. Once again, I sat on the panel after the screening, this time with Jeffrey and pioneering HIV physician, Dr. Michael Gottlieb. I was so excited by the fuss being made over me that I didn't hesitate to take off my mask for the panel as well as the photo opportunities. Because of chemotherapy, my immune system was weak, and I'm pretty sure this is where I caught COVID.

Once again, I learned fame does not solve my problems. In this case, the allure of fame helped cause a *major* problem. Still, I must admit to a joyful delight in the idea that in some circles, I am famous.

Many people have asked me, "Why do you keep surviving what kills other people?" I have thought about that a lot over the years, and honestly, I don't really know. As I wrote in my Gilbert and Sullivan song takeoff, maybe my survival was a miracle or maybe it was an anomaly. Whatever the reason, I feel deeply grateful to be alive. So many gay men of my generation did not get to grow old. What a privilege to have reached the age of seventy, still dancing with joy.

There's a Native American saying I learned from death and dying teacher and author Stephen Levine. I've often used it in my talks and sermons about AIDS: "The quality of life is not measured by the length of life, but by the fullness with which we enter into each present moment."

None of us have any guarantees that we will be here tomorrow. All any of us have is this moment. So in this moment, I rejoice that I have survived all I survived, because I would not have wanted to miss a single moment of all that I have lived to see. In this moment, I feel deep gratitude and joy.

When I stop to think of all I've survived, I can't help but think of the moment when Tammy Faye told me, "We want you to beat this thing." I replied, "I will, with Jesus's help." Little did I realize that I would indeed beat AIDS. I've survived candidiasis, hepatitis, pneumonia, herpes, shingles, a rare tropical foot fungus, stage 4 lymphoma, Kaposi's sarcoma, AIDS, valley fever, adrenal insufficiency, partial paralysis, wasting syndrome, painfully inflamed eyes, pancreatitis, gall bladder removal, spinal stenosis, type 2 diabetes, sepsis, C-diff, MRSA, COVID-19, and pneumonia again, not to mention depression and my addictions to alcohol, marijuana, and nicotine. Although I'm now battling stage 4 stomach cancer, I have every confidence that God is with me and will be with me through all the treatments and their side effects. As I sing in my "Medical Anomaly" song, "It's certainly a miracle for anyone with faith to see." Even if someone is not a person of faith, that person would have to admit that I've beaten the odds repeatedly. I believe that has a lot to do with my faith. To paraphrase the apostle Paul, I am convinced that there is nothing in this life, not alcoholism, nor drug addiction, nor stage 4 cancer, nor HIV/AIDS, nor COVID-19, nor death itself that can separate us from the healing love of God.

ACKNOWLEDGMENTS

THIS MEMOIR WOULD NOT HAVE BEEN POSSIBLE IF NOT FOR THE MANY people who helped me get it across the finish line.

My gratitude list begins with my friend since 1956, Tripp Royce, for his continual encouragement to put my story down in book form. Furthermore, I am most grateful to his sister, Amanda Royce-Hale, who offered her services as a professional editor. She saw me through the first four drafts and provided constantly solid advice on editing it down from eight hundred pages to under three hundred pages. She was helpful in so many ways, not the least of which was her invaluable help with grammar, style, and narrative while always staying positive and encouraging.

My brilliant physician and dear friend Alexandra M. Levine, MD, MACP, provided me with great direction in getting the medical facts correct. Her memories of the past four decades of our professional and personal relationship were invaluable in getting my story right. Of course, the ways she has kept me alive through all the ups and downs of living with AIDS all these years are what made this book possible to begin with. How can I ever express adequate thanks for repeatedly saving my life?

I am grateful to my literary agent, George Greenfield at Creative Well, for taking me on, for guiding me through a professional editorial process, and for patiently shepherding the memoir through more than a few presentations to potential publishers. I am particularly thankful to my dear friend Christina Britton Conroy for bringing George and me together.

I greatly appreciate my editor, Richard Brown, senior executive editor of religion and spirituality at Rowman & Littlefield Publishers, whose expert guidance in making revisions and preparing the memoir for publication was matched in every way by his kindness.

I'm also extremely grateful to Jaylene Perez, assistant acquisitions editor at Rowman & Littlefield. She has done an enormous amount of heavy lifting in getting my manuscript ready for production. I don't know how I would have done this without her.

My assistant, Julian Armaya, has been invaluable in doing a lot of the detail work that my current battle with cancer has not allowed me to accomplish myself: securing rights and permissions for photographs and quotes, and formatting the manuscript chief among them. Hiring him was one of the smartest decisions I've made in writing this volume.

I appreciate so many others who encouraged me and supported me throughout the several years it took to write this: my beloved niece Jen Pieters; my dear cousins Rick, David, and Nancy Pieters; Stacy Markel; Karen Jackson; and Cherie Sprole Boice. There are numerous long-distance friends to whom I'm indebted for their support and encouragement: Christie Hefner, Emily Golden, Valerie Slivinski, David Maier, Jan Powell, Betsy Pfau, Nancy Radclyffe, Barb Freeman, and Donna Baker-Hartwell. Locally, Timothy Smith, Solomon Trager, and Barbara Wilder have been invaluable friends in setting down my memories and improving my writing. Numerous friends from the Gay Men's Chorus of Los Angeles, Founders Metropolitan Community Church, and my recovery support network have also been there for me through the ups and downs of writing my memoir.

Alison Arngrim has been one of the most supportive, caring friends I could hope for throughout this process. She not only supported me through COVID-19 by doing my laundry every week and often cooking for me, freeing me up to write, but she also offered invaluable advice from the experience of writing her memoir, *Confessions of a Prairie Bitch: How I Survived Nellie Oleson and Learned to Love Being Hated*. She's kept me laughing through it all.

So many people have supported me through this, and I thank each one whether or not I have mentioned them here. I have thoroughly enjoyed the process of writing, editing, and bringing the book to publication. A profound thanks to all who have contributed to this undertaking!

About the Author

The Rev. Dr. Steve Pieters (1952–2023) was a long-term survivor of AIDS. Diagnosed with Gay-Related Immune Deficiency in 1982, and AIDS/Kaposi's Sarcoma and stage four lymphoma in 1984, he was told he would not survive to see 1985. His remarkable story of recovery serves as an inspiring example of healing and hope. Best known for his 1985 interview with Tammy Faye Bakker on *Tammy's House Party*, he is featured in the 2000 documentary *The Eyes of Tammy Faye*, and he is portrayed in the 2021 feature film *The Eyes of Tammy Faye*, for which Jessica Chastain won the 2022 Oscar for Best Actress. The grandson of two of the first missionaries to Korea, Rev. Pieters was born and raised in Lawrence, Massachusetts, where his father chaired the mathematics department at nearby Phillips Academy. Ordained by the Metropolitan Community Churches, a primarily LGBT denomination, he served as their field director of AIDS ministry during the worst years of the AIDS crisis. His work in AIDS ministry is part of the LGBT collection at the Smithsonian National Museum of American History.

Rev. Pieters' final manuscript was approved by the publisher on the very day he fell ill and went back into the hospital, unknowingly, for the last time. He was passionate about sharing this memoir to inspire others to find hope and strength in the face of great challenges. His mantra through it all was "I keep on dancing."